Practical Chinese Medicine

Contents

Introduction to Traditional Chinese Medicine 4
      The Origins of Traditional Chinese Medicine 4
  Western Medicine versus Chinese Medicine 5
Tuina Chinese Medical Acupressure 7
  Tuina – a definition 7
Contra-indications 9
Indications 10
Yin and Yang 11
    The Five Aspect's of Yin & Yang Relationship. 11
    Clinical expressions of disharmony between Yin and Yang 12
The Five Elements 13
The Vital Substances 16
    The Concept of Qi in Chinese Medicine 16
      Types of Qi 17
    Functions of Qi in the Body 18
    Pathology of Qi 19
Blood (Xue) 19
    Blood - Qi relationship 19
      Blood Pathology 20
Body Fluids 21
Essence (Jing) 21
Shen 21
The Zang Fu 22
    Ancient anatomical knowledge 22
    The Heart (Xin) 23
    The Pericardium (Xin Bao) 24
    The Liver (Gan) 24
    The Spleen (Pi) 26
    The Lung (Fei) 27
    The Kidney (Shen) 28
    The Gallbladder (Dan) 31

- The Stomach (Wei) 31
- The Small Intestine (Xiao Chang) 31
- The Large Intestine (Da Chang) 32
- The Urinary Bladder (Pang Guang) 32
- The San Jiao 32

Traditional Chinese Medicine Diagnostics 35
- Diagnostic methods 35

The Six Exogenous Factors 36
The Seven Emotional Factors 39
Internal Causes of disease 41
Diagnostic Methods 42
- Observation of the Tongue 45

Listening (Auscultation) and Smelling (Olfaction) 47
- Palpating the Pulse 52

Differentation of Patterns of Disharmony 58
Eight principles 58
Lung Patterns of Disharmony 68
Large Intestine Patterns of Disharmony 70
Stomach Patterns of Disharmony 70
Spleen Patterns of Disharmony 72
Heart Patterns of Disharmony 74
Small Intestine Patterns of Disharmony 76
Urinary Bladder Patterns of Disharmony 76
Kidney Patterns of Disharmony 77
Gall Bladder Patterns of Disharmony 78
Liver Patterns of Disharmony 79
Complicated Patterns of Disharmony 82
The Meridian, Channels, Collaterals and Acupoints 88
Methods of Locating Acupoints 92
Lungs 94
Large Intestine 96
Stomach 99
Spleen 104
Heart 107
Small Intestine 108
Urinary Bladder 111
Kidney 117
Gall Bladder 120
Liver 124
Pericardium 126
San Jiao 128
Du 131
Ren 134
Extra Points 135

Practical Chinese Medicine

Section 1

Introduction to Traditional Chinese Medicine

Introduction to Traditional Chinese Medicine

"The sage submits to the law of Yin and Yang energy, for its variations dominates the beginning and end and decides the life and death of everything. To live in harmony with Yin and Yang means health, happiness and life, to act contrary means disease, illness and death. This is the reason the sage will treat those who are not yet diseased. To treat after one is diseased is like digging a well after one is thirsty or forging weapon's after the battle has begun"

This was quoted by Qi Bo an advisor to Huang Di, the Yellow Emporer, recorded in the Huang Di Nei Jing, one of the most important texts of Chinese medicine compiled 2,200 years ago.

The emphasis of Chinese medicine is on prevention, although today, most of the patients seen in the Traditional Chinese Medicine practitioner's clinic have come as a last resort. They knock yet another door to find an answer to their malady. They present with a symptom or number of symptoms. They may even have the medical term for their illness, i.e. Arthritis, dysmenorrhoea, asthma, psoriasis, or any of the other numerous illnesses. Practitioners of Chinese medicine have little use for this label as they take a holistic view of the person and each sign and symptom is looked at, in relation to the whole body in order to identify the cause and treatment of the problem.

Culture plays an important role in the development of any healing or medical system as it presents the philosophy that defines the way the system works. Where Western science breaks everything down to its constituent parts including medicine and disease (known as reductionism), Traditional Chinese Medicine strives to see the whole picture, nothing is excluded, and nothing is evaluated or understood without reference to the whole. In Traditional Chinese Medicine everything is interdependent or viewed within the "holistic" health picture.

In Traditional Chinese Medicine, there are four main schools or areas of medical skills, namely Herbal Therapy, Acupuncture, Tuina Chinese Medical Massage and Medical Qi Gong exercise. A "practitioner of Traditional Chinese Medicine" will study all or will specialise in just one medical skill, which includes the affects of constitution, diet, lifestyle and environment on the body.

The Origins of Traditional Chinese Medicine

"History is continuous, as one piece of fuel is consumed, the flame passes to another"
(trad.)

In ancient times, say around 4,000 years ago, before the arrival of professional physicians, people would visit the mountain hermits or Shamans, who advised diet, herbs and specific exercise to the suffering patient. One of the concepts to emerge from this period was that of a vital substance called Qi. This "vitality or energy" became an integral part of all Chinese medical thinking. It is the vital energy that circulates throughout the universe. It permeates the air we breathe, and the food we eat. It is the life force that starts the heart beating and initiates our first breath after leaving our mother's womb.

In order to maintain balance or homeostasis, the body's Qi must run smoothly. The diagrams of the Qi meridians show 14 channels that spread throughout the body. Qi flows along this network of meridians. 12 of these meridians are located bilaterally with each pair associated with a different organ system.

Over these 4,000 years, the ancient Chinese learned that by stimulating certain areas and points on the surface of the body, they could influence how our bodies deal with disharmonies. Chinese medicine believes that we have the ability to heal ourselves of many of the illnesses that humans and animals suffer. As with the Western concept of homeostasis, Traditional Chinese Medicine strives to achieve harmonious equilibrium in the body by balancing Yin & Yang, a profound concept that can describe the balance in every phenomenon in existence. One legend has it that acupuncture and Tuina evolved as early Chinese healers studied the puncture wounds of Chinese warriors, noting that certain points on the body created interesting results when stimulated. Tuina is the non-invasive form of acupuncture, as Chinese physicians determined that stimulating points on the body with massage and pressure could be effective for treating certain problems.

The first references to massage treatment for disease are found inscribed on bones and tortoise shells, which were used in divination practice from the Yin and Shang Periods (1600 – 1100BC). These references are written in "jiaguwen", the earliest form of writing in China. Massage is also recorded in one of the oldest text of Chinese medicine, *The Huang Di Nei Jing translated to Yellow Emperor's Classic of Internal Medicine*, dating back at least 2,000 years ago. (c.? - 200 BC), comprising the Su Wen (simple questions) and Ling Shu (spiritual axis)

Spring Autumn and Warring States (770 – 221BC).

Confucius (551 – 479BC) established a "code of conduct" on the harmony that exists between the forces of nature that made a significant contribution to Chinese Medicine. Anmo "massage" appears in other medical works, expanding on treatment techniques and principals. The relationship between Anmo and medicinal ointments are illustrated during this time. Bian Que (407 – 310BC) is asserted to be China's first eminent doctor, a master of all medical skills, expert in the use of herbs, acupuncture, Anmo and Qi Gong. When patients wish to thank their doctor, they present him or her with a framed calligraphy that states "Bian Que is not dead, but alive in this practice".

Lao Zi (571 –? BC) the father of Daoism established the theory of cosmic law based on Shen Nong's opposing principals and the concept of Yin Yang was concieved.

Tuina has been known by other terms in ancient times such as "Anqiao", "Anfu", and "Anmo". The name Tuina did not come into the record books until the Ming Period 1368 – 1644 AD, where it appeared in a book on pediatric disorders. The term is used today to distinguish massage or acupressure therapy based on the theories of Traditional Chinese Medicine, from popular folk massage, which is simply called "Anmo". Today Tuina is a general practice delivered in modern and traditional hospitals alongside allopathic medicine, in traditional hospitals, in conjunction with allopathic medicine.

Western Medicine versus Chinese Medicine

Science versus Tradition

Western and Chinese medicines are as different as east and west. The Western medicinal approach is to view the interplay of disease with the person or animal at a microscopic level. It pays particular attention to the symptoms of the disease process, however a major and fundamental flaw is that it rarely looks at the affect of constitution, diet, lifestyle or environemnt on the person's health. Pharmacuticals are then prescribed to deal with these symptoms. These medicines are normally syntheic and not a naturally occuring substance. They are scientifically researched and the affects of which are observed in laborotory conditions, however in most cases without researching the long term affects of these medicines. Treatment is based on the symptom of the problem and the cause is secondary. It could also be said that Western medicine is very quick to use surgery to cure certain disease without looking at alternative methods of treatment. A headache is treated with the same drugs no matter what, and if that does not work, the use of surgery is considered.

The Chinese approach looks at illness as the result of an imbalance of emotional, lifestyle, social, diet, environmental factors and the constitution of the persons various body organs. The symptoms we experience are just the body's attempts to restore harmony or homeostasis. Traditional Chinese treatments involve assisting the patients own natural healing abilities back to a normal working condition. Threatment may include: Tuina acupressure therapy or acupuncture, taking herbal medicine, making lifestyle changes (e.g. a mother staying home for a month before and after a birth) or altering the diet (perhaps light eating or fasting for a day or avoiding certain foods). The patient is encouraged to take more responsibility for their own health.

In addition, instead of waiting until illness occurs, the Chinese medical practitioner recommends certain herbs as part of the daily diet. Herbs are described as strong foods in China and this is why the older generation Chinese, believe in making and drinking soup with every meal.

> *"The traditional Chinese concept of health is simple, not measured by checking chemical levels in Blood and urine"* (Ted J. Kapchuk)

The Chinese view it differently; they look at the whole person. They take all the symptoms and also signs, like Tongue and Pulse diagnosis. They look at the built and psychology of the patient (emotions; angry, sad, happy, worry, fear etc.) and then weave everything into a Pattern of Disharmony. The Chinese do not distinguish mental from physical illness, everything is connected, and both the cause & manifestation are treated.

Following are three cases of males with medically confirmed headaches. You will note that each, with the exception of headache, has different symptoms. Each of the following would have different Chinese treatments, which has excellent results in treating headache.

Example of patterns of disharmony for headaches:

1st. Patient	Clinical Manifestations: Headache, Worse with pressure, Red complexion, full deep voice, Assertive personality, Constipation, Dark urine	*Tongue:* Yellow coating *Pulse:* Full & wiry
2nd. Patient	Clinical Manifestations: Headache, red cheek bones, tired in the afternoon, no thirst, Sweaty palms, nervous & Fidgety, Constipation, Insomnia	*Tongue:* Dry *Pulse:* Thin & rapid
3rd. Patient	*Clinical Manifestations:* Headache, Better with pressure, Pale face, timid personality, abdominal distention,	*Tongue:* Pale *Pulse:* Empty (feels like a balloon, Hollow inside)

There are many more Patterns of Disharmony where headache is the central symptom. All these patients had a diagnosis of Headache with different treatment protocols offered to each.

Traditional Chinese Medicine will never compete with Western Medicine nor will it compete with any other healing discipline. It is a complimentary health therapy that has developed by empirical observation over thousands of years. Through trial and error the Chinese documented all medicinal treatments. They observed that by stimulating or placing a needle into a certain point they influenced certain symptoms. They are still developing new points, today, a recent one, is used to help the patient give up smoking. In the past, the Needles used varied from stone ones at the start, which were very painful, to the modern clinically clean disposable needles.

Four Diagnostics
Observation
Asking/Hearing
Smelling/Tasting
Palpation

Tuina Chinese Medical Acupressure

Tuina, Traditional Chinese Medicinal Acupressure is one of the four main areas of Chinese medical healthcare, **Chinese herbals, Acupuncture, Tuina and Medical Qi Gong** that have evolved over a three thousand year period from the accumulated knowledge of Chinese treatment methods. Its therapeutic ideology is based on systematic Traditional Chinese Medicine theories covering Yin Yang, Five Phase, Zang Fu, and particularly the theory of the meridians or channels. Clinical treatment takes into consideration the Four Diagnostic Methods, 8 Principles of Diagnosis, and Pattern Identification.

Tuina – a definition

"Tuina is the study and practice of a series of Chinese manual clinical techniques, which are used to prevent and treat disease, based on the principals of Traditional Chinese Medicine". In Tuina, the same Qi points as in acupuncture are used, but are stimulated with finger, thumb, knuckle, elbow pressure instead of with the insertion of needles. The pressure of the manipulation either acts on the body directly or on the channels to regulate diseased organs and tissue. Tuina is used to prevent and treat disease by using a variety of different kinds of manipulation to activate the channels, balance Yin & Yang, regulate the circulation of Qi and Blood, and normalise the function of the Zang Fu. Literally the terms "Tui" means to push or move along and "Na" means to hold or grasp.

A Comprehensive Therapy

Tuina therapy may be used in the treatment of internal and external conditions, traumatic injury, and musculo-skeletal, gynaecological, obstetrics, and paediatric diseases as well as disorders of the eye, ear, nose, and throat. In addition, it can strengthen the body's resistance to disease and prevent invasion of pathogens in healthy people, and especially in the middle aged, elderly and weak.

Simplicity

Most of the manipulations introduced are easy to learn and suitable not only for the experienced medical practitioner, but also for the lay person as long as he or she becomes familiar with the principals of Traditional Chinese Medicine. This is particularly true of paediatrics. Tuina can be performed not only by a physician but also by the parents of the child.

Safe and free from harmful side effects.

Tuina is an external therapy. The manipulations are performed on the surface of the body. This allows the patient to avoid medicines or invasive surgical procedures which may cause other kinds of physical damage. Tuina has almost no side effects if the diagnosis and manipulation are correct. It is very effective for relief of pain.

Inexpensive and convenient

Tuina requires almost no equipment or special medical facilities, so it is an inexpensive therapy. It may be performed anywhere the patient needs medical care, even at home. Costly and difficult hospital visits and care can therefore be avoided.

In common with all Traditional Chinese Medicine therapies, Tuina has its own specific benefits and advantages in practice and treatment. It is becoming more and more popular world-wide as a result.

Foundation of Tuina

There are four aspects that constitute an effective and beneficial Tuina clinical treatment, and these are the foundation of each student's competence and development to master practitioner level.

a) **Appropriate Duration** - i.e. the manipulation techniques are required to last for reasonable period of time.

b) **Appropriate force** – i.e. the practitioner should apply certain amount of force when employing the manipulation. The degree of force mainly depends on the constitution of the patient, the nature of the disease, and location of the disease.

c) **Appropriate rhythm** - i.e. the techniques employed should have good rhythm. Try to avoid using sudden fast or sudden slow rhythm, and sudden strong and sudden light for implementing the techniques.

d) **Gentleness** - i.e. Good Tuina techniques are light but not shallow, strong but not clumsy. Respect the client and the techniques and avoid aggressive force. In addition, try to be natural when changing between different techniques.

A successful and competant practitioner will always bear these aspects in mind while practicing Tuina. Practice and more practice is the key to the competence in achieving these requirements.

Practical Chinese Medicine

Contra-indications and Precautions

"Protect your Patient and your Professional Reputation"

A contraindication is a specific condition or health state in which Tuina should not be used because it. Contraindication is the opposite of indication, which is a reason to use a certain treatment.

1. Severe cardiac, pulmonary, and encephalopathic disease, or extreme constitutional weakness and other special cases where manipulation would be unbearable.

2. A recent history of bleeding or diseases of the Blood, which might lead to internal bleeding after manipulation.

3. Local skin lesions or skin diseases such as leprosy, tinea, scalds, or burns where the skin may be damaged or the condition aggravated by manipulation.

4. Acute communicable diseases; erysipelas, osteomyelitis, bone tuberculosis.

5. Acute spinal injury or other injuries without a clear-cut diagnosis.

6. Pregnancy beyond three months, menstruation, or postpartum lochia.

7. Psychosis or intoxication. Or after over eating

8. Benign and malignant tumours.

9. Severe degenerative disease – severe osteoporosis.

Indications

Here are some of the conditions that Tuina are said to be an effective treatment for. This list is not exhaustive as there are many other chronic and acute conditions that have been effectively treated by Tuina.

Musculo-skeletal diseases and trauma

Sprains and contusions in the soft tissues, dislocation and subluxation *(an incomplete dislocation)* of the joints, non infectious inflammation in the joints, stiff neck, †cervical spondylosis, periarthitis of the shoulder, lumbar sprain, prolapsed of the lumbar intervertebral disc and the sequelae of fractures.

Internal diseases

Epigastric pain, headache, insomnia, chronic bronchitis, cholecystitis, hypertension, cardiac disorders, sequelae *(a condition following as a consequence of a disease)* of CVA *(cardiac vascular accident)*, chronic diarrhoea or constipation.

External diseases

The early stage of mastitis, bed sores, post operative adhesions of the bowel.

Gynaecological and obstetric disease, Dysmenorrhoea, irregular menstruation, PID (pelvic inflammatory disease), post partum separation of the pubis.

Paediatric disease

Fever, cough, diarrhoea, dysentery, vomiting, malnutrition, constipation, retention of urine, night crying, bedwetting, torticollis.

Disease of the eye, ear, nose and throat

Numbness of the tongue, difficulty swallowing, sore throat, myopia *(short-sightedness, nearsightedness)*, strabismus *(cross-eyed, squint)*, presbyopia *(loss of sight in the elderly)*, rhinitis.

Yin and Yang

The philosophy of Yin & Yang is the single most important and distinctive theory of Traditional Chinese Medicine. It is said that all phenomenon including Chinese medical physiology, pathology and treatment can, eventually be broken down to Yin & Yang. The concept is extremely simple, yet very profound. You can seemingly understand it on a rational level, and yet, continually find new expressions of it in clinical practice and indeed, in life. (Maciocia, 1997)

The theory of Yin & Yang, together with that of Qi, pervades Chinese philosophy over the centuries and is radically different to any western philosophical idea. *In general, western logic is based upon the opposition of contraries which is fundamental premise of Aristotelian logic. According to this logic, contraries (such as "The table is square" and "The table is not square") cannot both be true. This has dominated western thought for over 2,000 years. The Chinese concept of Yin & Yang is radically different to this system of thought: Yin and Yang represent opposite but complementary qualities. Each thing or phenomenon could be itself and it's contrary. Moreover Yin contains the seed of Yang and vice versa, so that, contrary to Aristotelian logic, A can also be non-A..* (Giovanni Maciocia).

Yin & Yang can be used to express all things and phenomenon in existence. They are two opposing yet complementary qualities and are in constant motion. Yin contains the seed of Yang and Yang contains the seed of Yin.

The Five Aspect's of Yin & Yang Relationship.

Opposition: Yin & Yang are both opposites, but this is relative to the subject matter i.e. an amateur athlete is Yang compared to a couch potato, but Yin compared to a professional athlete.

Yin & Yang as opposites.

Yin	Yang
Water	Fire
Cold	Hot
Quite	Restless
Soft	Hard
Inhibition	Excitement
Slowness	Rapidity
Descending	Ascending
Inside	Outside
Slow	Fast

Interdependence:

Yin & Yang are totally interdependent in that there cannot be one without the other. i.e.

	Yin		Yang
There is no	Night	without	Day
There is no	Rest	without	Activity
There is no	Cold	without	Hot

Mutual Consumption:

The important part of making this diagnosis is to attempt to differentiate between Full Heat and Empty Heat, and between Full Cold and Empty Cold.

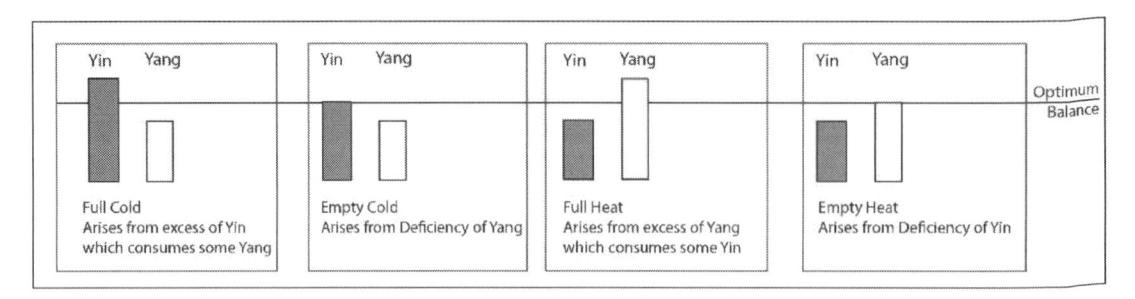

Yin Yang	Yin Yang	Yin Yang	Yin Yang	
Full Cold
Arises from excess of Yin which consumes some Yang	Empty Cold
Arises from Deficiency of Yang	Full Heat
Arises from excess of Yang which consumes some Yin	Empty Heat
Arises from Deficiency of Yin	Optimum Balance

Inter-transformation:

Yin is constantly transforming into Yang and vice versa i.e. A jogger starts out on a run, the body is cold (Yin), after running for a while the body heats up (Yang) and after relaxation the body cools again (Yin).

Infinite Divisibility:

Within one you can always find the other. The seed of one is always found in the other.

Yin and Yang are the single most important principles of Traditional Chinese Medicine. The Chinese characters (above) for Yin and Yang are related to the cloudy and sunny side of a hill. Yang is considered the light and energetic quality while Yin is the dark and slow. The two are opposites, yet they cannot survive without each other, nothing is totally Yin or totally Yang, because Yang contains the seed of Yin and vice versa. The small black and white spots in the Yin Yang symbol represent this. Yin and Yang can measure every facet of life

Clinical expressions of disharmony between Yin and Yang

Excess Yang

Headache, signs of activity, restlessness, heat, thirst, rapid pulse, red tongue.

Deficiency of Yang

Chills, cold limbs, lassitude, no thirst, clear frequent urination, loose stools, tongue is pale and wet, pulse is weak and deep.

Deficiency of Yin

caused by consumption of Body Fluids or Kidney & Liver Yin Deficiency; afternoon fever, malar flush, 5 palm heat, night sweat, Dryness of throat and mouth, dry stools, dry tongue, yellow or no coat, rapid thready pulse,

Excess Yin

Rarely seen in clinic. This can appear as Oedema but the cause is related to other factors.

The Five Elements

The Yin and Yang philosophy was further refined into the system of the five Elements to gain a deeper understanding of how the body, Mind and spirit work. Five Elements (or Five Phases) theory is found recorded in Silk scrolls from the Warring States period (476-221BC).

The microcosm of the body is linked to the universe and is affected by the daily and seasonal cycles of nature. (Think about the seasonal affective disorder which manifests itself in winter or when the light is not sufficient). The individual and the world are changing all the time. But Chinese believe that these changes are occurring in certain order and in cycles. (We can think about these like our economic cycles or agricultural cycles. A period of growth is always followed by a period of stagnation or unemployment. In the stock market, a bull market is always followed by a bear market etc.) In the same way, a seed planted in spring blooms in summer, seeds itself in late summer to autumn, dies in winter, and a new seed grows again in spring. It is part of a never-ending cycle and each phase has its role to play in maintaining the balance of nature. The same process of change occurs within the body. Cells grow and die to make way for new cells, and body systems depend upon each other in a similar way to the seasons, working together to ensure the balanced functioning of the body, Mind and spirit and the healthy flow of vital energy.

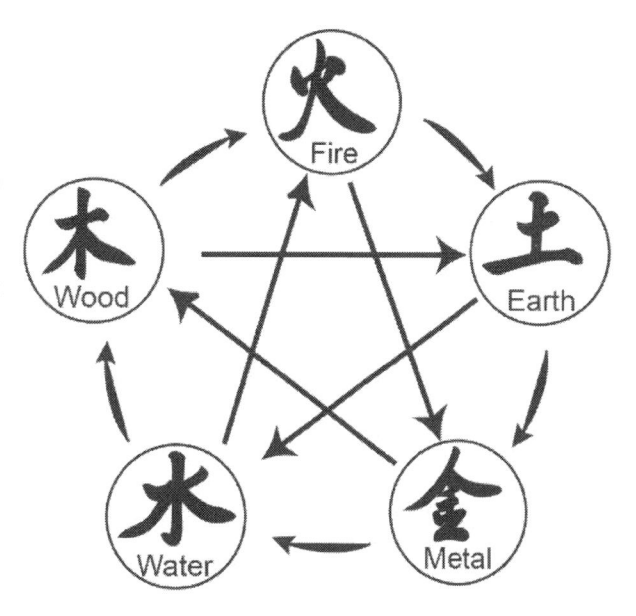

The theory of the Five Elements is an attempt to classify phenomena into a cycle of natural processes. The theory is very simple and based on common sense, that it "Oriental" common sense, as it is most difficult to interpret Oriental culture with a Western frame of reference. The translation comes from "Wu Xing". Wu is the number five and Xing means "walk" or "move" and perhaps more appropriately, it implies a process. Therefore "Wu Xing" are five kinds of processes; hence the Five Elements.

Below as a list of the Elements and their related qualities and functions.

	Wood	**Fire**	**Earth**	**Metal**	**Water**
Season	Spring	Summer	Late Summer	Autumn	Winter
Yin Organ	Liver	Heart	Spleen	Lungs	Kidney
Yang Organ	Gallbladder	Small Intestine	Stomach	Large Intestine	Urinary bladder
Color	Green/ Blue	Red	Yellow	White	Black
Emotion	Anger	Joy	Pensive	Grief/ Sad	Fear
Voice	Shouts	Laughs	Sings	Weeps	Groans
Taste	Sour	Bitter	Sweet	Pungent	Salty
Tissues	Tendons	Blood Vessels	Muscle	Skin	Bones
Orifice	Eyes	Tongue	Mouth	Nose	Ears
Climate	Windy	Hot	Damp	Dry	Cold
Manifests on	Nails	Face	Lips	Body Hair	Hair (head)

It is somewhat a misconception to call the theory Five "Elements" as this implies organic or inorganic matter, however each Phase is normally headed by the elements, Wood, Fire, Earth, Metal and Water, for documentation purposes.

The Five Elements can be used to describe the annual cycle in terms of biological growth and development. Wood corresponds to spring, Fire to summer, Metal to autumn and Water to winter, while Earth represents the transition between each season and is commonly referred to as late summer. An example of the Five Elements cycle is that spring, turns into summer, summer into autumn and autumn into winter.

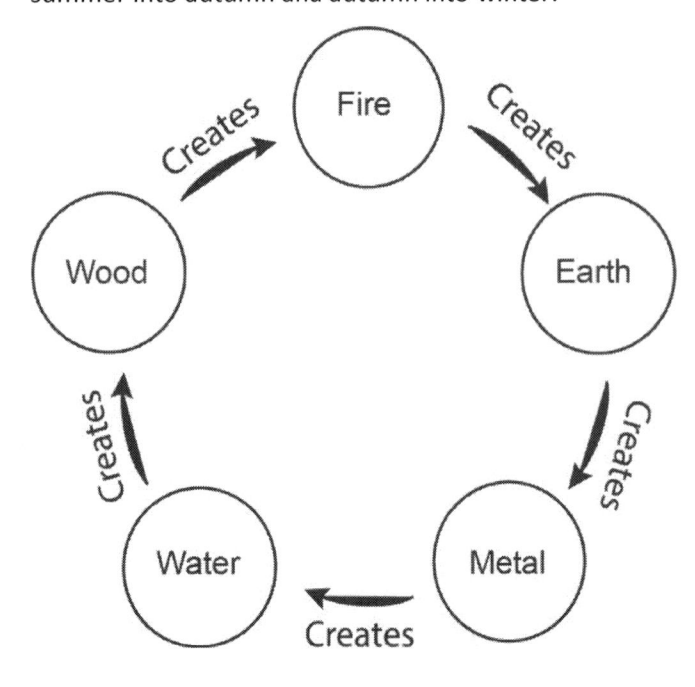

Each person's physical and mental constitution can be described as a balance of the Elements in which one or more may naturally dominate. The proportion of the Elements in a person determines his or her temperament. Oriental medicine considers the ideal condition as one in which all the five Elements are in balance or in harmony.

For thousands years or more the Oriental cultures observed both the external environment and the internal one, and from this study the relationship between the Elements was discovered, and two cycles of action determined. The Creative Cycle and the Controlling Cycle represent the primary actions of the Elements. The Controlling cycle is often mistakenly referred to as the destructive cycle, whereas, all life needs to operate within certain boundaries and this cycle provides them.

Think of a steam engine. The Creative cycle would be the guy shovelling fuel in, it burns, heats the tank and the pressure raises. If no governing valve is fitted the whole thing will explode. Such is life; the Controlling cycle gives us the opportunity to regulate our own existence.

Wood is said to be the mother of Fire and the child of Water. (Water allows wood to grow, wood provides fuel for the Fire). Using these relationships one can describe all possible Yin-Yang imbalances within the body. The thrust of five Phase diagnosis is to isolate and treat the imbalanced Phase, because an imbalanced Phase is like a weak link in your energetic chain that can undermine the strength of your Mind, body and spirit. We can see that Fire creates (feeds) Earth which creates (feeds) Metal and so on.

The pentagram pattern of arrows in the center represent the Controlling cycle. Fire controlling Metal controlling Wood etc. Each Phase has hundreds of attributes.

The Controlling cycle is a supporting role and should not be seen as restraining the other Phase as that would imply disharmony.

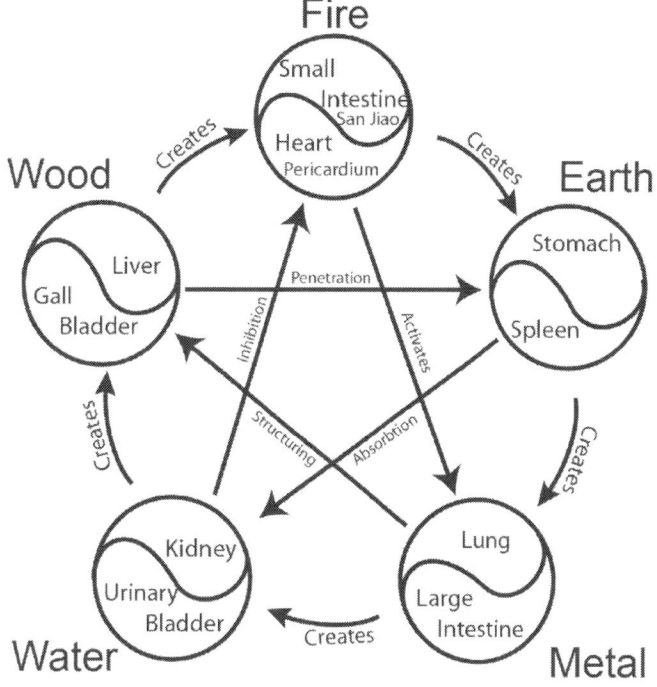

The Vital Substances

The four substances are Qi, Blood, Fluids, and Essence (Jing). Shen is also included in this group.

Qi

The Concept of Qi in Chinese Philosophy, has occupied Chinese philosophers of all times, right from the beginning of Chinese civilization to our modern times. It is the vital energy that circulates throughout the universe. It fills the air we breathe, and the food we eat. It is the life that starts the heart beating and our first breath after leaving our mother's womb.

It is clearly indicated, in the Chinese symbol for Qi (vapour, steam, & rice), that Qi can be as rarefied and immaterial as vapour, and as dense and material as rice. It also indicates that Qi is a subtle substance (steam, vapour) deriving from a coarse one (rice) just as steam is produced by cooking rice.

It is very difficult to translate the word "Qi" and many different ones have been proposed, none of which approximates the essence of Qi exactly. It has variously been translated as "energy", "material force", "matter", "ether", "matter-energy", "vital force", "life force", "vital power", "moving power". The reason it is so difficult to translate the word "Qi" correctly, lies precisely in its fluid nature whereby Qi can assume different manifestations and be different things in different situations.

The way "Qi" is translated also depends on the particular view point taken. Most modern physicists would probably agree that Qi may be termed energy since Qi expresses the continuum of matter and energy as it is now understood by modern particle physics.

Qi is at the basis of all phenomena in the universe and provides continuity between coarse, material forms and tenuous, rarefied non-material energies. Qi produces the human body just as water becomes ice. As water freezes into ice, so Qi coagulates to form the human body. When ice melts it becomes water. When a person dies, he or she becomes spirit again.

The Concept of Qi in Chinese Medicine

Chinese philosophers and doctors saw the interrelationship between the universe and human beings and considered the human being's Qi as a result of the interaction of the Qi of Heaven and Earth. A human being results from the Qi of Heaven and Earth. The union of the Qi of Heaven and Earth is called human being. This stresses the interaction between the human being's Qi and natural forces. Chinese Medicine emphasises the relationship between human beings and their environment and takes this into account in determining aetiology, diagnosis, and treatment.

Traditional Chinese Medicine aims to restore the smooth flow of Qi by stimulating Qi points. It has been shown by scientific research that stimulating these points triggers the body's production of endorphins, naturally occurring substances that ease pain and induce euphoric feelings.

In particular, two aspects of Qi are especially relevant to medicine:

- Qi is an energy which manifests simultaneously on the physical and spiritual level.
- Qi is in a constant state of flux and in varying states of aggregation. When Qi condenses, energy transforms and accumulates into physical shape.

Types of Qi

According to the Chinese there are many different "types" of human Qi, ranging from the tenuous and rarefied, to the very dense and coarse. All the various types of Qi, however, are ultimately one Qi, merely manifesting in different forms.

Within the body there are two basic types of Qi. Original Qi is the Qi that we are born with. It is essentially limited and the quality and amount of this Qi represents our basic constitution. Post Heaven Qi, on the other hand, is derived from the foods we eat and the air that we breathe. The quality of Post Heaven Qi depends on our lifestyle habits such as food quality, balance of emotions, physical exercise and so on.

Pre Heaven Qi is inherited from our parents, it is formed at conception and stored in the Kidneys. It determines our basic constitution, strength and vitality. It can be conserved but it cannot be replenished. It is made up of Essence (Jing) and Yuan Qi.

Post Heaven Qi can be stored and replenished and is composed of Gu Qi (Food Qi) Kong Qi (Air Qi), Zong Qi (Gathering Qi), Zhen Qi (True Qi)

The Formation of Qi

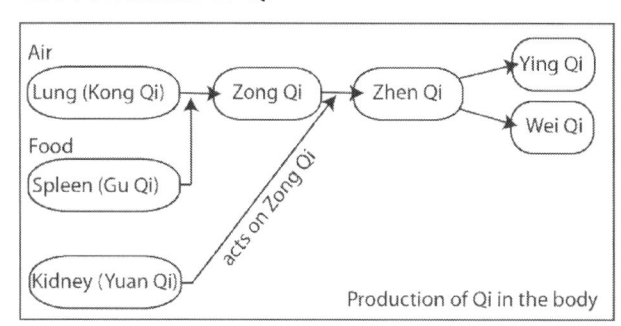

While we use the word Qi to mean energy, it is clear from the Chinese medical theories that there are many aspects and differentiations of Qi. Different types of Qi vary in how they are used by the body and what imbalances are caused by a deficiency. For example, Essence (Jing) deficiency in children may present with signs of slow growth and poor mental development, whereas, a person with a deficiency of Wei Qi may experience frequent colds and/or infections. The various types of Qi and their corresponding sources, functions, distributions and relevance are described below:

Essence

Essence (Jing) is derived from parents and supplemented by Post Heaven Qi. It is responsible for growth, reproduction and development. It is stored mainly in the Kidneys. Weak Jing in children may lead to poor bone development, slow learning or poor concentration. Weak Jing in the elderly may lead to deafness, osteoporosis or unclear thinking.

Yuan Qi

Yuan Qi (Original Qi) is derived from Essence (Jing), its function is to promote and stimulate functional activities of organs. It also acts as the foundation/catalyst for the production of Zhen Qi. It originates in the Ming Men between Kidneys (Du-04), and circulates via the San Jiao, pools in the meridians at the Yuan Source points. Deficiencies in Yuan Qi may lead to poor development of Post Heaven Qi.

Gu Qi

Gu Qi (Food Qi) originates from the action of the Spleen on the food in the Stomach. Some aspects of Gu Qi are transformed into Blood, but most it combines with Kong Qi to form Zong Qi. It arises in the Stomach & Spleen and is moved to the chest where it is further distributed. Good quality food and a strong Stomach & Spleen are important to generate energy. Weaknesses in the Spleen may lead to bloating, distension, fatigue, loss of appetite, etc.

Kong Qi

Ong Qi (Air Qi) originates from the air received by the Lungs. It is distributed from the chest. Good quality air and good breathing practices are essential for the formation of energy.

Zong Qi

Zong Qi (Gathering Qi) is a combination of Gu Qi & Kong Qi. It nourishes the Heart and Lungs. It aids the Lungs in their role of respiration and circulating energy throughout the body. It assists the Heart in circulating Blood through the Vessels. It is stored in the chest. With a deficiency of Zong Qi you will see the Heart and Lung most affected. Low energy, weak voice, poor circulation in the extremities, etc.

Zhen Qi

Zhen Qi (True Qi) is derived from Zong Qi when acted upon by Yuan Qi. Its function is to circulate in the meridians and nourish the organs. It originates in the chest and is distributed throughout the body by respiration. Made up of Ying Qi & Wei Qi. Deficiencies indicate either an imbalance in the functioning of the creation of Post Heaven Qi or in a declining amount of Yuan Qi.

Ying Qi

Ying Qi (Nutritive Qi) nourishes the organs and helps to produce Blood. It circulates in the main meridians. It flows with the Blood in the main meridians and within the Blood Vessels. This is the aspect of Qi that is stimulated with Acupressure and Acupuncture.

Wei Qi

Wei Qi (Defensive Qi) helps to protect the body, warms the surface of the body and regulates body temperature by opening & closing the pores. It is distributed on the surface of the body and within the muscles and skin, but not within the meridians and its circulation is dependent on the Lungs. People who catch colds easily or often have Wei Qi deficiency. Deficiency may also make it difficult to regulate body temperature.

Functions of Qi in the Body

Generally speaking, the Qi serves several vital functions within the body. When imbalances arise, they are seen as disruptions in the functions of Qi. A prolapse, for example, is seen as a disruption in the ability of Qi to provide the raising and stabilizing function on a particular organ. In this case certain acupuncture points which have a strong lifting and stabilizing effect such as Du-20 may be used to help rebalance the body.

The functions of Qi are:

- Activation: Qi assists in the formation and transformations within the body, for example the transformation of food into Qi and Blood. Qi helps to control homeostasis and provides warmth for the body. It activates our 1st breath.

- Protection: It defends the body from external pathogens

- Containment: Qi holds organs in their place, keeps Blood in the Vessels, governs the removal of fluids

- Transportation: Qi is the foundation of all movement and growth in the body.

Pathology of Qi

Qi Deficiency

Qi in traditional Chinese medicine represents energy, movement, motivational force. When we experience a lack of energy, this can be called a Qi Deficiency.

The Spleen, Lung, Kidney and to a lesser extent Heart are involved in the production of Qi, and any disharmony within any of these Zang Fu (Internal Organs), can result in a deficiency of Qi.

The clinical manifestations can include: tiredness, fatigue, lethargy, apathy, exhaustion, disillusionment, dislike to speak, spontaneous sweating, and all these manifestations are made worse on exertion or with exercise. *It is not necessary for the patient to experience all these manifestations. When diagnosing according to Traditional Chinese Medical theory, it cannot be over emphasised the importance of a holistic clinical picture, which includes all symptoms and signs of disharmony.*

Qi Sinking

One of the functions of the Spleen is raising Qi within the body. If Spleen Qi is deficient it can sink, causing prolaspe of the organs. Qi deficiency signs with down-bearing sensation in abdomen.

Qi Stagnation

The Liver is the primary Zang, responsible for moving Qi and when there is disharmony effecting the Liver, Qi can fail to move and stagnate. Clinical manifestations, which normally include some sort of pain, or distension or "stuck feeling" can include: Distended or dull ache in hypochondrium and chest, sighing, hiccup, abdominal distention, feeling of difficulty in swallowing, melancholy, moodiness, fluctuation of mental state, unhappiness, and feeling of lump in throat, painful periods, and distention of breasts before periods, pre menstrual tension, and irritability.

Qi Rebellious

Qi can flow in the wrong direction. This is called "rebellious Qi". For example, Stomach Qi failing to descend and flowing upwards, causing nausea, vomiting, coughing, and belching.

Blood (Xue)

In Chinese medicine has a different meaning than the western Medicine. In Chinese Medicine, it is a form of Qi, a very dense and material one, but Qi nevertheless. Moreover Blood is inseparable from Qi itself. Qi infuses life into Blood; without Qi, Blood would be an inert fluid. Blood sustains the physical mass of the body, it includes a kind of Qi, and also has a non material aspect to it.

The main function of Blood is that of moistening and nourishing the body, it complements the nourishing action of Qi. The Blood ensures that the body tissues do not dry out. For example, Liver Blood moistens the eyes and the sinews, so that the eyes can see properly and the sinews are flexible and healthy.

Blood is also important in another way, it provides the material foundation for the Spirit (Shen). Blood is part of Yin and it houses and anchors the Shen. Blood embraces the Spirit (Shen) and provides the harbour within the Spirit (Shen) can flourish.

Blood - Qi relationship

The Blood Qi relationship is very close. Blood is a kind of Qi, albeit a dense one. Qi is Yang compared to Blood. Qi and Blood are inseparable.

This can be seen in clinical signs following a serious haemorrhage: often in these cases, after a massive loss of Blood, the person develops signs of Qi deficiency, such as breathlessness, sweating, and cold limbs (from Yang deficiency).

On the other hand, after prolonged and heavy sweating (which depletes Qi), one may develop signs of Blood (Xue) deficiency, such as pallor, numbness, dizziness and palpitations.

Four aspects of the Qi - Blood relationship

Qi generates Blood

- Food Qi is the basis of Blood.

Qi moves Blood

- Qi is the motive force for Blood, without Qi, Blood would be an inert material. This is brought home to us in the traditional saying "When Qi moves, Blood follows" and also in "If Qi stagnates, Blood congeals".

Qi holds Blood

- In the Vessels, thus preventing haemorrhage. This is especially true of Spleen Qi.

Blood nourishes Qi

- Qi needs the nourishing qualities of Blood. Blood provides a dense material which prevents Qi from "floating".

"Qi is the commander of Blood, Blood is the mother of Qi"

The Formation of Blood

There are two separate cycles of Blood formation in the body. The Pre-Heaven cycle uses the action of Kidney Yuan Qi to produce Marrow which produces Blood.

The Post-heaven Qi cycle uses Foods and Fluids (Gu Qi) transformed by the Spleen. The Spleen sends this Food Qi upwards to the Lung, and through the pushing action of Lung Qi, this is sent to the Heart, where it is transformed into Blood.

The Formation of Blood

Blood Pathology

Blood deficiency

If there is insufficient Blood to nourish the Zang Fu and Meridians then disharmony resulting in clinical manifestations such as: pale complexion, pallor, pale lips, pale thin and dry tongue, insomnia, dizziness, vertigo, blurring of vision, palpitations, numbness of hands and feet,

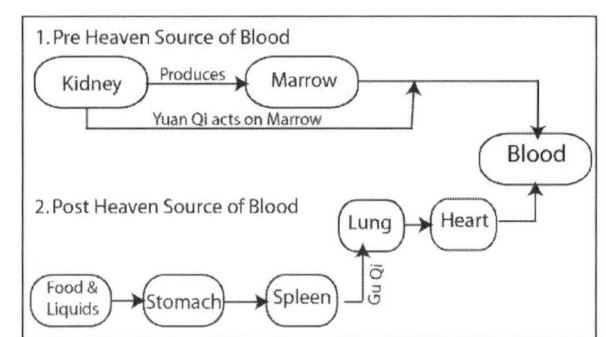

Cause: When there is weakness of the Spleen and Stomach, or Excessive Blood loss, or Drastic emotional changes that consume Body Fluids,

Blood Heat

Blood can be hot, this is mostly due to Liver (Gan) Heat.

Blood Stasis

The Blood can fail to move properly and stagnate. This may be caused by stagnation of Qi, by Heat, or by Cold.

Body Fluids

Fluids (Jin-Ye) are all the fluids except Blood and they moisturise the organs, skin, mucus membrane, eyes, etc. They lubricate the joints, nourish the Brain, Marrow & Bones. They are divided into two categories, (Jin) Pure and (Ye) Impure.

Jin is Pure (thinner, clearer, Watery) and Ye is impure (turbid, heavy, dense)

Impure Fluids are sent inwards and down, pure Fluids are sent deeper and down.

Essence (Jing)

is the basis of all organic life. Essence (Jing) is the blueprint for mental and bodily development.

Essence (Jing) is divided into three aspects.

>Pre Heaven a pre natal substance received from our parents.

>Post Heaven a post natal substance created by food and air.

>Kidney (Shen) Essence (Jing) which is the total Essence (Jing) of the body.

Shen

Shen is the spirit of the person, the ability to think and reason and is often described as the Mind. Shen characterises the forces that shape our personality including mental and spiritual aspects. The Heart houses Shen although the other Zang Fu Organs have connections to Shen. Dsturbances of Shen generally refer to emotional and mental disorders. While Shen is often referred to as the spirit, it should not be confused with the religious idea of the spirit; it is more about a person's mental vitality. Our Shen allows us to think and discriminate, and shapes our personality.

The Zang Fu

Zang Fu is the general term for the organs of the human body, and includes the six Zang organs, the six Fu organs and the Extraordinary Fu organs. The Heart, Lung, Spleen, Liver, Kidney and Pericardium are known as the six Zang organs. The Gallbladder, Stomach, Small Intestine, Large Intestine, Urinary Bladder and San Jiao are known as the six Fu organs. The Brain, Marrow, Bones, Vessels, Gallbladder and Uterus are known as the "Extraordinary Fu" organs. Since the Pericardium is a protective membrane of the Heart, the "Extraordinary Fu" organs pertain respectively to the other Fu organs, it is generally called five Zang and six Fu organs.

The main physiological functions of the Zang organs are to manufacture and store essential substances, including vital Essence (Jing), Qi, Blood and Body Fluids. The main physiological functions of the Fu organs are to receive and digest food, and transmit and excrete the wastes. The eleventh chapter of Su Wen (Plain Questions) says: The so called five Zang organs store pure essential Qi without draining it off, and for this reason they can be filled up but cannot be over filled. The six Fu organs transmit Water and food without storing them, and for this reason they may be over supplied but cannot be filled up

Although the Zang organs are different from the Fu organs in terms of physiological activities, there is a structural and functional connection by the way of meridians and collaterals between individual Zang and Fu organ, between the Zang and Fu organs collectively and between the Zang Fu organs on the one hand, and the five sense organs and tissues on the other.

The theory of the Zang Fu organs considers the physiological functions and pathological changes of the Zang and Fu organs, as well as their interrelationships. This theory was called "Zang Xian" by ancient doctors. "Zang" refers to the interior location of the Zang Fu organs, and "Xian" denotes their manifestations or "image." In other words, the Zang Fu organs are located on the inside of the body, but their physiological activities and pathological changes are reflected on the exterior. The book Classified Classics by Zhang Jiebin (1562 - 1639) states "The Zang Fu organs are situated interiorly and manifested exteriorly therefore the theory of the Zang Fu organs is called Zang Xiang."

There are two main aspects to the theory of the Zang Fu organs. Firstly the study of the physiological functions and pathological changes of the Zang Fu organs, tissues and their interrelationships. Secondly the physiology and pathology of vital Essence (Jing), Qi, Blood and Body Fluids, as well as the relationship between these on the one hand and the Zang Fu organs on the other.

Ancient anatomical knowledge

The twelfth chapter of Ling Shu (Miraculous Pivot) says: "A man is about eight Chi tall in average, the external size of the body is measurable because its skin and flesh are visible, and also his pulse may be taken in different regions. The Tongue and Pulse are considered the Pillars of Diagnosis because they allow us to see inside the body. The Zang Fu have been observed by the external manifestations of their functions. Each clinical picture are measured by asking, listening, observing, smelling and palpating.

Observation of physiological and pathological phenomena. An example is the development of the theory that the skin and hair are connected with the nose and Lung, through observation of cases of common Cold due to invasion of the exterior of the body by pathogenic Cold. Typical symptoms of nasal obstruction, runny nose, chills, fever and cough demonstrate this connection.

An example is the development of the theory of the Kidney dominating bone. In the treatment of fracture, application of the method of invigorating the Kidney may hasten the healing of bone.

Zang (organs)	**Fu (organs)**
Heart (*Xin*)	Small Intestine (*Xiao Chang*)
Pericardium (*Xin Bao*)	San Jiao
Liver (*Gan*)	Gallbladder (*Dan*)
Spleen (*Pi*)	Stomach (*Wei*)
Lung (*Fei*)	Large Intestine (*Da Chang*)
Kidney (*Shen*)	Urinary Bladder (*Pang Guang*)

The Heart (Xin)

The Heart is situated in the thorax and its meridian connects with the Small Intestine with which it is internally externally related. The main physiological functions of the Heart are: dominating the Blood and Vessels, manifesting on the complexion, housing the Mind, and opening into the tongue.

Dominating the Blood and Blood Vessels and manifesting on the face.

This means that the Heart is the motive force for Blood circulation, whereas the Blood Vessels are the physical structures which contain and circulate the Blood. The Blood circulation relies on cooperation between the Heart and the Blood Vessels, with the Heart being of primary importance. In the forty - fourth chapter of Su Wen (Plain Questions) it is stated: *"The Heart dominates the Blood and Blood Vessels"*

The functions of the Heart in propelling the Blood relies on Heart Qi. When the Heart Qi is strong, the Blood will circulate normally in the Vessels to supply the whole body. Since the Heart, Blood and Vessels are interconnected and there are many Vessels on the face, the health or decline of the Heart Qi and the amount of Blood circulating will be reflected in changes in both the pulse and complexion. If the Heart Qi is vigorous and the Blood ample, the pulse will be regular and strong and the complexion rosy. When the Heart Qi and Blood are deficient, the pulse will be thready and weak, and the complexion pale. As the ninth chapter of Su Wen (Plain Questions) says: "The glory of the Heart is manifested on the face, since the Blood fills up the Vessels."

Housing the Mind

The word "Mind" has the broad meaning of the outward appearance of the vital activities of the whole body, and the narrow meaning of consciousness, e.g. spirit and thinking. The theory of the Zang Fu organs holds that thinking is related to the five Zang organs and principally to the physiological functions of the Heart. The seventy - first chapter of Ling Shu (Miraculous Pivot) says: *"The Heart is the residence of the spirit."* The eighth chapter in the same book also says: *"The Mind is responsible for the performance of activities."*

This shows that mental activities and thinking have their foundation in the functions of the Heart. Spirit, consciousness, thinking, memory and sleep are therefore all related to the function of the Heart in housing the Mind. Blood is the main material basis for mental activities. It is controlled as well as dominated and regulated by the Heart. So the function of the Heart in housing the Mind is closely related to that of the Heart in controlling the Blood and Vessels. Therefore it is stated in the same chapter, "The Heart dominates Vessels and the Vessels house Mind"

Opening into the tongue

"Opening" refers to the close structural, physiological and pathological relationship between a particular Zang and one of the sense organs. The tongue is connected to the Heart Meridian interiorly and via this connection the Heart dominates the sense of taste and the speech. When the function of the Heart is normal, the tongue will be rosy, moist and lustrous, the sense of taste will be normal, and the tongue will move freely. On the other hand, disorders of the Heart will reflect on the tongue. For example, deficiency of Heart Blood may give rise to a pale tongue, flaring up of Heart Fire may give rise to redness of the tongue tip and ulceration of the tongue body; stagnation of Heart Blood may give rise to a dark, purplish tongue body or purplish spots on the tongue. The saying: "the Heart opens into the tongue" and "the tongue is the mirror of the Heart" reflect this close physio / pathological relationship.

The Pericardium (Xin Bao)

The Pericardium, known as "xin bao luo" is a membrane surrounding the Heart. Its meridian connects with the San Jiao with which it is externally internally related. Its main function is to protect the Heart. When pathogenic Qi invades the Heart, the Pericardium is always the first to be attacked, and invasion of the Pericardium by pathogenic Qi will often affect the normal function of the Heart. For example, invasion of the interior by pathogenic mild Heat, which gives rise to symptoms of mental derangement such as coma and delirium, is described as "invasion of the Pericardium by pathogenic Heat," although the clinical manifestations are the same as those of the Heart. For this reason, the Pericardium is not generally regarded as an independent organ, but as an attachment to the Heart.

The Liver (Gan)

The Liver is situated in the right hypochondriac region. Its meridian connects with the Gallbladder with which it is internally externally related. Its main physiological functions are storing Blood, maintaining the free flow of Qi, and controlling the tendons, manifesting in the nails and opening into the eye.

Storing Blood

The Liver stores Blood and regulates the volume in circulation. The volume of Blood circulating in various parts of the body changes according to different physiological needs. During vigorous movement and other daytime activities, the Blood is released from the Liver, increasing the volume of Blood in circulation. During rest and sleep, the volume of Blood required decreases and part of the Blood remains in the Liver. As Wang Bing said in the explanation on the tenth chapter of Su Wen (Plain Questions): *"The Liver stores Blood ... the Blood circulates in the Vessels during exertion and remains in the Liver during rest."*

Because of its function of regulating the volume of circulating Blood, the Liver is closely related to all the activities of the Zang Fu organs and tissues. When the Liver is diseased, dysfunction of the Liver in storing Blood will affect the normal activities of the body, and lead to pathological changes of the Blood itself. For example, deficiency of Liver Blood may give rise to blurred vision, spasm and convulsion of the tendons and muscles, numbness of the four limbs and amenorrhoea in females.

Maintaining the Smooth smooth flow of Qi

The Liver is responsible for the unrestricted, free going, and harmonious functional activity of all the Zang Fu organs, including itself. The normal character of the Liver is to "flourish" and to dislike depression. Stagnation of Liver Qi due to emotional changes may affect the function of the Liver in maintaining the smooth flow of Qi, manifesting in the following three ways:

The Liver and emotional activity

In addition to the Heart, emotional activity is closely related to the Liver Qi. Only when the function of the Liver in maintaining the free flow of Qi is normal can the Qi and Blood is harmonious and the Mind at ease. Dysfunction of the Liver, therefore, is often accompanied by emotional changes such as mental depression or excitement. When Liver Qi stagnates, for example, there may be mental depression, paranoia, or even weeping, when Liver Qi is hyperactive, there may be irritability, insomnia, dream-disturbed sleep, dizziness and vertigo. Whilst dysfunction of the Liver often leads to emotional changes, at the same time prolonged excessive mental irritation often leads to dysfunction of the Liver in maintaining the free flow of Qi.

The Liver function and digestion

The Liver function of maintaining the free flow of Qi is related not only to the ascending and descending function of the Stomach and Spleen, but also to the secretion of bile. The Liver therefore has an important influence on digestion. Dysfunction of the Liver may affect the secretion and excretion of bile, and the digestive function of the Spleen and Stomach, resulting in dyspepsia. When the Liver fails to maintain the free flow of Qi, there may be symptoms of stagnation of Liver Qi such as distending pain of the chest and hypochondrium, mental depression or irritability. If the descending function of the Stomach is affected, there may also be belching, nausea and vomiting, and if the Spleen's function of transportation and transformation is affected, there may be abdominal distension and diarrhoea. The former is called "attack of the Stomach by Liver Qi" and the latter "disharmony of the Liver and Spleen."

The Liver function and Qi and Blood

The Blood circulation relies upon the propelling function of Qi. Although the Heart and Lung play the main role in the circulation of Qi and Blood, the function of the Liver in maintaining the free flow of Qi is also needed to prevent stagnation of Qi and Blood. Stagnation of Qi and Blood due to the failure of the Liver in maintaining the free flow of Qi may lead to stuffiness and pressure in the chest, distending or pricking pain in the hypochondriac region, dysmenorrhoea, and even the formation of palpable mass.

Controlling the tendons and ligaments and manifesting in the nails

The sinews today called tendons and ligaments are the main tissues linking the joints and muscles and dominating the movement of the limbs. Since the Liver nourishes the tendons of the whole body to maintain their normal physiological activities, when Liver Blood is consumed, it may deprive the tendons of nourishment and give rise to weakness of the tendons, numbness of the limbs, and dysfunction of the joints in contraction and relaxation. When the tendons are invaded by pathogenic Heat of the Liver, there may be convulsion of the four extremities, †opisthotonus and clenching of the teeth.

Manifesting in the nail mean that the state of the Yin and Blood of the Liver affects not only the movement of the tendons but also the condition of the nails. When Liver Blood is ample, the tendons and nails are strong, and when Liver Blood is deficient, the tendons will be weak and the nails soft and thin, withered, or even deformed and chipped. The tenth chapter of Su Wen (Plain Questions) therefore says: "The Liver controls the tendons and manifests in the nails."

Opening into the eye

In the eightieth chapter of Ling Shu (Miraculous Pivot), it says: "The essential Qi of the Five Zang and six Fu organs flows upward to enter into the eyes to generate vision."

Of the five Zang and six Fu organs, the Liver is the main organ affecting the eyes and vision. The Liver stores Blood and its meridian ascends to connect with the eyes. Therefore, the seventeenth chapter of Ling Shu (Miraculous Pivot) says: "The Liver Qi is in communication with the eyes."

Whether the Liver function is normal or not often reflects on the eye. For example, deficiency of the Yin and Blood of the Liver may lead to Dryness of the eyes, blurred vision or even night blindness. Wind heal in the Liver Meridian may give rise to redness, swelling and pain of the eyes.

The Spleen (Pi)

The Spleen is situated in the middle Jiao. Its meridian connects with the Stomach, with which it is internally externally related. Its main physiological functions are governing transportation and transformation, controlling Blood, dominating the muscles and limbs, opening into the mouth and manifesting on the lips.

Governing transportation and transformation

Transportation implies transmission and transformation implies digestion and absorption. This function of the Spleen involves transportation and transformation of Water and food on the one hand, and of Dampness on the other.

The function of the Spleen in transporting and transforming essential substances refers to the digestion, absorption and transmission of nutrient substance. Since Water and food are the main source of the nutrient substance required by the body after birth, as well as being the main material base for the manufacture of Qi and Blood, the Spleen is considered to be the main Zang organ for the manufacture of Qi and Blood. When Spleen Qi is vigorous, digestion, absorption and transmission are normal. Deficiency of Spleen Qi and dysfunction of the Spleen in transportation and transformation may lead lo poor appetite, abdominal distension, loose stools, lassitude, emaciation and malnutrition.

The function of the Spleen in transporting and transforming Dampness refers to the Spleen's role in Water metabolism. The Spleen transports the excess fluid of the meridians, tissues and organs and helps discharge it from the body. It ensures that the various tissues of the body are both properly moistened and at the same time free from retention of Dampness. Dysfunction of the Spleen in transportation and transformation may lead to retention of Dampness, with such clinical manifestations as oedema, diarrhoea, Phlegm and retained fluid.

The Spleen's functions of transporting and transforming Water and food on the one hand, and Water Damp on the other are interconnected, and failure of the transportation and transformation function may give rise to clinical manifestations of either. The transportation and transformation function of the Spleen relies on Spleen Qi, which is characterized by ascending. If the Spleen Qi does not ascend, or indeed sinks, there may be vertigo, blurred vision, and prolapse of the rectum after prolonged diarrhoea, or prolapse of various other internal organs. Treatment is aimed at strengthening the ascending function of Spleen Qi.

Controlling Blood

Controlling Blood means that the Spleen Qi has the function of keeping the Blood circulating in the Vessels and preventing bruising. When the Spleen Qi is strong, the source for the manufacture of Blood will also be strong, there will be ample Qi and Blood in the body and the Blood will be prevented from leaving the vessels. If the Spleen Qi is weak and fails to control Blood, there may be various kinds of haemorrhage, such as bloody stool, uterine bleeding and †purpura.

Dominating the muscles and four limbs

The Spleen transports and transforms the Essence (Jing) of food and Water to nourish the muscles and the four limbs. Adequate nourishment ensures well - developed muscles and proper function of the limbs. If nourishment is inadequate, the muscles of the four limbs will. Be weak and soft. The forty - fourth chapter of Su Wen (Plain Question) therefore says: "The Spleen is in charge of muscles."

Opening into the mouth and manifesting on the lips

The Spleen's function of transportation and transformation is closely related to food intake and the sense of taste. When the Spleen functions normally, there will be good appetite and a normal sense of taste, when there is dysfunction of the Spleen, there will be poor appetite, impaired sense of taste and a sticky, sweetish sensation in the mouth due to retention of pathogenic Damp in the Spleen.

The Spleen dominates muscles, and the mouth is the opening of the Spleen. For this reason, the lips reflect the condition of the Spleen's function of transporting and transforming Water and food. When the Spleen is healthy, there will be ample Qi and Blood and the lips will be red and lustrous. Deficiency of Spleen Qi will lead to deficiency of Qi and Blood, and the lips will be pale or sallow.

The Lung (Fei)

The Lung situated in the thorax, communicates with the throat and opens into the nose. It occupies the uppermost position among the Zang Fu organs, and is known as the "canopy" of the Zang Fu organs. Its meridian connects with the Large Intestine with which it is internally externally related. Its main physiological functions are dominating Qi, controlling respiration, dominating dispersing and descending, dominating skin and body hair and regulating the Water passages.

Dominating Qi and controlling respiration

Dominating Qi has two aspects: dominating the Qi of respiration and dominating the Qi of the whole body.

Dominating the Qi of respiration means that the Lung is a respiratory organ through which the Qi from the exterior and the Qi from the interior are able to blend together. Through the Lung, the human body inhales clear Qi from the natural environment and exhales waste Qi from the interior of the body. This is known as "getting rid of the stale and taking in the fresh." The fifth chapter of Su Wen (Plain Questions) says; "The Qi of heaven is in communication with the Lung."

Dominating the Qi of the whole body means that the function of the Lung in respiration greatly influences the functional activities of the whole body and is closely related to the formation of Zong Qi, which is formed from the combination of the essential Qi of Water and food, and the clear Qi inhaled by the Lung. It accumulates in the chest, ascends to the throat to dominate respiration, and is distributed to the whole body in order to maintain the normal functions of the tissues and organs. The tenth chapter of Su Wen (Plain Questions) says: "All kinds of Qi belong to the Lung."

When the function of the Lung in dominating Qi is normal, the passage of Qi will be unobstructed and respiration will be normal and smooth. Deficiency of the Lung Qi may lead to general lassitude, feeble speech, weak respiration and shortness of breath.

Dominating dispersing, skin and hair

Dispersing here means distributing. It is by the dispersing function of the Lung that defensive Qi and Body Fluids are distributed to the whole body to warm and moisten the muscles, skin and hair. The thirtieth chapter of Ling Shu (Miraculous Pivot) says: "Qi refers to the substance that originates in the upper Jiao, spreads the essential part of Water and food, warms the skin, fills up the body and moistens the hair, like irrigation by fog and dew."

The skin and hair, located on the surface of the body and including the sweat glands, serve as a protective screen to defend the body from exogenous pathogenic factors. The skin and hair are warmed and nourished by Wei (defensive) Qi and Body Fluids distributed by the Lung, which controls respiration. The pores of the skin also have the function of dispersing Qi and regulating respiration. Traditional Chinese medicine says: "the Lung dominates skin and body hair" and "the pores are the gate of Qi."

The close physiological relationship between the lung, skin and hair means that they often affect each other pathologically. For example, exogenous pathogenic factors often invade the Lung through the skin and hair, giving rise to symptoms such as aversion to Cold, fever, nasal obstruction and cough, reflecting failure of the Lung in dispersing. If Lung Qi is deficient, failure of the Lung in dispersing the Qi of Water and food can result in the skin becoming pale and sallow and lead to deficiency of the anti-pathogenic Qi and hence susceptibility to catching Cold. When Lung Qi fails to protect the surface of the body, there may be frequent spontaneous perspiration.

The Lung dominates descending and regulates the Water passages

As a general rule, the upper Zang Fu organs have the function of descending, and the lower Zang Fu organs the function of ascending. Since the Lung is the uppermost Zang organ, its Qi descends to promote the circulation of Qi and Body Fluids through the body and to conduct them downwards. Dysfunction of the Lung in descending may lead to upward rebellious of Lung Qi with symptoms such as cough and shortness of breath.

Regulating the Water passages means to regulate the pathways for the circulation and excretion of Water. The role of the Lung in promoting and maintaining Water metabolism depends on the descending function of Lung Qi. Dysfunction may result in †dysuria, †oliguria and oedema.

Opening into the nose

The nose is the pathway for respiration. The respiratory and olfactory functions of the nose depend on Lung Qi. When Lung Qi is normal, the respiration will be free and the sense of smells acute. Dysfunction of the Lung in dispersing, for example, due to invasion by Wind Cold, will lead to nasal obstruction, runny nose, and †anosmia. Excessive pathogenic Heat in the Lung will lead to shortness of breath and vibration of the ala nasi.

Since the throat is also a gateway of respiration and an organ of speech, through which the Lung Meridian passes, the flow of Qi and the speech are directly affected by the state of the Lung Qi. When the Lung is diseased, it usually causes pathological changes in the throat, such as hoarse voice and †aphonia.

The Kidney (Shen)

The Kidneys are located at either side of the lumbers, which is therefore described as "the home of the Kidney." The Kidney Meridian connects with the Urinary Bladder with which it is internally externally related. Its main functions are: to store Essence (Jing) and dominate human reproduction and development, dominate Water metabolism and the reception of Qi, produce Marrow to fill up the Brain, dominate bone, manufacture Blood, manifest in the hair, open into the ear, and dominate anterior and posterior orifices.

Storing Essence (Jing) and dominating development and reproduction

"Essence (Jing)" is the material base of the human body and of many of its functional activities. Kidney Essence (Jing) consists of two parts: Pre-Heaven and Post-Heaven. Pre-Heaven Essence

(Jing) is inherited from the parents, and Post-Heaven Essence (Jing) is transformed from the essential substances of food by the Spleen and Stomach. The Pre-Heaven and Post-Heaven Essence (Jing) relies on, and promotes, each other. Before birth, Pre-Heaven Essence (Jing) has prepared the material base for Post-Heaven Essence (Jing). After birth, Post-Heaven Essence (Jing) constantly replenishes Pre-Heaven Essence (Jing). Of the two, Post-Heaven Essence (Jing) is the most important.

The function of the Kidney in reproduction and development relies entirely on Kidney Qi. In other words, the ability to reproduce, grow and develop is related to the prosperity or decline of the essential Qi of the Kidney.

In childhood the essential Qi of the Kidney develops gradually and manifests in changes in the skin and hair. It flourishes in adolescence and at this time males will have seminal emission and females the onset of menstruation, reflecting the ripening of the sexual function. In old age the essential Qi of the Kidney declines, reproductive ability and sexual function finally disappear, and the body begins to fail. The first chapter of Su Wen (Plain Questions) says; "At the age of fourteen, a woman will begin to menstruate, her Ren Meridian begins to flow, and the Qi in the Chong Meridian begins to flourish. That is why she is capable of becoming pregnant.... At the age of forty - nine, the Qi of the Ren Meridian declines, the Qi of the Chong Meridian becomes weak and scanty, the sexual energy becomes exhausted and menstruation stops, with the result that her body becomes old and she can no longer become pregnant."

It also says: "At the age of sixteen, the Kidney Qi of a man becomes even more abundant, his sexual function begins to develop, and he is filled with semen that he can ejaculate. When he has sexual intercourse with a woman, she can have children. At the age of fifty six, sexual energy begins to decline, the semen becomes scanty, and the Kidney weak, with the result that all parts of the body begins to age. At the age of sixty four teeth and hair are gone."

These quotations clearly reflect the role played by the Kidney in dominating human growth, development and reproduction. This is why the Kidney is considered to be "the Pre-Heaven foundation" and why traditional Chinese medicine attaches such great importance to it.

The essential Qi of the Kidney includes Kidney Essence (Jing) and the Kidney Qi transformed from Kidney Essence (Jing). The transformation of Kidney Qi from Kidney Essence (Jing) relies on the evaporating function of Kidney Yang upon Kidney Yin. Both Kidney Yin and Kidney Yang take the essential Qi stored in the Kidney as their material base. The essential Qi of the Kidney therefore involves both Kidney Yin and Kidney Yang.

Kidney Yin is the foundation of the Yin fluid of the whole body, which moistens and nourishes the Zang Fu organs and tissues. Kidney Yang is the foundation of the Yang Qi of the whole body, which warms and promotes the functions of the Zang Fu organs and tissues. Yin and Yang are both lodged in the Kidney, which was therefore said to be "the house of Water and Fire" by the ancients. According to their nature, Essence (Jing) is Yin, and Qi is Yang, so Kidney Essence (Jing) is sometimes called Kidney Yin and Kidney Qi is sometimes called Kidney Yang. Kidney Yin and Kidney Yang both restrict and promote each other in the human body so as to maintain a dynamic physiological balance. Once this balance is disrupted, pathological changes due to imbalance of Yin and Yang in the Kidney will manifest. If Kidney Yin is deficient through exhaustion, it will fail to control Yang, which becomes hyperactive. Typical symptoms are Heat sensations of the chest, palms and soles, afternoon fever, night sweats, and seminal emission in males or sexual dreams in females. If Kidney Yang is deficient, leading to failure in warming and promoting, there may be symptoms such as lack of spirit, coldness and pain in the lumbar region and knees, aversion to Cold, Cold limbs, and impotence in men and frigidity and infertility in women. If Kidney deficiency is not accompanied by obvious Cold symptoms, it is usually called Kidney Qi Deficiency or Kidney Essence (Jing) Deficiency.

Dominating Water metabolism

Dominating Water metabolism means that the Kidney plays an extremely important role in regulating the distribution of Body Fluids. Such a function relies on the Qi activity of the Kidney. When the Qi activity of the Kidney is normal, then the "opening and closing" of the Kidney will also be normal. The Stomach first receives Water, and then transmitted by the Spleen to the Lung, which disperses and descends it. Part of the fluid reaches the Kidney where it is further divided into two parts - the clear and the turbid by the Qi activity of Kidney Yang. The clear fluid is transmitted up to the Lung from which it is circulated to the Zang Fu organs and the tissues of the body. The turbid flows into the Urinary Bladder to form urine, which is then excreted. The function of the Kidney dominates this whole metabolic process. If the Kidney fails to open and close, then disturbance of Water metabolism such as oedema or abnormal urination will occur.

Receiving Qi

Receiving Qi means that the Kidney assists the Lung in its function of receiving and descending the Qi. The book Direct Guidebook of Medicine states: "The Lung is the governor of Qi and the Kidney is the root of Qi."

In other words, respiration depends not only on the descending function of the Lung, but also on the Kidney's function of reception and control. Only when the Kidney Qi is strong can the passage of Qi in the Lung be free, and the respiration smoothes and evens. If Kidney Qi is weak, the root of the Qi is not firm, and the Kidney will fail to receive Qi, giving rise to shortness of breath and difficult inhalation, which is worse after movement.

Dominating bone, manufacturing Marrow to fill up the Brain and manifesting in the hair

The Kidney stores Essence (Jing), which produces Marrow. The Marrow develops in the bone cavities and nourishes their growth and development. When Kidney Essence (Jing) is sufficient, the bone Marrow has a rich source of production and the Bones are well nourished, firm and hard. If the Kidney Essence (Jing) is deficient, it will fail to nourish the Bones, leading to weakness and soreness of the lumbar region and knees, weakness or even atrophy of the feet, and underdevelopment. Since the Kidney dominates bone, and the teeth are the surplus of bone, ample Kidney Essence (Jing) will result in strong healthy teeth, whilst deficiency of Kidney Essence (Jing) will lead to loose or even falling teeth.

The Marrow consists of two parts: spinal Marrow and bone Marrow. The spinal Marrow ascends to connect with the Brain, which is formed by the collection of Marrow. The thirty - third chapter of Ling Shu (Miraculous Pivot) therefore states: "The Brain is the sea of Marrow."

Essence (Jing) and Blood promote each other. When the Essence (Jing) is sufficient, then Blood will flourish. The nourishment of the hair is dependent on a sufficient supply of Blood, but its vitality is rooted in the Kidney Qi. The hair, therefore, is both the surplus of Blood on the one hand, and the outward manifestation of the Kidney on the other. Growth or loss of hair, its lustre or withering is all related to the condition of the Kidney Qi. During the prime of life, the Kidney Qi is in a flourishing state and the hair is lustrous, in old age the Kidney Qi declines and the hair turns white and falls. The tenth chapter of Su Wen (Plain Questions) states: "The Kidney dominates bone and manifests on the hair."

Opening into the ear and dominating anterior and posterior orifices

The function of the ear in dominating hearing relies on nourishment by the essential Qi of the Kidney. The ear therefore pertains to the Kidney. When the essential Qi of the Kidney is sufficient, the ear is well nourished and hearing is acute. When the essential Qi of the Kidney is deficient, it will fail to ascend to the ear leading to tinnitus and deafness.

Anterior orifice refers to the urethra and genitalia, which have the function of urination and reproduction. Posterior orifice refers to the anus, which has the function of excreting the faeces. Although the discharge of urine is a function of the Urinary Bladder, it also relies on the Qi activity of the Kidney, as do the reproductive function and the excretion of faeces. Decline or deficiency of Kidney Qi, therefore, may give rise to frequency of urination, †enuresis, †oliguria and †anuria; seminal emission, impotence, premature ejaculation and infertility in reproduction.

The Gallbladder (Dan)

The Gallbladder is attached to the Liver with which it is externally - internally related. Its main function is to store bile and continuously excrete it to the intestines to aid digestion. When the function of the Gallbladder is normal, its Qi descends. Since the bile is bitter in taste and yellow in colour, upward rebellious of Gallbladder Qi may give rise to a bitter taste in the mouth, vomiting of bitter fluid, and failure to aid the Stomach and Spleen in digestion, resulting in abdominal distension and loose stools. Since this function of the Gallbladder is closely related to the Liver's function of maintaining the free flow of Qi, it is said that the Liver and Gallbladder together have the function of maintaining the free flow of Qi. Similarly, the relation of the Liver to emotional changes is shared by the Gallbladder, and this is often taken into account in the clinic when treating symptoms such as fear and palpitations, insomnia and dream - disturbed sleep.

Although the Gallbladder is one of the six Fu organs, unlike the other five it stores bile and does not receive Water or food. For this reason it is also classified as one of the "Extraordinary Fu."

The Stomach (Wei)

The Stomach is located in the epigastrium. It connects with the oesophagus above, and with the Small Intestine below. Its upper outlet is the cardiac, called Shangwan, and its lower outlet is the pylorus - known as Xiawan. Between Shangwon and Xiawan is Zhongwan. These three areas together make up the epigastrium. The Stomach Meridian is connected with the Spleen with which it is externally - internally related. Its main function is to receive and decompose food (Rotten and Ripen food). Food enters the mouth, passes through the oesophagus, and is received by the Stomach where it is decomposed and transmitted down to the Small Intestine. Its essential substances are transported and transformed by the Spleen to supply the whole body. The Stomach and Spleen, therefore, act in conjunction and are the main organs carrying out the functions of digestion and absorption. Together they are known as the "Post-Heaven foundation."

When the function of the Stomach is normal, its Qi descends. If the descending function is disturbed, there will be lack of appetite, distending pain in the epigastrium, nausea and vomiting.

The Small Intestine (Xiao Chang)

The Small Intestine is located in the abdomen. Its upper end connects with the Stomach, and its lower end with the Large Intestine. The Small Intestine Meridian communicates with the Heart with which it is externally - internally related. Its main functions are reception and digestion. It receives and further digests the food from the Stomach, separates the clear from the turbid, and absorbs essential substance and part of the Water from the food, transmitting the residue of the food to the Large Intestine, and of the Water to the Urinary Bladder. Since the Small Intestine has the function of separating the clear from the turbid, dysfunction may not only influence digestion, but also give rise to an abnormal bowel movement and disturbance of urination.

The Large Intestine (Da Chang)

The Large Intestine is located in the abdomen. Its upper end connects with the Small Intestine via the ileocecum, and its lower end is the anus. The Large Intestine Meridian communicates with the Lung with which it is externally - internally related. The main function of the Large Intestine is to receive the waste material sent down from the Small Intestine, absorb its fluid content, and form the remainder into faeces to be excreted. Pathological changes of the Large Intestine will lead to dysfunction in this transportation function, resulting in loose stools or constipation.

The Urinary Bladder (Pang Guang)

The Urinary Bladder is located in the lower abdomen. Its meridian connects with the Kidney with which it is externally - internally related. The main function of the Urinary Bladder is the temporary storage of urine, which is discharged from the body through Qi activity when a sufficient quantity has been accumulated. This function of the Urinary Bladder is performed with the assistance of the Kidney Qi. Disease of the Urinary Bladder will lead to symptoms such as anuria, urgency of urination and dysuria, failure of the Urinary Bladder to control urine may lead to frequency of urination, incontinence of urine and enuresis

The San Jiao

The San Jiao is located "separately from the Zang Fu organs and inside the body." It is divided into three parts: the upper Jiao, middle Jiao and lower Jiao. Its meridian connects with the Pericardium with which it is externally - internally related. Its main functions are to govern various forms of Qi, and serve as the passage for the flow of Yuan Qi and Body Fluids. Yuan Qi originates in the Kidney, but requires the San Jiao as its pathway for distribution in order to stimulate and promote the functional activities of the Zang Fu organs and tissues of the whole body. The chapter Sixty - sixth Question of Classics on Medical Problems, therefore, says: "The San Jiao is the ambassador of Yuan Qi. It circulates the three Qi and distributes them to the five Zang and six Fu organs."

The digestion, absorption, distribution and excretion of food and Water are performed by the joint efforts of various Zang Fu organs, including the San Jiao. The chapter The Thirty - first Question in the book of Classics on Medical Problems says: "The San Jiao is the passage of Water and food."

It is also mentioned in the eighth chapter of Su Wen (Plain Questions): "The San Jiao is the irrigation official who builds Waterways."

The upper, middle and lower Jiao combine with their related Zang Fu organs and each function differently in order to carry out the digestion, absorption, distribution and excretion of Water and food. The upper Jiao dominates dispersion and distribution. In other words, in combination with the distributing function of the Heart and Lung, the upper Jiao distributes the essential Qi of Water and food to the whole body in order to warm and nourish the skin and muscles, tendons and Bones, and regulate the skin and pores. This function is described in the eighteenth chapter of Ling Shu (Miraculous Pivot): "The upper Jiao is like a fog."

Here *fog* is used to describe the all pervading vapour like state of the clear and light essential Qi of Water and food.

The middle Jiao dominates digestion of Water and food and refers to the functions of the Spleen and Stomach in digesting food, absorbing essential substance, evaporating Body Fluids, and transforming nutrient substance into nutrient Blood. This function is described in the same chapter: "The middle Jiao looks like a froth of bubbles."

A froth of bubbles" here refers to the appearance of the decomposed state of digested food.

The lower Jiao dominates the separation of the clear from the turbid and the discharge of fluid and wastes from the body. This process mainly involves the urinary function of the Kidney and Urinary Bladder, and the defecation function of the Large Intestine. The same chapter states: "The lower Jiao looks like a drainage ditch."

In other words, the turbid Water continuously flows downward to be discharged. If the Water passage in the lower Jiao is obstructed, there may be urinary retention, dysuria and oedema.

Clinically, the terms upper, middle and lower Jiao are often applied to generalize the functions of the internal organs of the chest and abdominal cavity. Above the diaphragm is the upper Jiao, which includes the Heart and Lung, between the diaphragm and umbilicus is the middle Jiao which includes the Spleen and Stomach; and below the umbilicus is the lower Jiao, which includes the Kidney, Intestines and Urinary Bladder.

Practical Chinese Medicine

Section 2

Diagnostics

Traditional Chinese Medicine Diagnostics

Diagnostic methods

In TCM there are four diagnostic methods:

- **Observation (Inspection)** is a method of diagnosis in which the doctor understands and predicts the pathological changes of internal organs by observing abnormal changes in the patient's vitality, colour, appearance, secretions and excretions.

- **Listening (Auscultation)** and Smelling (olfaction) refer to listening and smelling.

- **Asking (Inquiring)** is asking the patient or the patient's companion about the disease condition in order to understand the pathological process. Inquiring covers a wide range of topics: Chills and fever, Perspiration, Appetite, Thirst, Taste, Defecation, Urination, Pain, Sleep, Menstration, and Leucorrhoea.

- **Palpation** is a method of diagnosis in which the pathological condition is detected by palpating, feeling and pressing certain areas of the body. It is discussed under the headings of feeling the pulse and palpation of different parts of the body

Differentiation of Patterns

Differentiation of patterns is the method in traditional Chinese medicine of recognizing and diagnosing diseases. This method entails making a comprehensive analysis of the symptoms and signs, in order to clarify their internal relationships. There are a number of methods in traditional Chinese medicine for differentiating patterns

Aetiology & Pathogenesis

The subject of aetiology is the study of the causative factors of disease, whilst the study of pathogenesis concerns the actual bodily processes whereby disease occurs, develops and changes. Traditional Chinese medicine holds that there is normally a state of relative equilibrium between the human body and the external environment on the one hand, and among the Zang Fu organs within the body on the other hand. This equilibrium is not static, but is in a state constant self-adjustment, and in this way the normal physiological activities of the body arc maintained, if external influences exceed the powers of adaptability of the organism, or if the body itself is unable to adjust to changing conditions, then this relative equilibrium will be lost, and disease will develop. Whether a disease occurs or not, whilst associated with the presence of the various causative factors, is primarily determined by the physiological adaptability of the body to the natural environment. This is the basic viewpoint of traditional Chinese medicine regarding pathogenesis.

Aetiology

Numerous factors can cause disease, and these include the six exogenous factors, the seven emotions, improper diet, over work, lack of physical exercise, traumatic injuries, bites by insects or wild animals, as well as stagnated Blood and Phlegm fluid. The symptoms and signs of any disease reflect the pathological reactions of the affected body to certain causative factors. The causative factors, therefore, are studied both as the objective causes of disease, and in the specific ways they affect the body. On the basis of this understanding, traditional Chinese medicine is able to identify the causative factors of disease by analyzing the clinical manifestations. This is known as "seeking the causative factors by differentiating symptoms and signs."

The study of aetiology, therefore, is based on developing a profound understanding of the characteristic clinical manifestations produced by each causative factor.

The Six Exogenous Factors	The Seven Emotional Factors
Improper diet	Overstrain, stress or lack of physical exercise
Traumatic Injury and Insect or Animal Bites	Phlegm Fluid and Stagnant Blood

The Six Exogenous Factors

Wind, Cold, Summer Heat, Damp, Dryness and Fire (mild Heat and Heat) are the six climatic changes found in nature. Under normal conditions, they do not produce pathological changes in the body and are thus known as the "six types of Qi" in the natural environment. These six types of Qi will only cause disease if either the climatic change is extreme or sudden, or if the body's resistance is low. When responsible for inducing disease, these six types of Qi are known as "the six exogenous pathogenic factors"

All the six pathogenic factors, when affecting the body, invade from the exterior via the skin, mouth or nose. For this reason, the pathological reactions they induce are known as "exogenous diseases"

Diseases due to the six exogenous factors are closely related to seasonal changes in the weather and to living environment. For example, Heat patterns mostly occur in Summer, Cold patterns in winter, and Damp patterns are usually caused by prolonged exposure to Damp. Another term for these patterns is "seasonal diseases"

Each of the six exogenous pathogenic factors may affect the body singly or in combination. Examples are common Cold due to pathogenic wind and Cold, or hi patterns due to pathogenic wind, Cold and Damp, etc. In the process of causing disease, the six exogenous factors may influence each other, and may also, under certain conditions, transform into each other. For example, pathogenic Cold may transform into Heat in the interior of the body, and prolonged Summer Heat may result in Dryness by consuming the Yin of the body, etc. The properties of the six exogenous factors and their specific pathological influences on the body are described as follows:

• Wind	• Cold
• Summer Heat	• Damp
• Dryness	• Fire (mild Heat and Heat)

Wind

Wind is the predominant Qi of spring but may also occur in any of the four seasons. Wind may easily invade the body after sweating, or whilst sleeping.

Wind is the primary exogenous pathogenic factor in causing disease, since Cold, Damp, Dryness and Heat all depend on wind to invade the body, it is stated in the forty - second chapter of Su Wen (Plain Questions) "Wind is the leading causative factor of many diseases."

Pathogenic wind can not only combine with the other five exogenous factors, but also with Phlegm to form wind Phlegm. Facial paralysis, for example, is mostly seen as a consequence of the obstruction of wind Phlegm in the meridians.

Wind is a Yang pathogenic factor and is characterized by "upward and outward dispersion." It can therefore easily invade the upper part of the body, i.e. the head and face and the exterior portion of the body, leading to impairment of the opening and closing of the pores. Clinical manifestations are headache, nasal obstruction, itching or pain in the throat, facial puffiness, and aversion to wind and sweating.

Wind in nature blows in gusts and is characterized by rapid changes. Migratory symptoms, rapid changes and abrupt onset of disease, therefore, mark disorders caused by pathogenic wind. The migratory joint pain of wandering bi, for example, which is caused by pathogenic wind, is known as wind. [1]Urticaria caused by pathogenic wind is characterized by itching of the skin and wheals that appear and disappear from place to place.

Constant movement characterizes wind. Moving pathogenic wind in the body can cause dizziness, vertigo, tinnitus, convulsions and opisthotonus. Examples are [1]tetanus and deviation of the mouth and eyes with spasm of the facial muscles.

Cold

Cold, the predominant Qi of winter, may occur in other seasons but not as severely. Thin clothing, exposure to Cold after sweating, being caught in rain and wading in water in Cold winter can give rise to invasion of pathogenic Cold.

Cold is a Yin pathogenic factor that consumes the Yang Qi of the body. As a result the warming function of the body will be impaired, resulting in symptoms such as Cold limbs, Cold pain in the epigastria and abdominal regions, diarrhea containing undigested food, increased flow of clear urine, etc.

Contraction and stagnation, resulting in impairment of the opening and closing of the pores, spasmodic contraction of tendons and meridians, and impaired circulation of Qi and Blood characterize Cold. Accompanying symptoms include pain, aversion to cold, lack of sweating and restricted movement of the limbs.

Dryness

Dryness is the predominant Qi of autumn, and in China often occurs in this season which is usually very dry.

Dryness consumes Body Fluids resulting in Dryness of the nose and throat, dry mouth with thirst, chapped skin, withered body hair, constipation and reduced urination.

Pathogenic Dryness often impairs the function of the Lung, the "delicate" Zang, which has the function of dispersing, descending and moistening. Dryness invades the Lung through the nose or mouth. When lack of moisture impairs the dispersing and descending functions of the Lung, there may be a dry cough with scanty sticky or bloody sputum.

Heat (Fire and mild Heat)

Heat caused by excess of Yang Qi, often occurs in summer, but may be seen in other seasons. Fire, mild Heat and Heat vary in degree. Of the three, Fire is the most severe and mild Heat the least severe, yet they all share similar characteristics. The terms of Fire Heat and mild Heat, therefore, are often used to describe their common features.

Fire is a Yang pathogenic factor characterized by burning and upward direction. Clinical manifestations include high fever, restlessness, thirst, sweating, mouth and tongue ulcers, swollen and painful gums, headache and congestion of the eyes. Restlessness, insomnia, mania, emotional excitement and coma or delirium may occur if pathogenic Fire disturbs the Mind.

Pathogenic Fire often consumes Yin fluid. Burning pathogenic Fire Heat can consume Yin fluid and force it to the exterior of the body, leading to insufficiency of Body Fluids. Clinically, apart from high fever, there may be thirst with desire to drink, dry lips and throat, constipation and deep - yellow scanty urine.

Invasion by Fire stirs up wind and causes disturbance of Blood. Excess of Fire Heat affects the Liver Meridian and deprives the tendons and meridian of nourishment, thus stirring up the Liver wind. Clinical manifestations include high fever, coma, and convulsion of the four limbs, neck rigidity, opisthotonus and upward staring of the eyes. These symptoms are known as "extreme Heat stirring up wind."

When pathogenic Fire Heat disturbs Blood, it speeds up Blood circulation and gives rise to very rapid pulse. In severe cases, Blood is forced out of the Vessels, leading to †epistaxis, spitting of blood, bloody stool, haematuria, uterine bleeding and menorrhagia. Pathogenic Heat may stay in and rot the Blood and flesh, thus creating †carbuncle, Furuncle, boil and ulcer.

Summer Heat

Summer Heat is the predominant Qi of Summer, and unlike the other exogenous factors, is only seen in its own season. Summer Heat diseases are induced by excessively high temperatures, overexposure to the blazing sun whilst working, and working or staying for too long in poorly ventilated places.

Summer Heat, characterized by extreme Heat, is a Yang pathogenic factor that is transformed from Fire. Clinical manifestations characterized by Yang Heat include high fever, restlessness, thirst, profuse sweating and a surging pulse.

Upward direction, dispersion and consumption of Body Fluids characterize Summer Heat. It usually affects the head and eyes, causing dizziness and blurred vision. Due to its dispersing function, pathogenic Summer Heat may cause the pores to stay open. The excessive sweating that causes may consume Body Fluids resulting in thirst with a strong desire to drink, dry mouth and tongue, scanty deep - yellow urine. In addition, there will be symptoms of Qi deficiency such as reluctance to speak and lassitude. Severe invasion of Summer Heat may disturb the Mind, resulting in sunstroke with the symptoms of sudden collapse and coma.

Since summer is often characterized by high humidity, pathogenic Summer Heat is frequently combined with pathogenic Damp. Clinical manifestations of Summer Heat and Damp include dizziness, heaviness in the head, suffocating sensation in the chest, nausea, poor appetite, loose stools and general lassitude, in addition to fever restlessness and thirst.

Damp

Damp is the predominant Qi (energy) of late summer, which is the period between summer and autumn. In China this represents the hot, rainy, damp and humid season. Many conditions related to invasion by pathogenic Damp occur at this time. Damp conditions may also develop when living in Damp conditions and places, wearing clothes made Damp by sweat or rain, frequent exposure to Water and prolonged rainy periods.

Damp is characterized by heaviness and turbidity. Patients often complain of dizziness, a heavy sensation in the head as though it had been wrapped in a piece of cloth, heaviness of the body as though it were carrying a heavy load, and soreness, pain and heavy sensations in the joints. There may be turbid discharges from the body, such as oozing sores, weeping eczema, profuse weeping leucorrhoea with a foul odor, turbid urine and stools containing mucus and even Blood.

Damp is also characterized by viscosity and stagnation. Patients affected by pathogenic Damp usually have a sticky or greasy tongue coating, a sticky stool that is difficult to excrete and obstructed urination. Conditions due to pathogenic Damp tend to be prolonged and stubborn, such as fixed Bi syndrome, Damp fever (intestinal typhoid) and eczema.

Damp is Yin in nature and damages Yang. It easily obstructs Qi circulation. Clinical manifestations may include a sensation of fullness in the chest, epigastric distention, difficult

Insect or animal bites including the bites of poisonous snakes, wild beasts and rabid dogs may result in bleeding, pain and broken skin in mild cases, and toxicosis or even death in severe cases.

Internal Causes of disease

Phlegm Fluid and Stagnant Blood

Phlegm fluid and stagnant Blood are the pathological products of dysfunction of the Zang Fu organs. Both of them, however, having been produced, Further affect the Zang Fu organs and tissues - either directly or indirectly and cause numerous diseases. Phlegm fluid and stagnant Blood are therefore considered to be a kind of pathogenic factor

Phlegm fluid

Phlegm fluid results from accumulation of Body Fluids due to dysfunction of the Lung, Spleen and Kidney and impairment of Water metabolism. Phlegm is turbid and thick, whilst retained fluid is clear and dilute. The term Phlegm fluid is the short form of the combination of the two. Diseases caused by Phlegm fluid include numerous patterns involving either substantial or non-substantial Phlegm fluid. Clinical manifestations vary according to the area of the body affected. Retention of Phlegm in the Lung, for example, may cause cough with profuse sputum and asthmatic breathing. Phlegm afflicting the Heart may lead to palpitations, coma and depressive and manic psychosis, obstruction of the meridians, bones and tendons by Phlegm may cause tuberculosis of the cervical lymph nodes, subcutaneous nodules, and inflammation of deep tissues, numbness of the limbs and body, and hemiplegia.

Phlegm fluid affecting the head and eyes may cause dizziness, vertigo, and blurred vision. Accumulation of Phlegm and Qi in the throat may lead to a "foreign body sensation." Retained fluid attacking the skin and muscles may cause oedema, general aching and a heavy sensation of the body, retention of fluid in the chest and hypochondrium may cause cough, asthmatic breathing, distention and pain, retained fluid spreading to the Stomach and intestines may lead to nausea, vomiting of sticky fluid, discomfort in the epigastrium and abdomen, and borborygmus

Diseases caused by Phlegm fluid cover a wide range, referring not only to those with such symptoms as visible sputum, but also to those with clinical manifestations characterized by Phlegm fluid. General clinical manifestations include spitting of profuse sputum or sticky fluid, a rattling sound in the throat, a full sensation in the epigastric and abdominal regions, vomiting, dizziness and vertigo, palpitations, a sticky tongue coating and a wiry rolling pulse

Stagnant Blood

Stagnant Blood is mainly caused by impaired Blood circulation due to either Cold or deficiency or stagnation of Qi. Traumatic injuries may cause internal bleeding which accumulates and is not dispelled, leading to stagnant Blood.

The clinical manifestations of stagnant Blood vary according to the area affected. Stagnant Blood in the Heart, for example, may result in a suffocating sensation in the chest, cardiac pain and green purplish lips. Stagnant Blood in the Lung can cause chest pain and haemoptysis. Stagnant Blood in the gastrointestinal tract can lead to haematemesis and Bloody stool. Stagnant Blood in the Liver may cause hypochondriac pain and palpable masses in the abdomen. Stagnant Blood in the Uterus can cause dysmenorrhoea, irregular menstruation, and a dark red menstrual flow with clots. Stagnant Blood on the body surface may cause a purplish or green color of the skin and subcutaneous haematoma

Diseases due to stagnant Blood, although they can be varied, share certain common characteristics:

- Pain which is worse with pressure and stabbing in nature
- Bleeding which is deep or dark purple in color containing clots
- Ecchymoses or petechiae, accompanied by pain in the affected parts, indicate stagnant Blood retained in the superficial portion of the body. The tongue may be deep purple in color or show purple spots
- There may be fixed purplish masses accompanied by pain

Additional

In addition to the Six Exogenous Pathogenic Factors occurring in nature, there also exist some extremely infectious noxious epidemic factors. Although the characteristics of these are similar to those of mild - Heat and Heat, they are severely toxic and can result in the sudden onset of severe diseases such as plague. The medical literature of Traditional Chinese medicine describes epidemics of many diseases recognized by modern medicine, such as smallpox, cholera, diphtheria and toxic dysentery.

In addition to diseases caused by the six exogenous pathogenic factors, there are many diseases caused by functional disturbances of the Zang Fu organs, which nevertheless share similar clinical manifestations. These pathological changes are therefore referred to as Endogenous Wind, Cold. Damp, Dryness and Fire (Heat) in order to avoid ambiguity. Descriptions of these pathogenic factors are ignored here and are covered in the chapter on the differentiation of patterns of the Zang Fu organs.

Diagnostic Methods

In TCM there are four diagnostic methods, namely:

Observation or Inspection

Is a method of diagnosis in which the doctor understands and predicts the pathological changes of internal organs by observing abnormal changes in the patient's vitality, colour, appearance, secretions and excretions. In their long-term medical practice, the Chinese physicians realized the close relationship between the external part of the body, especially the face and tongue, and the Zang Fu organs. Any slight changes appearing in these areas can tell pathological conditions in various parts of the body. Inspection of the exterior of the body, therefore, is of much help in diagnosis.

- Observation of the vitality
- Observation of the color
- Observation of the appearance
- Observation of the five sense organs
- Observation of the tongue

Listening and Smelling (Auscultation and olfaction)

Inquiring

Is asking the patient or the patient's companion about the disease condition in order to understand the pathological process. Inquiries are made systematically with questions focused on the chief complaint of the patient according to the knowledge necessary in differentiating a pattern. Inquiring covers a wide range of topics.

• Chills and fever	• Perspiration
• Appetite	• Thirst
• Taste	• Defecation
• Urination	• Pain
• Sleep	• Menses
• Leukorrhea	•

Palpation

Is a method of diagnosis in which the pathological condition is detected by palpating, feeling and pressing certain areas of the body. It is discussed under the headings of feeling the pulse and palpation of different parts of the body.

Feeling the pulse

Palpation of the epigastrium

Palpation of the abdomen

Palpation of the acupuncture points

As human body is an organic entity, its regional pathological changes may affect the whole body, and the pathological changes of the internal organs may manifest themselves on the body surface. The Medical Book by Master of Danxi says: "One should observe and analyse the external manifestations of the patient in order to know what is happening inside the body, for the disease of internal organs must have its manifestations on the body surface." Inspection, auscultation and olfaction, inquiring and palpation are the four approaches to understand the pathological conditions. They can not be separated, but relate to and supplement one another. In the clinical situation, only by combining the four can a comprehensive and systematic understanding of the condition of the disease be gained and a correct diagnosis made. Any inclination to one aspect while neglecting the other three is one-sided, therefore, is not suggested.

Observation of the Vitality

Vitality is the general manifestation of the vital activities of the human body, and the outward sign of relative strength of Qi and Blood of the Zang Fu organs, which take essential Qi as the basis. By observing vitality, one may get a rough idea of the strength of the antipathogenic Qi of the human body and severity of the disease; this is highly significant for the prognosis.

If the patient is fully conscious and in fairly good spirits, responds keenly with a sparkle in the eyes, the patient is vigorous and the disease is mild. If the patient is spiritless with dull eyes and sluggish response or even mental disturbance, the patient lacks vigor and the disease is severe.

Observation of the Color

Both the color and luster of the face are observed. There are five discolorations, namely, blue, yellow, red, pale and dark gray. Observation of the luster of the face is to distinguish whether the complexion is bright and moist or dark and haggard.

People of different races have different skin colors, and there is wide variation among people of the same race. However, a lustrous skin with natural color is considered normal.

The color and luster of the face are the outward manifestations of the relative strength of Qi and Blood of the Zang Fu organs. Their changes often suggest various pathological conditions. Observation of these changes is valuable for diagnosing disease. Here are the descriptions of the indications of the five discolorations.

A red color often indicates Heat patterns, which may be of deficiency type or of excess type. When the entire face is red, it is a sign of a Heat pattern of excess type resulting from either exposure to exogenous pathogenic factors with the symptom of fever, or hyperactivity of Yang of Zang Fu organs. The presence of malar flush accompanied by tidal fever and night sweating suggests an interior Heat pattern due to Yin deficiency.

A pale color indicates Cold patterns of deficiency type and loss of Blood. A pale complexion is often due to Yin excess or Yang deficiency. A bright white face with a puffy, bloated appearance is a sign of deficiency of Yang Qi. If the pale face is withered, it signifies Blood deficiency.

A yellow color indicates patterns of deficiency type and Damp patterns. When the entire body, including the face, eyes and skin, is yellow, it is jaundice. If the yellowness tends toward bright orange, it is called Yang jaundice resulting from Damp Heat. If the yellow is smoky dark, it is called Yin jaundice resulting from either Cold Damp or long - term stagnation of Blood. A pale yellow complexion without brightness is a sign of deficiency of both Qi and Blood.

A blue color indicates Cold patterns, painFul patterns, stagnation of Blood and convulsion. A pale complexion with a blue tinge is seen in a pattern of excessive Yin and Cold with the symptom of severe pain in the epigastrium and abdomen. Blue purplish face and Ups with the intermittent pain in the pericardial region or behind the sternum are due to stagnation of the Heart Blood. Blue purplish face and lips accompanied by high fever and violent movement of the limbs in children are signs of infantile convulsion.

A dark grey color indicates deficiency of the Kidney and stagnation of Blood. A pale and dark complexion accompanied with lumbar soreness and Cold feet suggests insufficiency of the Kidney Yang. A dark complexion without brightness, accompanied by scaly skin signifies prolonged stagnation of Blood.

Generally speaking, a lustrous and moist complexion indicates that the disease is mild, Qi and Blood are not deficient, and the prognosis is good ; whilst a dark and haggard complexion suggests that the disease is severe, essential Qi is already injured, and the prognosis is poor.

As to the clinical significance of the color of secretions and excretions, such as nasal discharge, sputum, urine and vaginal discharge, those clear and white in color generally denote deficiency and Cold, while those turbid and yellow in color indicate excess and Heat.

Observation of the Appearance

Appearance refers to the body shape which can be described as strong, weak, heavy or thin; and to the movement and posture related to disease.

OverWeight with mental depression mostly suggests deficiency of Qi and excess of Phlegm Damp. A thin person with dry skin indicates insufficiency of Blood. Great loss of Weight in the course of a long illness indicates the exhaustion of the essential Qi.

The patient's movement and posture are outward manifestations of the pathological changes. There is a variation of movement and posture in different diseases. But on the whole, an active patient is usually manifesting a Yang pattern, whilst a passive manner is usually Yin. For instance, a patient suffering from the Lung pattern of excess type with excessive Phlegm is likely to sit there with the extended neck ; whilst a patient with deficiency of Qi manifesting as shortness of breath and dislike of speaking tends to sit there facing downward.

Violent movement of the four limbs is mostly present in wind diseases such as tetanus, acute and chronic infantile convulsion. The occurrence of weakness, motor impairment and muscular atrophy of the limbs suggests Wei patterns. The presence of pain, soreness, heaviness and numbness in the tendons, Bones and muscles accompanied by swelling and restricted movement of the joints points to Bi patterns. The appearance of numbness and impaired movement of the limbs on one side of the body indicates hemiplegia or wind stroke.

Observation of the Five Sense Organs

Observation of the eye.

The Liver opens into the eye, and the essential Qi of the five Zang and six Fu organs all goes up into the eye. Therefore, abnormal changes in the eye are not only associated with the Liver, but also reflect the pathological changes of other Zang Fu organs. Apart from the expression of the eye, attention should also be paid to the appearance, color and movement of the eye. For instance, redness and swelling of the eye are often due to wind Heat or Liver Fire. Yellow sclera suggests jaundice. Ulceration of the canthus denotes Damp Heat. Upward, straight forward or sideways staring of the eye is mostly caused by disturbance of Liver wind.

Observation of the nose.

This is to observe the appearance and discharge of the nose. The flapping of the ala nasi is often present in asthmatic breathing due to either Heat in the Lung or deficiency of Qi of both the Lung and Kidney. Clear nasal discharge is due to exposure to wind Cold, whilst turbid nasal discharge to wind Heat. Prolonged turbid nasal discharge with stinking smell suggests chronic rhinitis or chronic sinusitis.

Observation of the ear.

Due attention is paid to the color of the ear and conditions of the internal ear. Dry and withered auricles, burnt black in color, present in the patient with a prolonged or severe illness, are due to consumption of the Kidney Essence (Jing) not allowing it to nourish upwards. Purulent discharge in the ear, known as Tin Er (suppurative infection of the ear), is mostly caused by Damp Heat of the Liver and Gallbladder.

Observation of the gums.

Pale gums indicate deficiency of Blood. Redness and swelling of the gums are due to flaring up of the Stomach Fire. If redness and swelling of the gums are accompanied by bleeding, it is due to injury of the Vessels by the Stomach Fire.

Observation of the lips and mouth.

This is to observe the changes of the lips and mouth in color, moisture and appearance. Pale lips denote deficiency of Blood. Blue purplish lips suggest either retention of Cold or stagnation of Blood. Dry lips, deep red in color, indicate excessive Heat. Sudden collapse with open mouth is deficiency, whilst sudden collapse with lock jaw is excess.

Observation of the throat.

The focus is on abnormal changes of the throat in color and appearance. Redness and swelling of the throat with soreness denote accumulation of Heat in the Lung and Stomach. Redness and swelling of the throat with yellow or white ulcer spots are due to excessive toxic Heat in the Lung and Stomach. A bright red throat with a mild soreness suggests Yin deficiency leading to hyperactivity of Fire. If there occurs a false membrane over the throat, which is greyish white in color, hard to remove, bleeds following forceFul rubbing and regrows immediately, it indicates diphtheria resulting from Heat in the Lung consuming Yin.

Observation of the Tongue

Also known as tongue diagnosis, is an important procedure in diagnosis by inspection. It provides primary information for the Chinese physicians to make diagnosis.

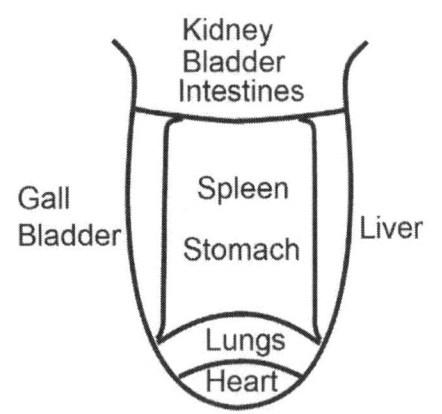

Physiology of the tongue

The tongue directly or indirectly connects with many Zang Fu organs through the meridians and collaterals. The deep branch of Heart Meridian of Hand-ShaoYin goes to the root of the tongue; the Spleen Meridian of Foot Tai-Yin traverses the root of the tongue and spreads over its lower surface; the Kidney Meridian of Foot-ShaoYin terminates at the root of the tongue. So the essential Qi of the Zang Fu organs can go upward to nourish the tongue, and pathological changes of the Zang Fu organs can be reflected by changes in tongue conditions. This is why the observation of the tongue can determine the pathological changes of the internal organs.

Tongue Colour

Pale: Deficiency of Yang or Blood.
Yang deficiency: slightly wet and swollen
Blood deficiency: slightly dry
Liver-Blood deficiency: if Pale on sides or slightly orangey

Red: Heat

If coating:	Full-Heat
If no coat:	Empty-Heat
Red tip on Red tongue:	Heart-Fire or Empty Heart-Heat
Red sides:	Liver-Fire or Gall-Bladder Heat. If sever – swollen side
Red centre:	Stomach-Heat

Red points or spots always mean Heat, but also can indicate Blood stasis

Red points:

On tip: Heart-Heat,
On sides: Liver-Heat,
On roof: Heat in the Lower Jiao, around centre: Stomach-Heat

Deep Red: condition is more sever

Purple: always Blood-Stasis. 2 types:

Reddish-Purple: Heat and stasis of Blood – develops from Red
Bluish Purple: Cold and stasis of Blood – develops from Pale
Purple on sides: Liver-Blood stasis
Purple in centre: Blood stasis in the Stomach

Blue: Interior Cold giving rise to Blood stasis.

Tongue Shape

Thin:	If Pale – Blood deficiency
	If Red and Peeled – Yin deficiency
	Both cases indicate chronic condition
Swollen:	If Pale – Dampness deriving from Yang deficiency
	If Red – retention of Damp-Heat
Stiff:	Interior Wind
Flaccid:	deficiency of Body Fluids
Long:	tendency towards Heat and in particular Heart Heat

        Short: If Pale & Wet – Interior Cold
                            If Red & Peeled – deficiency of Yin
        Cracked: Either deficiency of Yin or Full-Heat
                            Short horizontal cracks – Stomach Yin deficiency
                            Long midline crack to tip – Heart pattern
                            Shallow wide crack in midline (not to tip) Stomach Yin Def.
                            Short transversal cracks on sides – chronic Spleen Qi Def.
Quivering: Chronic Spleen Qi deficiency or Wind
Deviated: interior Wind
    Tongue Coating
    Indicate state of Fu organs, and in particular the Stomach
    Normal coating should be thin & white
    Thick Coat: presence of pathogenic factor. Thicker the coat stronger Pathogenic Factor
    No Coat: deficiency of Stomach Yin and/or Kidney Yin
    If Red & no Coat – Kidney Yin deficiency
    White: Cold pattern
    Yellow: Heat
    Grey or Black: can indicate Cold or Heat, depending on dry or wet
Moisture
    Indicate state of Body Fluids
    Normal tongue: slightly moist – Body Fluids are intact
    Red body and Dry – Heat has started to injure Body Fluids
    Dry with no coat – Empty Heat
    Dry with coat – Full Heat
    Too Wet – Yang Qi is not transforming fluids and Dampness accumulates
    Sticky – Dampness

Listening (Auscultation) and Smelling (Olfaction)

Listening to the speech

In general, speaking lustily indicates patterns of excess type, while speaking feebly and in low tones indicates those of deficiency type. A hoarse voice or loss of voice in a severe case may be of deficiency type or of excess type. If they are present in exogenous diseases with a sudden onset, they are of excess type. Chronic or recurrent onset in endogenous diseases are of deficiency type.

Incoherent speech in loud voice accompanied by impaired consciousness indicates a pattern of excess type due to disturbance of the Mind by Heat. Repeated speech in feeble voice accompanied by listlessness suggests a pattern of deficiency type of the Heart resulting from severe damage of the Heart Qi.

Listening to the respiration

Feeble breathing indicates deficiency of Qi. Forceful and coarse breathing accompanied by a loud voice suggests a pattern of excess type due to excessive pathogenic Heat in the interior.

Feeble asthmatic breathing accompanied by shortness of breath indicates deficiency of the Qi of the Lung and Kidney, pertaining to deficiency type asthma. Coarse asthmatic breathing in loud tones with the preference for exhalation suggests retention of pathogenic factor in the Lung impairing the functions of Qi. This belongs to asthma of excess type.

Listening to the cough

Cough is the manifestation of dysfunction of the Lung in dispersing and descending leading to upward rebellious of Qi. Cough in a coarse voice indicates a pattern of excess type; cough in a feeble voice suggests a pattern of deficiency type. Unproductive cough or cough with a small amount of thick sputum implies injury of the Lung by pathogenic Dryness or Dryness of the

Lung due to Yin deficiency.

Smelling (olfaction)

Stench smell of a secretion or excretion usually indicates Heat patterns of excess type; less stinking smell suggests Cold patterns of deficiency type; foul and sour smell implies retention of food. Different odorous should be identified in order to deduce the nature of the disease. The source of the odor should also be traced for determining the locality of the disease.

Asking (Inquiring)

Chills and Fever

Apart from confirming the presence of chills and fever, we need to ask such questions as which is more severe, when they occur and what symptoms and signs accompany them, for this information is necessary for further differentiation of patterns

Chills accompanied by fever. Simultaneous occurrence of chills and fever at the beginning of the disease indicates exogenous exterior pattern. It is the manifestation of invasion of the body surface by the pathogenic factor and its contending with the antipathogenic Qi. Exterior patterns resulting from exposure to pathogenic wind Cold usually manifest as severe chills and mild fever with the accompanying symptoms and signs such as absence of sweating, headache and general aching, and a superficial and tense pulse. Exterior patterns due to invasion by pathogenic wind Heat are characterized by mild chills and severe fever; the patient also reveals thirst, sweating and a superficial and rapid pulse.

Alternate chills and fever: The patient may notice alternate attacks of chills and fever. This is the representative symptom of intermediate patterns. The patient may also complain of a bitter taste in the mouth, thirst and Fullness and stuffiness in the chest and hypochondrium. High fever following chills occurring at a definite time of the day suggests malaria.

Fever without chills: Fever may occur without chills. Persistent high fever with aversion to Heat instead suggests interior Heat patterns of excess type due to transmission of the pathogenic factors from the exterior to the interior with excessive Heat in the interior. The accompanying symptoms and signs are proFuse sweating, severe thirst and a surging pulse. If fever occurs or becomes worse at a fixed hour of the day just like the sea waves, it is known as tidal fever. Tidal fever in the afternoon or evening, accompanied by night sweating and a red tongue with little moisture indicates deficiency of Yin; afternoon fever with constipation and Fullness and pain in the abdomen suggests excess Heat of the Yang ming Meridian.

Chills without fever: The subjective feeling of chills without fever indicates interior Cold pattern of deficiency type. The patient may also have chilled appearance, Cold limbs and a deep, slow and weak pulse.

Perspiration

The patient should, first of all, be asked whether sweating is present or not. Further inquiring deals with the feature of sweating and its accompanying symptoms and signs.

Absence of sweating in exterior patterns indicates invasion by pathogenic Cold; presence of sweating in exterior patterns suggests either exterior patterns of deficiency type resulting from exposure to pathogenic wind, or exterior Heat patterns due to invasion by pathogenic wind Heat. The accompanying symptoms and signs are considered in differentiation.

Sweating that occurs during sleep and stops upon wakening is known as night sweating. It usually indicates deficiency of Yin with hyperactivity of Yang Heat. The patient may also present tidal fever and a red tongue with little coating.

Frequent sweating which is worse on slight exertion is known as spontaneous sweating. It is a sign of deficiency of Qi and deficiency of Yang. The patient may also exhibit chills, restlessness and lassitude.

Profuse sweating accompanied by high fever, mental restlessness, thirst with preference for Cold drinks and a surging pulse indicates interior Heat patterns of excess type resulting from excessive Yang Heat in the interior expelling the sweat out. Ptofuse sweating accompanied by restlessness, feeble energy, Cold limbs and a deep and thready pulse in a severe case is a critical sign indicating total exhaustion of Yang Qi.

Appetite

Poor appetite present in the patient with a prolonged illness manifesting as emaciation, loose stools, lassitude and a pale tongue with a thin white coating indicates weakness of the Spleen and Stomach; poor appetite accompanied by stuffiness in the chest, fullness in the abdomen and a thick, sticky tongue coating suggests stagnation of Qi of the Spleen and Stomach caused by retention of food or retention of pathogenic Damp.

Excessive appetite and getting hungry easily in a skinny patient indicate excessive Stomach Fire.

Hunger with no desire to eat or eating a small amount of food suggests impairment of the Stomach Yin producing internal Heat of deficiency type.

Thirst

Lack of thirst during an illness suggests that Body Fluids is not consumed. It is present in Cold patterns or patterns in which pathogenic Heat is not noticeable. The presence of thirst indicates consumption of Body Fluids or retention of Phlegm Damp in the interior preventing Body Fluids from ascending. Further analysis is based on features of thirst, amount of drinks to be taken and the accompanying symptoms and signs.

Taste

A bitter taste in the mouth usually indicates hyperactivity of the Fire of the Liver and Gallbladder.
A sweetish taste and stickiness in the mouth imply Damp Heat in the Spleen and Stomach.
Sour regurgitation means retention of Heat in the Liver and Stomach.
Tastelessness points to deficiency of the Spleen with its impaired function of transportation.

Defecation

Constipation due to Dryness of stool usually indicates accumulation of Heat or consumption of Body Fluids.
Loose stool suggests deficiency of the Spleen or retention of Damp in the Spleen.
Watery stool with undigested food implies deficiency of Yang of the Spleen and Kidney.
Bloody stool with mucus and tenesmus results from Damp Heat in the intestines and stagnation of Qi in the intestinal tract.

Urination

Yellow urine generally indicates Heat patterns, while clear and proFuse urine indicates absence of the pathogenic Heat in an illness, or Cold patterns.

Turbid urine suggests downward inFusion of Damp Heat or downward leakage of turbid Essence (Jing).

Red urine implies injury of the Vessels by Heat.

Clear urine increased in volume means infirmity of the Kidney Qi and dysfunction of the Urinary Bladder in controlling urine, while scanty yellow urine with urgent and painful urination means downward inFusion of Damp Heat into the Urinary Bladder.

Dribbling urination or retention of urine in a severe case is present not only in patterns of deficiency type due to exhaustion of the Kidney Qi with its impaired function of controlling urine, but also in patterns of excess type caused by obstructed Qi activities of the Urinary Bladder due to downward inFusion of Damp Heat, stagnant Blood or stones.

Pain

Pain is one of the most common symptoms complained of by the patient. Apart from a thorough understanding of the history and accompanying symptoms and signs, the nature and locality of pain must be asked. Differentiation of the nature of the pain is significant for deducing its etiology and pathology, while identification of the locality of the pain helps determine diseased Zang Fu organs and meridians.

Nature of the pain

Distending pain: Distending pain manifesting as severe distension, mild pain and moving from place to place is a typical sign of Qi stagnation. It often occurs in the chest, epigastric, hypochondriac and abdominal regions. But headache with a distending sensation in the head is due to upward disturbance by Fire and Heat.

Pricking pain: Pricking pain, sharp in nature and fixed in location, is a sign of stagnation of Blood. It usually occurs in the chest, epigastric, hypochondriac and lower abdominal regions.

Weighty pain: Pain with a heavy sensation is a sign of Damp blocking Qi and Blood, as Damp is characterized by heaviness. It is often present in the head, four limbs and lumbar region.

Colicky pain: Colicky pain is a sign of abrupt obstruction of the Qi by substantial pathogenic factors.

Pulling pain: Pulling pain which is spasmodic in nature and short in duration often relates to the disorders of the Liver. It is caused by Liver wind.

Burning pain: Pain with a burning sensation and preference for coolness often occurs in the hypochondriac regions on both sides and epigastric region. It results from invasion of the collaterals by pathogenic Fire and Heat or from excessive Yang Heat due to r in deficiency.

Cold pain: Pain with a Cold sensation and preference for warmth often occurs in the head, lumbar, epigastric and abdominal regions. It is caused by pathogenic Cold blocking the collaterals or lack of warmth and nourishment in the Zang Fu organs and meridians due to deficiency of Yang Qi.

Dull pain: Dull pain is not severe. It is bearable lingering and may last for a long time. It is usually present in Cold patterns of deficiency type.

Hollow pain: Pain with a hollow sensation is caused by deficiency of Blood leading to emptiness of Vessels and retardation of Blood circulation.

Locality of the pain

Headache: Head is the meeting place of all the Yang meridians and Brain is the sea of Marrow. Qi and Blood of the five Zang and six Fu organs all go up into the head. If the pathogenic factors invade the head and block the clear Yang , or if stagnation of Qi and Blood in endogenous diseases blocks the meridians and deprives the Brain of the nourishment, headache will ensure. In cases of deficiency of Qi and Blood, head fails to be nourished, and the sea of Marrow becomes empty; headache due to this is of deficiency type. Headache due to disturbance of the clear Yang by the pathogenic factor is mostly of excess type.

Chest pain: As the Heart and Lung reside in the chest, chest pain indicates the pathological changes of the Heart and Lung.

Hypochondriac pain: The hypochondriac region is traversed by the Liver and Gallbladder Meridians. Obstruction or undernourishment of these meridians may produce hypochondriac pain.

Epigastric pain: Epigastrium (wan) refers to the upper abdomen in which the Stomach situates. It is divided into three regions, namely, Shangwan, Zhongwan and Xiawan (upper, middle and lower wan respectively). Epigastric pain may result from invasion of the Stomach by pathogenic Cold, retention of food in the Stomach or invasion of the Stomach by the Liver Qi.

Abdominal pain: Abdomen is divided into upper abdomen, lower abdomen and sides of the lower abdomen. The upper abdomen refers to the area above the umbilicus and pertains to the Spleen. The area below the umbilicus is the lower abdomen and pertains to the Kidney, Urinary Bladder, large and Small Intestines and Uterus. Both sides of the lower abdomen is traversed by the Liver Meridian of Foot - JueYin. So according to the locality of the pain, the diseased Zang Fu organs and meridians can be identified.

Abdominal pain caused by retention of Cold, accumulation of Heat, stagnation of Qi, stagnation of Blood, retention of food or parasitic diseases is excess in nature, while that caused by deficiency of Qi, deficiency of Blood or deficiency of Cold is deficiency in nature.

Lumbago: The Kidney resides in the lumbar region. Lumbago may result from obstruction of the meridians in the local area ; besides, deficiency of the Kidney failing to nourish the lumbar region is often the cause.

Pain in the four limbs: Pain in the four limbs may involve joints, muscles or meridians. It is caused by retardation of Qi and Blood circulation due to invasion of the exogenous pathogenic factors.

Besides, the duration of pain and its response to pressure should also be asked. Generally, persistent pain in a recent disease or pain which is aggravated by pressure indicates patterns of excess type. Intermittent pain in a prolonged illness or pain which is alleviated by pressure often occurs in patterns of deficiency type.

Sleep

Insomnia means either difficulty in falling asleep, or inability to sleep soundly, waking easily and being unable to fall asleep again. Insomnia accompanied by dizziness and palpitations usually indicates failure of Blood to nourish the Heart due to deficiency of both the Heart and Spleen. Insomnia accompanied by restlessness in Mind and dream - disturbed sleep suggests hyperactivity of the Fire of the Heart.

Difficulty in falling asleep due to an uncomfortable and empty sensation in the Stomach or gastric discomfort after a full meal implies derangement of the Stomach Qi leading to mental restlessness.

If lethargy is accompanied by dizziness, it indicates accumulation of Phlegm Damp in the interior. A situation of being half asleep with general lassitude suggests deficiency of the Heart and Kidney Yang.

Menstruation

Inquiring in this aspect covers menstrual cycle and period, amount, colour and quality of flow and the accompanying symptoms and signs. If it is necessary, questions concerning the date of the last menstrual period and age of menopause should be asked.

Menses of a shortened cycle, excessive in amount, deep red in color and thick in quality relates mainly to excessive Heat in the Blood; light colored menstrual flow proFuse in amount and thin in quality indicates failure of Qi to command Blood. A prolonged cycle with scanty purplish dark discharge or Blood clots suggests stagnation of Blood due to Cold; thin scanty and light-colored flow implies deficiency of Blood. Irregular menstrual cycle is a sign of disharmony of the Chong and Ren (Conception Vessel) Meridians due to obstruction of the Liver Qi.

Pre - menstrual or menstrual distending pain in the breasts and lower abdomen which intensifies on pressure means stagnation of Qi and Blood; Cold pain in the lower abdomen during the period points to stagnation of Blood due to Cold; dull pain in the lower abdomen during or after the period which is alleviated by pressure is due to deficiency of Qi and Blood.

Leucorrhea

Attention is paid to the color, amount, quality and smell of leucorrhoea

Watery leucorrhoea whitish in color and proFuse in amount indicates deficiency patterns and Cold patterns; thick leukorrhea yellow or red in color with offensive smell suggests excess patterns and Heat patterns

Palpating the Pulse

The location for feeling the pulse at the present time is above the wrist where the radial artery throbs. It is divided into three regions: cun, guan and chi. The region opposite to the styloid process of the radius (the bony eminence behind the palm) is known as guan, that distal to guan (i.e. between guan and the wrist joint) is cun and that proximal to guan is chi. There have been in different times various descriptions concerning the relationship between these three regions and their corresponding Zang Fu organs. They are fundamentally conformable. It is generally acknowledged that the three regions of cun, guan and chi of the left hand reflect respectively the conditions of the Heart, Liver and Kidney; and those of the right hand reflect the conditions of the Lung, Spleen and Kidney.

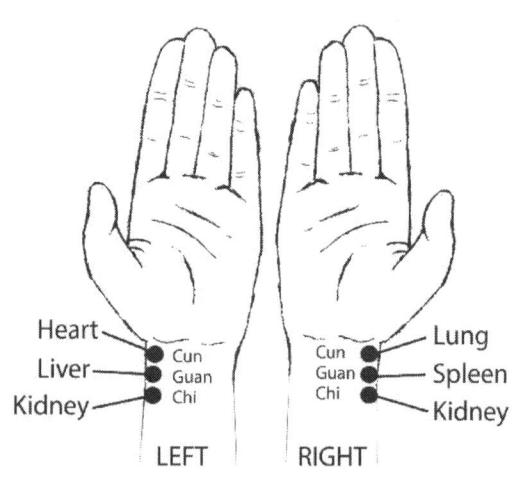

In feeling the pulse, let the patient take either sitting or supine position with the arm placed approximately on a level with the Heart, wrist extended and palm facing upward. This position facilitates smooth circulation of Qi and Blood. The practitioner by the side of the patient first locates the guan region with the middle finger, then the cun and chi regions with the index and ring fingers.

The three fingers are slightly flexed, presenting the shape of an arch. The finger tips are kept on the same horizontal level and the pulse is felt with the palmar side of the fingers. The space between each two fingers depends upon the height of the patient.

If the patient is tall and has long arms, it is desirable to separate the fingers accordingly. If the patient is short and has short arms, the three fingers are placed more closely. The method of "feeling the pulse in the guan region with one finger" is adopted in infantile cases, for a baby's pulse is not divided into these three regions. The pulse is palpated by exerting three different finger forces, first lightly (superficial palpation), then moderately (middle palpation) and finally heavily (deep palpation). Generally the finger pressure is of the same strength when exerted on the three regions at the same time and then feel each of the three regions separately according to the actual pathological conditions.

The pulse is differentiated in terms of; depth (superficial or deep), speed (rapid or slow), strength (forceful or weak), shape (thick or thready, soft or hard) and rhythm. Different conditions of the pulse indicate different patterns.

A normal pulse is smooth, even and forceful with the frequency of four beats per breath or between 60 and 70 beats per minute. However, the pulse may vary due to age, sex, and body constitution, emotional state and climatic changes. Due attention should be paid to distinguishing it from an abnormal pulse.

Clinical significance of abnormal pulse reading

Superficial or Floating pulse (Fu mai)

A floating pulse can be easily felt with gentle touch. It indicates exterior patterns, and is present at the early stage of exogenous diseases. Invasion of the body surface by the exogenous pathogenic factor creates its contending with Wei Qi. The pulsation is superficially situated, hence the floating pulse. A floating pulse may also be present in prolonged endogenous diseases. In this case, the pulse is superficial, large and weak, indicating outward floating of Yang Qi. This is a critical sign of the disease.

Deep or Sinking pulse (Chen mai)

A deep pulse is felt only on heavy pressure. It indicates interior patterns. If the pulse is deep and forceful, it indicates interior patterns of excess type. When the pathogenic factor invades the interior of the body, Qi and Blood circulation is blocked, presenting a deep and forceful pulse. If the pulse is deep and weak, it indicates interior patterns of deficiency type.

Slow pulse (chi mai)

The rate is slow, with less than four beats per breath (less than sixty beats per minute). A slow pulse indicates Cold patterns. Qi contracts and Blood flow stagnates on exposure to Cold. The retarded circulation of Qi and Blood produces a slow pulse. If the slow pulse is forceful, it indicates an interior pattern of excess type caused by retention of Yin Cold in the interior. If the slow pulse is weak, it indicates an interior pattern of deficiency type due to deficiency of Yang Qi.

Rapid pulse (shu mai)

The rate is quick, with more than five beats per breath (more than (ninety beats per minute). A rapid pulse indicates Heat patterns. Induced by pathogenic Heat, the Blood circulation is accelerated, the result being a rapid pulse. If excess Heat is retained in the interior and the antipathogenic Qi is still strong, their struggle will induce a rapid and forceful pulse. Deficiency of Yin in a prolonged illness produces deficiency - Heat in the interior, presenting a rapid and weak pulse. A rapid pulse may also be induced by outward floating of deficiency - Yang. In this case, the pulse feels rapid, large, weak and empty.

Empty (xu mai)

It is the general term for all the forceless pulses felt on the three regions at the three levels of pressure. The pulse indicates patterns of deficiency type due to deficiency of Qi and Blood. Deficiency of Qi and Blood implies weakness in activating Blood circulation, thus producing a pulse of deficiency type.

Full (shi mai)

It is the general term for all the forceful pulses felt on the three regions at the three levels of pressure. The pulse indicates patterns of excess type. The struggle waged by the strong antipathogenic Qi against the hyperactive pathogenic factor brings on excessive Qi and Blood, thus creating a pulse of excess type.

Surging pulse *(hong mai)*

A surging pulse is broad, large and forceful like roaring waves which come on powerfully and fade away. If a surging pulse lacks the momentum of roaring waves, it is called a large pulse. A surging pulse indicates excessive Heat, and often occurs together with a rapid pulse. Excessive Heat in the interior dilates the Blood Vessels and accelerates Qi and Blood circulation, thus producing a surging pulse.

Thin or Thready pulse *(xi mai)*

A thready pulse feels like a fine thread but is very distinct and clear. It indicates deficiency due to overstrain and stress or deficiency of Qi and Blood. It is often present in patients with weak body constitution in a prolonged illness manifesting as Yin deficiency and Blood deficiency. Deficiency of Yin and Blood means the inability to fill the Vessels. Qi is also deficient and unable to activate the Blood circulation, hence the thready pulse.

Slippery pulse *(hua mai)*

A rolling pulse feels smooth and flowing like pearls rolling on a dish. It indicates Phlegm and retained fluid, retention of food and excess Heat. When excess type pathogenic factor is retained in the interior, the Qi and Blood circulation is activated, resulting in a smooth and flowing pulse. This pulse often occurs in women during pregnancy, indicating sufficient and harmonious Qi and Blood.

Choppy pulse *(se mai)*

A choppy pulse feels rough and uneven. In the ancient classics it was described as scraping bamboo with a knife. It indicates deficiency of Blood, stagnation of Qi, stagnation of Blood, impairment of Essence (Jing). Stagnation of Qi and Blood means blockage of Vessels and impaired circulation of Blood. This condition produces a hesitant and choppy pulse. When the Essence (Jing) is impaired and Blood is insufficient, the Vessels are not filled and Blood circulation is retarded. This condition creates a choppy and weak pulse.

Wiry pulse *(xuan mai)*

A Wiry pulse feels taut, straight and long, giving the feeling of a string of a violin. It indicates disorders of the Liver and Gallbladder, painful patterns, and Phlegm and retained fluid. A Wiry pulse in disorders of the Liver and Gallbladder is due to disturbance of the Liver Qi tightening the Vessels; that in painful pattern is due to tightness of the meridians and Vessels; that in retention of Phlegm and fluid in the interior is due to dysfunction of Qi in transportation and Blood.

Tight or Tense pulse *(jin mai)*

A tense pulse feels tight and forceful like a stretched rope. It indicates Cold, pain and retention of food. As Cold is characterized by contraction, the Vessels contract on exposure to Cold, thus producing a tense pulse. The pulse is also present in painful patterns, for painful patterns are usually caused by pathogenic Cold.

Soft pulse *(ru mai)*

A soft pulse is superficial and thready, and hits the fingers without strength. It indicates Damp disorders. Pathogenic Damp is characteristically viscous and stagnant, its invasion of the Vessels blocks Qi and Blood and gives rise to a superficial, thready and forceless pulse.

Weak pulse *(ruo mai)*

A weak pulse is deep and thready, and hits the fingers without strength. It indicates various patterns due to deficiency of both Qi and Blood. When Blood is deficient, it fails to fill the Vessels: when Qi is deficient, the pulse is deprived of strength. So the pulse feels deep, thready and forceless.

Short (Duan Mai)

A short pulse does not reach (i.e. fill longitudinally) its location or range. Can be felt most clearly at the Guan position, more indistinct at the Cun and the Chi. Short and forceful indicates Qi Stagnation, Short and weak indicates Qi Deficiency.

Long (Chang Mai)

A Long pulse can be felt beyond its location. It can indicate an Excess Liver Yang, Yang and Heat Excess in the Interior, Strong Pathogenic factors. A long and smooth pulse can be normal (ping mai) for some people, the long characteristic is usually present with wiry.

Hurried pulse *(cu mai)*

A hurried or abrupt pulse feels hurried and rapid with irregular missed beats. It indicates excessive Yang Heat, stagnation of Qi and Blood, and retention of Phlegm or food. Excessive Yang Heat means failure of Yin to restrain Yang and thus produces an abrupt pulse. If this pulse is present in Heat patterns of excess type due to stagnation of Qi and Blood, retention of Phlegm or food, or swelling and pain, it is abrupt and forceFul. An abrupt and weak pulse is a sign

Knotted pulse (jie mai)

A knotted pulse is slow with irregular missed beats. It indicates excessive Yin, accumulation of Qi, retention of Cold Phlegm and stagnant Blood. Cold Phlegm and stagnant Blood block the Vessels, while excessive Yin means failure of Yang to arrive. Hence the knotted pulse.

Regularly intermittent pulse (Dai mai)

A regularly intermittent pulse is slow and weak with missed beats at regular intervals. It is associated with declining Zang Qi; it also indicates wind patterns, painful patterns and disorders due to emotional fear and fright, or traumatic contusions and sprains. The declining of the Qi of the Zang means insufficiency of Qi and Blood and may create discontinuation of Qi flowing in the Vessels. Therefore the pulse is slow and weak with regular missed beats at long intervals. The presence of a regularly intermittent pulse in wind patterns, painFul patterns and disorders due to emotional fear and fright or traumatic contusions and sprains is due to disturbance of the Heart Qi leading to discontinuation of the Qi flowing in the Vessels.

As the process of a disease is complex, the above described abnormal pulses do not often appear in their pure form, the combination of two pulses or more is often present. The condition of a number of pulses present at the same time is called complicated pulse. The indication of a complicated pulse is the combination of indications of each single pulse. For instance, a superficial pulse indicates exterior patterns, and a tense pulse indicates Cold patterns, a superficial and a tense pulse, therefore, indicates exterior Cold patterns. As a rapid pulse indicates Heat patterns, a superficial and rapid pulse indicates exterior Heat patterns.

Palpation of the Abdomen and Epigastrium

Abdominal and epigastrium pain which is alleviated by pressure is associated with deficiency, while that aggravated by pressure is related to excess. Abdominal distension and Fullness with tympanic note on percussion indicate stagnation of Qi if the abdomen does not feel hard on pressure and the urination is normal. If the abdomen feels like a rubber bag containing Water, and dysurine is present, it suggests accumulation of fluid. Immovable hard masses in the abdomen with pain at a definite site indicate stagnation of Blood. Unfixed soft masses oi the intermittent feeling of an indefinite mass in the abdomen with unfixed painFul areas indicate stagnation of Qi.

Palpation of acupuncture points

This method of palpation can be traced back to the early medical book The Internal Classic. One of its parts Ling Shu (Miraculous Pivot) says: "In order to see if the Back - Shu Point is located with accuracy, one may press the region to see if the patient feels sore or if the patient's original soreness gets relieved, in which case, the point has been located with accuracy". The Fifteenth chapter of the same book also states "When the Five Zang organs are diseased; the symptoms will manifest themselves in the conditions of the twelve Yuan (Source) Points with which they are connected". If we fully grasp the connections between the Zang organs and their corresponding Yuan (Source) Points as well as the latter's external manifestations, there will be no difficulty for us to understand the nature of the diseases of the Five Zang organs. Traditional Chinese Clinical practice in the recent years has demonstrated that during illness tenderness or sensative reactions may occur along the courses of the involved meridians or at certain points where the Qi of the meridian is converged. In gastralgia, for instance, tenderness may occur at Weishu (BL-21) and Zusanii (St-36) in disorders of the Liver there may be tenderness at Ganshu (BL-18) and Qimen (Liv-14): while in appendicitis, it may occur at Shangjuxu (St-37) the lower He-Sea Point of the Large Intestine. These signs may assist in making dignosis for disorders of internal organs.

Section 3

Pattern Identification

Differentation of Patterns of Disharmony

Differentiation of patterns is the method in traditional Chinese medicine of recognizing and diagnosing diseases. In accordance with the basic knowledge of traditional Chinese medicine, this method entails making a comprehensive analysis of the symptoms and signs obtained by applying the four diagnostic methods, in order to clarify their internal relationships, and ascertain their causes and nature as well as the relative strength of the antipathogenic Qi and pathogenic factor, and the direction of the pathological development. Differentiation of patterns and determination of treatment are inseparable, one relating to the other. The former is the premise and foundation of the later. The methods of treatment, so determined, may in turn test the validity of the differentiation. Correct differentiation is a prerequisite for applying appropriate methods and attaining anticipated results.

There are a number of methods in traditional Chinese medicine for differentiating patterns, including differentiation according to the theory of the:

Eight principles

• Exterior and interior	• Cold and Heat
• Deficiency and excess	• Yin and Yang

Qi

• Qi Deficiency	• Sinking Qi
• Qi Stagnation	• Rebellious Qi

Blood

• Blood Deficiency	• Blood Stasis (Stagnation)
• Heat in the Blood	

Zang Fu organs

• Lung	• Large Intestine
• Spleen	• Stomach
• Heart	• Small Intestine
• Kidney	• Urinary Bladder
• Liver	• Gallbladder

Complicated patterns

Deficiency of both the Heart and Spleen	Deficiency of the Qi of the Lung and Kidney
Deficiency of the Qi of the Lung and Spleen	Deficiency of the Yang of the Spleen and Kidney
Deficiency of the Yin of the Liver and Kidney	Deficiency of the Yin of the Lung and Kidney
Disharmony between the Heart and Kidney	Disharmony between the Liver and Stomach
Imbalance between the Liver and Spleen	Invasion of the Lung by the Liver Fire

Eight Principals

Of these, differentiation according to eight principles is the general method. Differentiation according to the theory of Qi and Blood and that according to the theory of Zang Fu organs are mainly concerned with endogenous diseases, while differentiation according to the theory of meridians and collaterals is principally concerned with disorders of meridians and collaterals. Each method has its own features and lays stress on a particular aspect while connecting with and supplementing the others. It is essential to understand and possess a thorough knowledge, through clinical practice, of the basic contents and characteristics of each method.

Exterior and Interior

The categories of exterior and interior form two principles, which are used to determine the depth of the diseased area and to generalize the direction of the development of a disease. The skin, hair, muscles and their interspaces, and the superficial portion of meridians and collaterals of the human body belong to the exterior, while the five Zang and six Fu organs pertain to the interior.

> Exterior Cold - Severe chills, mild fever, no sweating, absence of thirst, thin, white and moist tongue coating, superficial and tense pulse.
>
> Exterior Heat - Chills, fever, headache, general aching, thin tongue coating, superficial pulse. Mild chills, severe fever, no sweating or sweating, thirst, thin and yellow tongue coating, superficial and rapid pulse.
>
> Exterior deficiency - Sweating.
>
> Exterior excess - No sweating.

Exterior patterns

Exterior patterns refer to pathological conditions resulted from the invasion of the superficial portion of the body by exogenous pathogenic factors. They are marked by sudden onset of symptoms with short duration, and are often seen at the early stage of exogenous diseases. The chief manifestations are an intolerance to Cold (or wind), fever, a thin tongue coating and a superficial pulse. The accompanying symptoms and signs are headache, general aching, nasal obstruction and cough. Clinical manifestations may vary according to the invading pathogenic factors and the body constitution of the patient. They are manifested as Cold, Heat, deficiency and excess.

Interior patterns

Interior patterns refer to pathological conditions resulted from the transmission of exogenous pathogenic factors to the interior of the body to affect Zang Fu organs, or from the functional disturbances of Zang Fu organs. Interior patterns cover a wide range of pathological conditions and may occur in the following three conditions: transmission of persistent pathogenic factors from the exterior to the interior of the body to invade Zang Fu organs; direct attack on Zang Fu organs by exogenous pathogenic factors; drastic emotional changes, improper diet and overstrain and stress, all of which affect Zang Fu organs directly, leading to functional disturbances. For details of interior patterns, refer to the differentiation of deficiency and excess, and to the differentiation of patterns according to the theory of Zang Fu organs.

Differentiation of exterior and interior patterns.

The accompaniment of aversion to Cold with fever, and changes in tongue coating and pulse are highly significant for differentiating exterior and interior patterns in exogenous febrile diseases. Generally, fever accompanied by aversion to Cold suggests exterior patterns; fever with no aversion to Cold, or aversion to Cold with no fever indicates interior patterns. A thin and white tongue coating, possible with red tongue borders, is often seen in exterior patterns. The appearance of other abnormal qualities of tongue coating often indicates interior patterns. A superficial pulse suggests exterior patterns; a deep pulse suggests interior patterns.

The relationship between exterior and interior patterns.

In given conditions, exogenous pathogenic factors, if they are not expelled from the exterior of the body, may be transmitted to the interior, giving rise to interior patterns. This is known as "transmission from the exterior to the interior." Pathogenic factors in some interior patterns may be transmitted from the interior to the superficial portion of the body. This is known as "transmission from the interior to the exterior." The occurrence of the transmission mainly depends upon the relative strength of the pathogenic factor and antipathogenic Qi. The transmission of pathogenic factors from the exterior to the interior is often due to weakened body resistance to disease, or to hyperactivity of the pathogenic factors, improper care, or incorrect or delayed treatment. The transmission of interior pathogenic factors to the interior is often the result of correct treatment and care, and strengthened body resistance to disease. Generally speaking, the inward transmission of pathogenic factors indicates an aggravation of the disease, while the outward transmission represents a tendency of pathogenic factors in the interior being expelled, thus indicating an alleviation of the disease.

In the process of the development of disease, there is a condition known as "the exterior and interior being diseased simultaneously." This may appear at the early stage of a disease, when both exterior and interior patterns are seen at the same time. This also occurs when exogenous pathogenic factors are transmitted to the interior, while the exterior patterns are still present. Prolonged endogenous diseases complicated with recent exogenous diseases, or exogenous diseases inducing acute attacks of chronic endogenous diseases may also be the causes. As exterior and interior patterns are usually complicated with Cold, Heat, deficiency and excess, many different patterns are exhibited in " the exterior and interior being diseased simultaneously, " for example, exterior Cold complicated with interior Heat, exterior deficiency with interior excess, and exterior excess with interior deficiency.

Intermediate patterns. Intermediate patterns refer to pathological conditions in which exogenous pathogenic factors fail to be transmitted completely to the interior, while the antipathogenic Qi is not strong enough to expel the pathogenic factors to the body surface. The pathogenic factors thus remain between the exterior and interior. The chief clinical manifestations are alternate chills and fever, discomfort and Fullness in the chest and hypochondria, vomiting, anorexia, bitter taste in the mouth, dry throat, blurred vision and Wiry pulse. For details, refer to the ShaoYang Pattern in the chapter "Differentiation of Patterns According to the Theory of the Six Meridians."

Cold and Heat

Cold and Heat are the two principles used to differentiate the nature of a disease. According to the fifth chapter of Su Wen (Plain Questions) "Predominance of Yang gives rise to Heat, and predominance of Yin gives rise to Cold." Cold and Heat patterns are concrete manifestations of excess and deficiency of Yin Yang. Distinguishing between Cold and Heat patterns is important for guiding treatment.

Cold patterns

Pallor, aversion to Cold, absence of thirst or drinking a little hot drinks, loose stools, clear copious urination. Pale tongue with white and moist coating. Slow pulse.

Heat patterns

Red complexion, fever, thirst, preference for cold, constipation, deep yellow and scanty urine. Red tongue with yellow and dry coating. Rapid pulse.

Cold patterns and Heat patterns

Cold patterns are pathological conditions resulted from exposure to exogenous pathogenic Cold or from deficiency of Yang in the interior of the body. Heat patterns are pathological conditions caused by invasion of exogenous pathogenic Heat or by deficiency of Yin in the interior of the body.

Since Cold and Heat patterns are opposite in nature, the symptoms and signs they manifest are entirely different. Cold patterns are revealed by aversion to Cold, preference for warmth, tastelessness in the mouth, absence of thirst, pallor, Cold limbs, lying with the body curled up, loose stools, clear urine which is increased in volume, pale tongue, white and moist coating, slow or tense pulse. Heat patterns manifest as fever, preference for coolness, thirst with preference for Cold drinks, redness of face and eyes, irritability, restlessness, constipation, deep - yellow and scanty urine, red tongue with yellow and dry coating, and rapid pulse.

Deciding whether a pattern is of Heat or Cold nature cannot be based on one clinical manifestation alone. The correct conclusion is reached after careful observation of all the clinical manifestations. Of these, the presence of Cold, Heat and thirst and the conditions of complexion, four limbs, defecation, urination, tongue coating and pulse are the most important. Table 12 explains the differentiation of Cold and Heat conditions of excess type in interior patterns.

The relationship between Cold and Heat patterns

Although Cold patterns and Heat patterns are opposite in nature, they have a close relationship. They can exist simultaneously, manifesting as complicated patterns of Cold and Heat. In given conditions, they can also be transformed into each other, presenting either transformation of Cold patterns into Heat, or of Heat patterns into Cold. When the disease has developed to a very severe stage, patterns of true Heat and false Cold or true Cold and false Heat may appear.

Complicated patterns of Cold and Heat

The patient may have simultaneous signs of Heat in the upper half of the body, and of Cold in the lower half. The pattern like this is known as "Heat above with Cold below." This is one of the most frequently seen complicated patterns of Cold and Heat. Clinically the "Heat above" manifests as suffocation and Heat sensation in the chest and a frequent desire to vomit, whilst the "Cold below" presents abdominal pain which can be alleviated by warmth, and loose stools. The pattern is often due to a complicated etiology involving both Cold and Heat. This leads to a pathological disharmony of Yin and Yang of various Zang Fu organs, and manifests as excess of Yang in the upper part of the body and excess of Yin in the lower part. Other frequently seen complicated patterns are Cold on the exterior with Heat in the interior, and Heat on the exterior with Cold in the interior.

Transformation of Cold and Heat patterns

In transformation of a Cold pattern into Heat, the Cold pattern occurs first and gradually changes into a Heat pattern. An example is exposure to exogenous pathogenic Cold which may lead to an exterior Cold pattern and produce such symptoms and signs as fever, aversion to Cold, general aching, no sweating, white tongue coating and superficial and tense pulse. If this pathogenic Cold goes deep into the interior of the body and turns into Heat, Cold signs such as aversion to Cold will subside, but fever persists and other Heat signs such as irritability, thirst and yellow tongue coating will occur in succession. This indicates the transformation of exterior Cold into interior Heat. In transformation of a Heat pattern into Cold, the Heat pattern occurs first and gradually changes into a Cold pattern. An example is abrupt appearance of Cold limbs, pallor, and a deep and slow pulse in the patient with high fever, profuse sweating, thirst, irritability, and a surging and rapid pulse. These are the manifestations of the transformation of a Heat pattern into a Cold one. The mutual transformation of Cold and Heat patterns takes place in certain conditions, depending crucially on the relative strength of the pathogenic factor and antipathogenic Qi. Generally speaking, transformation of Cold into Heat results from a strengthening of the antipathogenic Qi and hyperactivity of Yang Qi. Constitutional deficiency of Yang, or exhaustion of Yang Qi during the course of a disease, may lead to a failure of the antipathogenic Qi in resisting the pathogenic factor, thus giving rise to transformation of a Heat pattern into a Cold one.

True and false phenomena in Cold and Heat patterns

True Heat with false Cold refers to a pattern in which there is Heat in the interior of the body and false Cold on the exterior. The pattern is manifested as Cold limbs, but a burning sensation in the chest and abdomen; no aversion to Cold, but aversion to Heat; and a deep but forceFul pulse. In addition, there is thirst with preference for Cold drinks, irritability, dry throat, foul breath, scanty, deep - yellow urine, constipation and a deep red tongue with yellow dry coating. In this pattern, excessive internal Heat binders the Yang Qi from reaching the exterior. True Cold with false Heat refers to a pattern in which there is real Cold in the interior and false Heat on the exterior. Clinical manifestations are feverishness of the body, flushed face, thirst and a superficial pulse. However, the patient wants to cover up the body in spite of the feverishness, wants to take warm drinks to relieve the thirst, and has a superficial and weak pulse. In addition, there are other Cold signs such as clear urine, loose stools and a pale tongue with white coating.

In this pattern, excessive Yin Cold in the interior forces the Yang Qi to the exterior. It is clear that the appearance of a disease does not necessarily reflect its essential nature in these types of patterns. CareFul observation and analysis should be made, if the false and true phenomena are to be differentiated accurately. Attention should be paid to the following points: Whether the pulse is forceFul or weak; whether the tongue is pale or red; whether the tongue coating is moist or dry; whether there is thirst or not; whether the patient likes Cold drinks or hot drinks; whether the chest and abdomen are warm or not; whether the urine is clear or yellow; and whether the patient wants to cover up the body or not.

Deficiency and Excess

Deficiency and excess are the two principles which are used to generalize and distinguish the relative strength of the antipathogenic Qi and pathogenic factor. According to the twenty-eighth chapter of Su Wen (Plain Questions), "hyperactivity of the pathogenic factor causes excess; consumption of essential Qi causes deficiency." Distinguishing whether a pattern is of deficiency type or of excess type forms the basis for the determination of promoting the antipathogenic Qi or eliminating the pathogenic factor in the treatment.

Deficiency refers to insufficiency of the antipathogenic Qi, and therefore patterns of deficiency type refer to pathological conditions resulted from deficiency of the antipathogenic Qi. Excess refers to hyperactivity of the pathogenic factor, and therefore patterns of excess type refer to pathological conditions in which the pathogenic factor is hyperactive, while the antipathogenic Qi remains strong.

Patterns of deficiency type

Insufficiency of the antipathogenic Qi of the human body may manifest as deficiency of Yin, deficiency of Yang, deficiency of Qi or deficiency of Blood, which may form different patterns. For patterns of Qi deficiency and Blood deficiency, refer to differentiation of patterns according to the theory of Qi and Blood.

Patterns of deficiency type

Emaciation, listlessness, lassitude, feeble breathing, dislike of speaking, pallor, palpitations, shortness of breath, insomnia, poor memory, spontaneous and night sweating, nocturnal emission, nocturnal enuresis, pain alleviated by pressure. Dry tongue with no coating or little coating. Pulse of deficiency type.

Patterns of Yang deficiency and patterns of Yin in deficiency. They generalize pathological conditions resulted from deficiency of Yang and Yin of the body. According to the inter-

consuming-supporting relationship of Yin and Yang, deficiency of Yang leads to a relative excess of Yin, and deficiency of Yin leads to a relative excess of Yang. In addition to the clinical manifestations of deficiency type, Cold signs are seen in deficiency of Yang, and Heat signs are seen in deficiency of Yin. However, they are essentially different from Cold and Heat patterns caused respectively by excess of Yin and excess of Yang.

Deficiency of Yin

Afternoon fever, malar flush, Heat sensation in the palms and soles, night sweating, Dryness of the throat and mouth, yellow urine, dry stools. Red tongue with little coating. Thready and rapid pulse.

Deficiency of Yang - Chills, Cold limbs, listlessness, lassitude, spontaneous sweating, absence of thirst, clear urine increased in volume, loose stools. Pale tongue with white coating. Weak pulse.

Patterns of excess type

In patterns of excess type, the clinical manifestations vary with the nature of the invading exogenous pathogenic factors and areas of the human body they invade. The following factors are mainly considered in distinguishing patterns of deficiency type from those of excess type: Body shape, spirit, strength of voice and breath, response to pressure on painFul areas, tongue coating and pulse.

Patterns of excess type

Sturdiness, agitation, sonorous voice, coarse breathing, distension and Fullness in the chest and abdomen, pain aggravated by pressure, constipation or tenesmus, dysuria. Thick and sticky tongue coating. Pulse of excess type.

The relationship between patterns of deficiency type and patterns of excess type. While patterns of deficiency type and patterns of excess type are essentially different, they are also interconnected, and one may affect the other. The clinical manifestations are described as follows.

Complication of deficiency and excess

When deficiency of the antipathogenic Qi and excess of the pathogenic factor manifest at the same time, this is known as a pattern complicated with deficiency and excess. Either deficiency of the antipathogenic Qi or excess of the pathogenic factor may predominate in complicated patterns. There are also complicated patterns in which deficiency of the antipathogenic Qi and excess of the pathogenic factor are on equal terms. Appropriate methods of treatment are determined on the basis of distinguishing which predominates and which is more urgent.

Transformation of deficiency and excess.

Although the pathogenic factor in patterns of excess type may gradually subside, the antipathogenic Qi is already injured due to delayed or incorrect treatment, thus transforming patterns of excess type into patterns of deficiency type. An example is a Heat pattern of excess type which manifests as high fever, thirst, sweating and superficial and rapid pulse. If the disease persists for a long time and consumes Body Fluids, this may transform into a pattern of deficiency type showing emaciation, pallor, feebleness, little tongue coating or no coating, and thready and weak pulse. In patterns of deficiency type, insufficiency of the antipathogenic Qi may impair the functions of certain Zang Fu organs in distribution and transformation, and produce endogenous pathogenic factors, thus eliciting various patterns of excess type. Excess resulting from deficiency like this is also known as deficiency complicated with excess, or as deficiency of the root cause with excess of manifestations. In deficiency of Qi of the Spleen and Lung, for example, dysfunction in transportation, transformation, dispersing and descending may produce endogenous pathogenic factors such as Phlegm, retained fluid, harmFul Water or Damp.

True and false phenomena in deficiency and excess

False phenomena may appear in patterns of deficiency type and those of excess type. Special care should be taken to distinguish them. True excess with false deficiency refers to a pattern of excess type which is accompanied by symptoms and signs similar to a pattern of deficiency type. An example is accumulation of Dryness and Heat in the intestines and Stomach, which binders circulation of Qi and Blood, and elicits such symptoms and signs as indifference, a Cold sensation of the body, Cold limbs, and deep and slow pulse. But Further examination of the patient will show a sonorous voice, coarse breathing, deep, slow but forceFul pulse, distension and Fullness in the abdomen, constipation, and red tongue with burnt - yellow coating. All this reveals that the accumulation of Dryness and Heat is the underlying cause of the pathological changes, while the symptoms and signs indicating the pattern of deficiency type are false phenomena.

True deficiency with false excess refers to a pattern of deficiency type which is accompanied by symptoms and signs similar to a pattern of excess type. Deficiency of Qi of the Spleen and Stomach, for example, may lead to weakness in transportation and transformation and give rise to distension, Fullness and pain in the abdomen and Wiry pulse. However, the distension and Fullness in the abdomen may be improved at times, while they usually persist in patterns of excess type. In addition, the abdominal pain is not aggravated by pressure, and is sometimes alleviated by pressure. The pulse is Wiry, but it is also weak on heavy palpation. So deficiency of the middle Jiao leading to dysfunction in transportation is the underlying cause of the pathological changes, while the distension, Fullness and pain in the abdomen indicating a pattern of excess type are false phenomena. Distinguishing between true and false phenomena in deficiency and excess requires careFul examination of the patient's pulse, tongue and other symptoms and signs. Factors such as the strength of the pulse, toughness of the tongue and response to pressure on the painFul area must be assessed. In addition, the causative factors of the disease and medication taken before should be considered.

Yin and Yang

Yin and Yang form a pair of principles used to generalize categories of patterns. Being the key link in the application of the eight principles, Yin and Yang are used to summarize the other three pairs of principles. Exterior, Heat and excess fall into the category of Yang, while interior, Cold and deficiency fall into the category of Yin. Yin and Yang are also used to explain some of the pathological changes of the Zang Fu organs and tissues, e.g. patterns of collapse of Yin, patterns of collapse of Yang , patterns of Yin deficiency, patterns of Yang deficiency.

Yin patterns and Yang patterns

Yin patterns refer to pathological conditions resulting from deficiency of Yang Qi in the body and retention of pathogenic Cold. Yang patterns refer to pathological conditions caused by hyperactivity of Yang Qi in the body and excess of pathogenic Heat. Patterns of deficiency type and Cold patterns come within Yin patterns; patterns of excess type and Heat patterns come within Yang patterns. Generally speaking, so far as clinical manifestations are concerned, those characterized by excitation, fidgeting, hyperactivity and bright complexion fall into the category of Yang patterns, while those characterized by inhibition, quiescence, hyperactivity and sallow complexion fall into the category of Yin patterns.

Collapse of Yin and collapse of Yang.

Collapse of Yin refers to pathological conditions resulting from massive consumption of Yin fluid. Collapse of Yang refers to pathological conditions caused by extreme exhaustion of Yang Qi in the body.

Both collapse of Yin and collapse of Yang are critical patterns in the process of a disease. They may result from the further aggravation of Yin deficiency and Yang deficiency. They may also occur as a result of an abrupt aggravation in acute diseases, e.g. severe vomiting and diarrhea or great loss of Blood may elicit collapse of Yin, and proFuse sweating may cause collapse of Yang.

As Yin and Yang depend upon each other, in the case of collapse of Yin, the Yang Qi has nothing to depend upon, and therefore it dissipates from the body. In collapse of Yang, Yin fluid is also consumed. However, the predominating factors in the two patterns are different, and corresponding methods of treatment must be adopted.

In addition to the various critical symptoms and signs of the disease which occur initially, sweating may be seen in the both patterns. The distinguishing points are described as follows:

Collapse of Yin - Sticky sweat, feverishness of the body, warm hands and feet, shortness of breath, irritability, restlessness, thirst with preference for Cold drinks. Red and dry tongue. Thready, rapid and weak pulse.

Collapse of Yang - ProFuse Cold sweat like pearls, coolness of the body, Cold hands and feet, feeble breathing, listlessness, absence of thirst or preference for hot drinks. Pale and moist tongue. Thready and fading pulse.

Pattern of deficiency of Qi.

The pattern of deficiency of Qi refers to pathological changes resulting from hypofunction of Zang Fu organs.

Clinical manifestations: Fatigue, tiredness, dislike of speaking, lassitude, spontaneous sweating, all of which are worse on exertion; a pale tongue, a pulse of deficiency type.

Etiology and pathology: This pattern is often due to weakness after long illness, feebleness in old age, improper diet, or excess of strain or stress. Insufficiency of the antipathogenic Qi and hypofunction of Zang Fu organs result in dislike of speaking and lassitude. Deficiency of Qi also implies weakness of Qi in propelling Blood normally, hence Qi and Blood fail to go upward to nourish the head and eyes, the result could be dizziness. In case of weakness of defensive Qi, it fails to control the opening and closing of pores, spontaneous sweating occurs. Because exertion further consumes Qi, it will also cause aggravation of the above symptoms. The pale tongue is a consequence of the deficient nutrient Qi which fails to go upward to nourish the tongue, and the deficient type pulse is due to weakness of Qi in moving Blood.

Pattern of sinking of Qi

Sinking of Qi is one of the pathological changes resulting from deficiency of Qi. It is characterized by a weakness in holding ability within the category of Qi deficiency. Since it often occurs in the middle Jiao, it is also known as "sinking of Qi of the middle Jiao."

Clinical manifestations: Fatigue, tiredness, lassitude, a bearing - down distending sensation in the abdominal region, prolapse of the anus or Uterus, gastroptosis and renal ptosis, a pale tongue, a pulse of the deficient type.

Etiology and pathology: The etiology of sinking of Qi is the same as that of deficiency of Qi. Fatigue, tiredness, lassitude, the pale tongue and pulse of the deficient type are common symptoms and signs in the pattern of deficiency of Qi. The bearing - down distending sensation in the abdominal region, prolapse of the anus or Uterus, gastroptosis and renal ptosis are all possible outcomes of weakness in holding ability.

Pattern of stagnation of Qi

The pattern of stagnation of Qi occurs when Qi in a certain portion of the body or of a specific Zang Fu organ is retarded and obstructed.

Clinical manifestations: Distension and pain.

Etiology and pathology: This pattern is often due to mental depression, improper diet, invasion of exogenous pathogenic factors, or sprains and contusions. Hindrance of Qi circulation is followed by obstruction of Qi, which is the primary cause of distension and pain. These symptoms have the following features: Distension is more severe than pain; both distension and pain wax and wane with no fixed position; and the onset is often related to emotions and the symptoms may be alleviated temporarily by belching or flatulence.

As stagnation of Qi has varied causes and may involve different Zang Fu organs, there exist, aside from distension, stuffiness and pain, separate clinical manifestations. For details, refer to the chapter dealing with differentiation of patterns according to the theory of Zang Fu organs.

Pattern of Rebellious Qi

In the pattern of rebellious Qi, there is a dysfunction of the Qi in ascending and descending which leads to upward disturbance of the Qi of Zang Fu organs. This pattern often refers to pathological changes resulting from upward disturbance of the Qi of the Lung and Stomach, and from excessive ascending of the Qi of the Liver.

Clinical manifestations: Upward disturbance of the Lung Qi manifests as coughing and asthmatic breathing. Upward disturbance of the Stomach Qi gives rise to belching, hiccups, nausea and vomiting. Excessive ascending of the Liver Qi causes headache, dizziness and vertigo, coma, hemoptysis and hematemesis.

Etiology and pathology: Upward disturbance of the Lung Qi is often due to invasion of exogenous pathogenic factors or to retention of Phlegm in the Lung. In either case, the Lung Qi fails in its function to disperse and descend, but instead ascends and disturbs, giving rise to coughing and asthmatic breathing.

Retention of fluid, Phlegm or food in the Stomach, of invasion of the Stomach by exogenous pathogenic factors may all block Qi circulation and deprive the Stomach Qi of its function in descending. Upward disturbance of the Stomach Qi produces belching, hiccups, nausea and vomiting.

Injury of the Liver by anger leads to excessive ascent of the Liver Qi and Further, to upward disturbance of Qi and Fire of the Liver, producing headache, dizziness and vertigo, and even coma, hemoptysis and hematemesis in severe cases.

Pattern of deficiency of Blood

The pattern of deficiency of Blood occurs when there is insufficient Blood to nourish Zang Fu organs and meridians.

Clinical manifestations: Pallor or sallow complexion, pale lips, dizziness, blurring of vision, palpitations, insomnia, numbness of the hands and feet, a pale tongue and a thready pulse.

Etiology and pathology: This pattern is often due to weakness of the Spleen and Stomach, hence Qi and Blood have an insufficient source, or due to excessive Blood loss, or drastic emotional changes which consume Yin Blood. Deficiency of Blood deprives the head, eyes and face of nourishment, causing dizziness, blurring of vision, pallor or sallow complexion and pale lips. Blood, failing to nourish the Heart, may lead to disturbance of the Mind, palpitations and insomnia appears. Numbness of the hands and feet originates from the lack of nourishment of meridians and collaterals. The pale tongue is a result of the deficiency of Blood depriving the tongue of nourishment, whilst the thready pulse is a consequence of insufficient Blood in the Vessels.

Pattern of stagnation of Blood

Stagnation of Blood refers to the accumulation of Blood in a local area due to hindrance of the Blood circulation or to extravasated Blood which has not been dispersed or immediately expelled from a fixed location in the body.

Clinical manifestations: Pain, mass tumors, hemorrhage, and ecchymoses or petechiae.

Etiology and pathology: There are many causes of stagnation of Blood, such as sprains and contusions, hemorrhage, retardation of Qi circulation leading to retardation of Blood circulation, deficiency of Qi causing a weakness in the normal movement of Blood, and invasion of the Blood system by pathogenic Cold or Heat.

Pain, which is the main symptom, occurs as a consequence of obstruction by stagnant Blood. The pain is fixed in location and stabbing in nature. Accumulation of stagnant Blood in the local area forms mass tumors which have fixed positions and are firm on palpation. Obstruction of Vessels by stagnant Blood does not permit Blood to circulate along the normal courses, and hence induces hemorrhage.

Hemorrhage of this sort occurs repeatedly and consists of purplish dark flow and may exhibit clots. Stagnation of Blood may also manifest with purplish spots on the skin and tongue.

Cold, Heat, excess and deficiency may all be causative factors of stagnation of Blood, hence patterns associated with these factors will be present along with the symptoms and signs listed above.

Pattern of Heat in the Blood

Heat in the Blood refers to the pattern which results either from endogenous Heat in the Blood system or from invasion of the Blood system by exogenous pathogenic Heat.

Clinical manifestations: Mental restlessness, or mania in severe cases, a dry mouth with no desire to drink, deep - red tongue, rapid pulse, possible occurrence of various hemorrhagic patterns, proFuse menstrual flow in women.

Etiology and pathology: This pattern is often due to either invasion of exogenous pathogenic Heat or to obstruction of Liver Qi turning into Fire. Hyperactivity of Heat in the Blood disturbs the Mind and results in mental restlessness or even mania in severe cases. Consumption of Yin Blood leads to a dry mouth, but since Heat is not in the Qi system, the patient does not want to drink. Excessive Heat accelerates the Blood circulation and hence a deep - red tongue and rapid pulse appear.

Hyperactive Heat in the Blood system easily causes injury of the Blood Vessels, the result of which is epistaxis, hemoptysis, hematemesis, hematuria and proFuse menstrual flow in women.

Acupuncture, Acupressure and moxibustion may regulate Qi and Blood. As stated in the first chapter of Ling Shu (Miraculous Pivot), "Fine needles are applied to clear obstructions in meridians and collaterals and to regulate Qi and Blood." Another medical classic Precious Supplementary Prescriptions holds, "All diseases start from stagnation of Qi and Blood. Needling may promote smooth circulation of Qi and Blood...." In acupuncture and acupressure clinics, suitable points are selected, and different techniques of needling and moxibustion are adopted to regulate Qi and Blood and to restore their harmonious states.

Lung Patterns of Disharmony

The Lung is the hub of vital energy. It dominates Qi, in particular, Zong (gathering) Qi, which is formed in the Lung, it controls respiration and takes charge of dispersing and descending, it relates externally to the skin and hair and opens into the nose. Pathological changes of the Lung mainly manifest as insufficiency of Zong (gathering) Qi and dysfunctions in respiration, dispersing and descending. As the Lung is a delicate organ and most susceptible to Cold or Heat, and it relates to the skin and hair, it is often the first organ to be affected when exogenous pathogenic factors invade the body.

Lung Qi Deficiency	Lung Yin eficiency
Invasion of the Lung by pathogenic wind	Retention of Phlegm Damp in the Lung
Retention of Phlegm Heat in the Lung	

Lung Qi Deficiency

Clinical manifestations: Feeble cough, shortness of breath which is worse on exertion, clear dilute sputum, lassitude, lack of desire to talk, low voice, aversion to wind, frigid appearance, spontaneous sweating, a pale tongue with thin, white coating and a weak pulse of the deficient type.

Etiology and pathology: This pattern is often due to a prolonged cough which damages the Qi and gradually leads to weakness of the Lung Qi. Or it may be due to overstrain and stress, or to weakness of Yuan (Source) Qi after a prolonged illness, either of which may cause insufficiency of Lung Qi and impairment of the Lung's function in dominating Qi. Feeble cough results from weakness of the Lung Qi and impairment of the Lung's function in dominating Qi and in descending. Shortness of breath and asthmatic breathing are the outcome of lack of Qi following impairment of the Lung's function in dominating Qi. Insufficiency of the Lung Qi does not allow the Qi to perform its function in distributing Body Fluids, the accumulation of which forms clear and dilute sputum. Weakness of Wei (defensive) Qi at the body surface produces aversion to wind, frigid appearance, spontaneous sweating. Lassitude, lack of desire to talk, low voice, a pale tongue with thin, white coating and a weak pulse of the deficient type are all signs of deficiency of Qi.

Lung Yin Deficiency

Clinical manifestations: Unproductive cough, cough with a small amount of sticky sputum, or cough with Blood tinged sputum; Dryness of the mouth and throat, afternoon fever, malar flush, night sweating, Heat sensations in the palms and soles, a red tongue with a small amount of coating and a thready, rapid pulse.

Etiology and pathology: This pattern is often due to a prolonged cough which consumes the Lung Yin; to overstrain and stress; or to invasion of exogenous pathogenic Dryness which causes insufficiency of the Lung Yin and, Further, the production of deficiency type Heat in the interior. Consumption of Yin deprives the Lung of moisture and allows upward disturbance of the Lung Qi, the result being cough with a small amount of sputum, Dryness of the mouth and throat. Injury of the Lung Vessels by cough produces Blood tinged sputum. Deficiency of Yin leads to hyperactivity of Fire, resulting in afternoon fever, malar flush, night sweating and Heat sensations in the palms and soles. A red tongue with a small amount of coating, and a thready rapid pulse are both signs of Heat due to deficiency of Yin.

Invasion of the Lung by pathogenic wind

Clinical manifestations: Invasion of the Lung by wind Cold displays such signs as cough with mucous sputum, absence of thirst, nasal obstruction, Watery nasal discharge; possible chills and fever; absence of sweating, headache, a thin, white tongue coating and a superficial, tense pulse. Invasion of the Lung by wind Heat generates cough with yellow purulent sputum, thirst, sore throat; possibly with Heat sensation of the body and aversion to wind; headache, a thin, yellow tongue coating and a superficial, rapid pulse.

Etiology and pathology: The pattern is due to invasion of the Lung system by exogenous pathogenic wind complicated with either Cold or Heat. Invasion of the Lung by wind Cold impairs the Lung's function in dispersing and descending and produces cough with mucous sputum. As the Lung opens into the nose, invasion of the Lung by pathogenic Cold affects the corresponding orifice and gives rise to nasal obstruction with Watery nasal discharge. Since the Lung is closely related to the skin and hair, invasion of the body surface by wind Cold causes disharmony of Ying (nutrient) Qi and Wei (defensive) Qi, producing chills and fever, absence of sweating, and Heat and body aches. A thin, white tongue coating and a superficial, tense pulse are both signs of wind Cold affecting the body surface. Invasion of the Lung by wind Heat impairs the function of the Lung in dispersing and descending, manifesting as cough with yellow purulent sputum. The consumption of Body Fluids by pathogenic Heat is the cause of thirst. Upward disturbance of wind Heat generates sore throat. The invasion of the body surface by wind Heat impedes Wei (defensive) Qi, which explains Heat sensation of the body, aversion to wind and headache. A thin, yellow tongue coating and a superficial, rapid pulse are both signs of wind Heat affecting the body surface.

Retention of Phlegm Damp in the Lung

Clinical manifestations: Cough with much frothy or white, sticky sputum, Fullness and stuffiness in the chest, gurgling with sputum in the throat, shortness of breath or asthmatic breathing; orthopnea in severe cases; a white, sticky tongue coating and a rolling pulse.

Etiology and pathology: This pattern is often due to recurrent attacks of cough following exposure to exogenous pathogenic factors. This impairs the Lung's function in disseminating Body Fluids, the accumulation the pattern may result from the dysfunction of the Spleen in transportation, which leads to the formation of Phlegm Damp. When this remains in the Lung, the above symptoms will be induced or become above symtoms will be induced or become worse on exposure to pathogenic wind Cold. Phlegm Damp blocks the passage of Qi and impairs the function of the Lung Qi, bringing on cough with much sputum, stuffiness in the chest, asthmatic breathing, gurgling with sputum in the throat, and in severe cases, orthopnea. Expectoration of frothy or white, sticky sputum, a white, sticky tongue coating and a rolling pulse are all signs of retention of Phlegm Damp in the interior.

Retention of Phlegm Heat in the Lung

Clinical manifestations: Cough, asthmatic and coarse breathing; flapping of ala nasi in severe cases; yellow, thick sputum or expectoration of foul smelling Bloody pus; chest pain on coughing, Dryness of the mouth, yellow urine, constipation, a red tongue with yellow, sticky coating and a rolling, rapid pulse.

Etiology and pathology: This pattern is often due to invasion of exogenous pathogenic wind Heat, or invasion of wind Cold which goes to the interior of the body and turns into Heat after a period of retention. Heat in the Lung changes Body Fluids into Phlegm by condensation. The Phlegm and Heat intermingle and impair the descending function of the Lung, the result being cough, asthmatic breathing, chest pain and yellow, thick sputum. Phlegm Heat blocks the Vessels of the Lung, which leads to decomposition and thereby produces pus, effecting expectoration of Bloody pus. Consumption of Body Fluids by pathogenic Heat gives rise to Dryness of the mouth and yellow urine. Failure of the Lung Qi in descending is the cause of constipation. A yellow, sticky tongue coating, a red tongue and a rolling, rapid pulse are all signs of retention of Phlegm Heat in the interior.

Large Intestine Patterns of Disharmony

The Large Intestine functions to transmit the waste products and excrete them from the body. Pathological changes of the Large Intestine mainly manifest as dysfunctions in transmission.

| Consumption of the fluid of the Large Intestine | Damp beat in the Large Intestine |

Consumption of the fluid of the Large Intestine

Clinical manifestations: Dry stools, constipation, Dryness of the mouth and throat, a red tongue with little moisture or with a dry yellow coating and a thready pulse.

Etiology and pathology: The pattern often occurs to people in old age, to women after deLivery, or in the late stage of a febrile disease when there is consumption of Body Fluids. Insufficiency of fluid in the Large Intestine leads to Dryness, thus constipation ensues. Dryness of the mouth and throat, a red tongue with little moisture or with a dry yellow coating and a thready pulse are all signs of deficiency type Heat due to consumption of fluids.

Damp Heat in the Large Intestine

Clinical manifestations: Abdominal pain, †tenesmus; Blood and mucus in the stools, or, diarrhea with yellow, Watery stools; a burning sensation of the anus; scanty deep - yellow urine; possible fever and thirst; a yellow, sticky tongue coating and a rolling, rapid pulse or soft, rapid pulse.

Etiology and pathology: Ibis pattern often occurs in summer and autumn when pathogenic Summer Heat, Damp and toxic Heat invades the intestines and Stomach. It may also be due to irregular food intake, excessive eating of raw and Cold food, or intake of unclean food, all of which may injure the Spleen, Stomach and intestines. Abdominal pain is the outcome of retention of pathogenic Damp Heat in the intestines, which results in retardation of Qi circulation. Damp Heat injures the Blood Vessels of the intestinal tract and thus creates Blood and mucus in the stools. Retention of Damp Heat in the Large Intestine impairs its function of transmission, eliciting diarrhea with yellow, Watery stools, burning sensation in the anus and scanty, deep yellow urine. Consumption of Body Fluids by excessive Heat gives rise to fever and thirst. A yellow, sticky tongue coating and a rolling, rapid pulse or a soft, rapid pulse is all signs of retention of Damp Heat in the interior.

Stomach Patterns of Disharmony

The Stomach functions to receive and digest food. When its Qi descends, its function is normal. So pathological changes of the Stomach often manifest as dysfunction of its Qi in descending and as poor digestion.

The Spleen and Stomach dominate reception, digestion, transportation and transformation by sending the "clear" upwards and bringing down the "turbid." They serve as the source of Qi and Blood, which nourish the whole body. That is why the Spleen and Stomach are called the "source of Post-Heaven constitution."

Damp Heat in the Spleen and Stomach	Hyperactivity of Fire in the Stomach
Insufficiency of the Stomach Yin	Retention of fluid in the Stomach due to Cold
Retention of food in the Stomach	

Damp Heat in the Spleen and Stomach

Clinical manifestations: Fullness and distension in the epigastrium and abdomen, loss of appetite, nausea, vomiting, bitter taste and stickiness in the mouth, heaviness of the body, lassitude ; bright yellow face, eyes and skin ; loose stools, scanty, yellow urine, a yellow, sticky tongue coating and a soft, rapid pulse.

Etiology and pathology: This pattern is often due to invasion of exogenous pathogenic Damp Heat. It may also result from excessive indulgence in greasy and sweet food, or alcoholic drinking, all of which may produce Damp Heat in the interior. Retention of Damp Heat in the Stomach and Spleen impairs their functions in reception, digestion, transportation and transformation, causing Fullness and distension in the epigastrium and abdomen, loss of appetite, nausea, vomiting and loose stools. Excessive Damp Heat gives rise to a sticky and bitter taste in the mouth and scanty yellow urine. As Damp is characterized by heaviness and viscosity, blockage of the Qi by Damp leads to heaviness of the body and lassitude. Damp Heat stirs up the bile which, therefore, permeates the muscles and skin, presenting bright yellow face, eyes and skin. A yellow sticky tongue coating and a soft rapid pulse are both signs of retention of Damp Heat in the interior.

Stomach Fire

Clinical manifestations: Burning sensation and pain in the epigastric region ; sour regurgitation and an empty and uncomfortable feeling in the Stomach; thirst with preference for Cold drinks; voracious appetite and getting hungry easily; vomiting, foul breath; swelling and pain or ulceration and bleeding of the gums; constipation, scanty yellow urine; a red tongue with yellow coating and a rapid pulse.

Etiology and pathology: This pattern may result from excessive eating of hot and greasy food which turns into Heat and Fire, or from emotional depression which leads to invasion of the Stomach by the Liver Fire. Hyperactivity of Fire in the Stomach burns Body Fluids and thus produces burning pain in the epigastric region and thirst with preference for Cold drinks. If obstruction of the Liver Qi turns into Heat, it may impair the function of the Stomach in descending, thus causing sour regurgitation and an empty and uncomfortable feeling in the Stomach. Hyperactivity of Heat in the Stomach may result in hyperfunction of the Stomach in digesting food, that is the reason for voracious appetite and getting hungry easily. Excessive Heat in the Stomach may make the Stomach Qi disturb upward, vomiting ensues. Since the Stomach Meridian traverses the gums, upward disturbance of the Stomach Fire along the meridian causes foul breath, swelling and pain or ulceration and bleeding of the gums. Constipation, scanty yellow urine, a red tongue with yellow coating, and a rapid pulse are all signs of hyperactivity of Fire and Heat in the interior.

Stomach Yin Deficiency

Clinical manifestations: Burning pain in the epigastric region, an empty and uncomfortable sensation in the Stomach, hunger with no desire to eat; or dry vomiting and hiccups; Dryness of the mouth and throat; constipation; a red tongue with little moisture and a thready rapid pulse.

Etiology and pathology: This pattern may be due to hyperactivity of Heat in the Stomach which consumes the Stomach Yin or to consumption of the Yin fluid by persistent pathogenic Heat at the late stage of a febrile disease. Consumption of the Stomach Yin deprives the Stomach of moisture and impairs its function of descending, the result being burning pain in the epigastric region, an empty and uncomfortable sensation in the Stomach, dry vomiting and hiccups. Insufficiency of fluid in the Stomach impairs the function of the Stomach in receiving food, the consequence is hunger with no desire to eat. With deficiency of Stomach Yin the fluids fail to be sent upward creating Dryness of the mouth anti throat. Constipation, a red tongue with little moisture and thready rapid pulse are all signs of deficiency of Yin producing interior Heat.

Retention of fluid in the Stomach due to Cold

Clinical manifestations: Epigastric Fullness and pain which are worse on exposure to Cold and better to warmth; reflux of clear fluid or vomiting after eating; a white, slippery tongue coating and a slow pulse.

Etiology and pathology: This pattern is often due to a constitutional deficiency of the Stomach Yang complicated by invasion of exogenous pathogenic Cold; or to intake of excessive raw and cold food which causes retention of Cold in the Stomach. Retention of Cold in the Stomach blocks the Stomach Qi and produces epigastric Fullness and pain, which is worse on exposure to Cold but better to warmth, for exposure to Cold, may aggravate the retention while exposure to warmth may disperse Cold and effect a smooth circulation of Qi. Impairment of Yang Qi in a prolonged disease implies inability of Yang Qi to distribute Body Fluids. Thus the retained fluid is formed. If the retained fluid remains in the Stomach and also disturbs upward, reflux of clear fluid and vomiting after eating follow. A white, slippery tongue coating and a slow pulse are both signs of deficient Yang complicated with retention of Cold and fluid in the interior.

Retention of food in the Stomach

Clinical manifestations: Distension, Fullness and pain in the epigastrium and abdomen, foul belching sour regurgitation, and anorexia. There may be vomiting and hesitant bowel movements. The tongue coating is thick and sticky, and pulse rolling.

Etiology and pathology: This pattern may be due to irregular food intake, voracious eating or eating of food which is difficult to digest. Retention of food in the Stomach blocks the Qi passage in the epigastrium and abdomen and thus causes distension, Fullness and pain there. Dysfunction in digesting food brings the turbid Qi upward, which is the cause of foul belching, sour regurgitation, anorexia and vomiting. Retention of the turbid part of the food blocks the Large Intestine and impairs its function in transmission, resulting in hesitant bowel movements. A thick, sticky tongue coating and a rolling pulse are both signs of retention of food.

Spleen Patterns of Disharmony

The Spleen functions to dominate transportation and transformation and control Blood. When its Qi ascends, its function is normal. So pathological changes of the Spleen often manifest as dysfunction in transportation and transformation and in controlling Blood and as sinking of the Spleen Qi.

The Spleen and Stomach dominate reception, digestion, transportation and transformation by sending the "clear" upwards and bringing down the "turbid." They serve as the source of Qi and Blood, which nourish the whole body. That is why the Spleen and Stomach are called the "source of Post-Heaven constitution."

Spleen Qi Deficiency	Spleen Yang Deficiency
Spleen not controlling Blood	Invasion of the Spleen by Cold Damp

Spleen Qi Deficiency

Clinical manifestations: Sallow complexion, emaciation, lassitude, dislike of speaking, reduced appetite, abdominal distension, loose stools ; or a bearing - down sensation in the abdominal region, viscera ptosis, prolapse of the anus ; a pale tongue with a thin, white coating and a slowing - down, weak or soft, thready pulse.

Etiology and pathology: The pattern is due to weakness after a prolonged illness, to overstrain and stress or to improper diet, all of which damage the Spleen Qi. Weakness of the Spleen Qi implies hypofunction in transportation and transformation, which gives rise to reduced appetite, abdominal distension and loose stools. Dysfunction of the Spleen in transportation and transformation produces an insufficient source of Qi and Blood, the result being sallow complexion, emaciation, lassitude and dislike of speaking. Weakness after a prolonged illness binders the Spleen Qi in ascending, and instead it sinks, resulting in bearing - down sensation in the abdominal region and possible prolapse of the Uterus, prolapse of the anus, gastroptosis or renal ptosis. A pale tongue with thin, white coating, and a slowing - down, weak pulse or a soft thready pulse are all signs of deficiency of Qi.

Spleen Yang Deficiency

Clinical manifestations: Pallor, the four limbs being not warm; poor appetite; abdominal distension which is worse after eating or dull pain in the abdominal region which is better with warmth and pressure; loose stools; a pale and delicate tongue with white coating and a deep, slow pulse.

Etiology and pathology: This pattern is a further development of deficiency of the Spleen Qi. It may also result from the intake of excessive raw and cold food or greasy and sweet food; or from excessive administration of herbs of Cold nature, both of which damage the Spleen Yang. Deficiency of the Spleen Yang impairs the Spleen's function in transportation and transformation, bringing on reduced appetite, abdominal distension and loose stools. Insufficiency of the Spleen Yang causes stagnation of Yin Cold and blockage of Qi, the result being a dull pain in the abdominal region. The patient likes warmth and pressure in a Cold pattern of deficiency type. Deficiency of the Spleen Yang is unable to warm up the Qi and Blood and to promote their smooth circulation, thus pallor ensues and the four limbs are not warm. A pale and delicate tongue with white coating and a deep slow pulse are both signs of deficiency of the Spleen Yang.

Spleen not controlling Blood

Clinical manifestations: Pale complexion, lassitude, dislike of speaking, purpura, Bloody stools, excessive menstrual flow, uterine bleeding, a pale tongue and a thready, weak pulse.

Etiology and pathology: This pattern is due to weakness after a prolonged illness, or to overstrain and stress, either of which may weaken the Spleen's function in controlling Blood. Deficiency of the Spleen implies impairment of its function in transportation and transformation, which produces an insufficient source of Qi and Blood that explains pale complexion, lassitude and dislike of speaking. Weakness of the Spleen Qi indicates inability of the Spleen to control Blood, which leaks from the Vessels and thus elicits purpura, Bloody stools, excessive menstrual flow and uterine bleeding. A pale tongue and a thready, weak pulse are both signs of deficiency of Qi and Blood.

Invasion of the Spleen by Cold Damp

Clinical manifestations: Fullness and distension in the epigastrium and abdomen, loss of appetite, sticky saliva, heaviness of the head and body, loose stools or diarrhoea, a white, sticky tongue coating and a soft pulse.

Etiology and pathology: This pattern may be due to wading in Water, being caught in the rain, sitting and sleeping in a Damp place or excessive eating of raw and cold food. The pattern may also result from excessive endogenous Damp. In all these cases, the Yang of the middle Jiao may be strained and the function of the Spleen in transportation and transformation impaired.

Invasion of the Spleen by Cold Damp impairs the Spleen's function in transportation and transformation, resulting in Fullness and distension in the epigastrium and abdomen, loss of appetite, loose stools or diarrhea. As Damp is characterized by heaviness and viscosity, blockage of the Cold Damp produces sticky saliva, and heaviness of the head and body. A white, sticky tongue coating and a soft pulse are both signs of excessive Damp in the interior.

Heart Patterns of Disharmony

The physiological functions of the Heart are dominating Blood and Vessels, and housing the Mind. Pathological changes manifesting as disturbance of Blood circulation and abnormal mental activities come within the diseases of the Heart. Since the Heart opens into the tongue, pathological changes of the tongue such as inflammation or ulceration of the tongue can be treated on the basis of differentiation of patterns of the Heart.

Heart Blood Deficiency	Heart Qi Deficiency
Mind disturbance	Hyperactivity of the Heart Fire
Stagnation of the Heart Blood	

Heart Blood Deficiency, Heart Yin deficiency

Clinical manifestations: Both deficiency of the Heart Blood and deficiency of the Heart Yin may manifest as palpitations, insomnia, dream - disturbed sleep and poor memory. If there are also pallor, pale lips, dizziness and vertigo, a pale tongue and a thready and weak pulse, this suggests deficiency of the Heart Blood. The accompaniment of mental restlessness, Dryness of the mouth, Heat sensation in the palms, and soles, tidal fever, night sweating, a red tongue and a thready and rapid pulse indicates deficiency of the Heart Yin.

Etiology and pathology: They often result from a weak body constitution, asthenia after a long illness or mental irritation which consumes the Heart Blood and Heart Yin. Insufficiency of Yin Blood deprives the Heart of nourishment, leading to palpitations and poor memory. Disturbance of the Mind results in insomnia and dream disturbed sleep. Blood deficiency with inability to nourish upwards may produce dizziness and vertigo, pallor, pale lips, and a pale tongue. The insufficient Blood in the Vessels is the cause of a thready and weak pulse. Insufficiency of the Heart Yin produces deficiency type Heat in the interior, which causes mental restlessness, Dryness of the mouth, Heat sensation in the palms and soles, malar flush, tidal fever, night sweating, a red tongue and a thready and rapid pulse.

Deficiency of the Heart Qi, deficiency of the Heart Yang

Clinical manifestations: Both deficiency of the Heart Qi and deficiency of the Heart Yang may exhibit palpitations and shortness of breath, which become worse on exertion, spontaneous sweating and a thready, weak pulse or a missed - beat pulse. Deficiency of the Heart Qi also manifests as listlessness, lassitude and a pale tongue with white coating. The accompaniment of chills, Cold limbs, cyanosis of lips and a pale, swollen and delicate tongue or a purplish dark tongue indicates deficiency of the Heart Yang. ProFuse sweating, Cold limbs, feeble breathing, a feeble fading pulse and mental cloudiness or even coma are all critical signs of prostration of the Heart Yang .

Etiology and pathology: They are usually caused by gradual declining of the Heart Qi after a long illness, damage of Yang Qi by an abrupt severe disease or weakness of the Qi of Zang due to old age or to Pre-Heaven deficiency. Insufficiency of the Heart Qi or Heart Yang implies weakness of the Heart in propelling the Blood, which explains palpitations and shortness of breath. As exertion consumes Qi, they become worse on exertion. Insufficiency of Blood in the Vessels due to weakness of Blood circulation leads to a thready and weak pulse. A missed beat pulse is produced by discontinuation of the Qi of Vessels due to weakness of the Heart in propelling the Blood. In case of deficiency of Qi and Yang, the muscles and body surface fail to be controlled, spontaneous sweating results. Deficiency of Qi leads to hypo function of Zang Fu organs, bringing on listlessness and lassitude. Deficiency of the Heart Yang deprives the Blood of warmth and gives rise to retardation of Blood circulation, the accompanying symptoms and signs being chills, Cold limbs, cyanosis of lips and a purplish dark tongue. Extreme deficiency of Yang creates an abrupt prostration and severe dissipation of Zong (gathering) Qi from the body with critical signs of profuse sweating, Cold limbs, feeble breathing, mental cloudiness or even coma, and a feeble fading pulse.

Mind Disturbance

("Phlegm misting the Heart" and "Phlegm - Fire disturbing the Heart")

Clinical manifestations: The pattern of "Phlegm misting the Heart" often displays mental depression and dullness, or incoherent speech, weeping and laughing without an apparent reason, or sudden collapse, coma and gurgling with sputum in the throat. A white, sticky tongue coating and a Wiry and rolling pulse are present.

The pattern of "Phlegm Fire disturbing the Heart" often exhibits derangement of the Mind, mania, aggressive and violent behavior, insomnia, dream - disturbed sleep, Hushed face, coarse breathing, constipation, deep - yellow urine, a yellow, sticky tongue coating and a rolling, rapid and forceFul pulse.

Etiology and pathology: The pattern of "Phlegm misting the Heart" is often due to mental depression which results in retardation of Qi circulation and consequent inability of Qi in distributing Body Fluids. The accumulation of Body Fluids forms Phlegm, which mists the Heart and produces the above symptoms and signs. Once the obstructed Qi turns into Fire, which changes Body Fluids to Phlegm by condensation, the Phlegm and Fire intermingle and disturb the Mind, the result would be the occurrence of excessive Phlegm Fire in the interior which manifests as mania, aggressive and violent behavior, insomnia, dream - disturbed sleep, a yellow, sticky tongue coating and a rolling, rapid and forceFul pulse

Hyperactivity of the Heart Fire

Clinical manifestations: Mental restlessness, insomnia, flushed face, thirst, ulceration and pain of the mouth and tongue, hot and deep yellow urine; hesitant and painFul urination in severe cases; a red tongue and a rapid pulse.

Etiology and pathology: The pattern is often due to mental depression which turns into Fire in prolonged cases; to retention in the interior of the body of exogenous pathogenic factors turning into Fire; or to excessive indulgence in pungent and hot food, cigarette smoking or alcoholic drinking, all of which produce Heat and Fire over a long period of time. The Heart Fire produced in the interior attacks the Heart and results in disturbance of the Mind, which is the cause of mental restlessness and insomnia. As the tongue is the sprout of the Heart, the hyperactive Heart Fire hares upwards and causes ulceration and pain of the mouth and tongue. Consumption of Body Fluids by Fire and Heat gives rise to thirst, hot and deep yellow urine, and even hesitant and painFul urination in severe cases. Flushed face, a red tongue and a rapid pulse are the outcomes of hyperactivity of pathogenic Heat which accelerates the Blood circulation.

Heart Blood Stagnation

Clinical manifestations : Palpitations, intermittent cardiac pain (stabbing or stuffy in nature in the pericardial region or behind the sternum) which often refers to the shoulder and arm, a purplish dark tongue or purplish spots on the tongue and a thready and hesitant pulse or a missed - beat pulse. In severe cases there may occur cyanosis of face, lips and nails, Cold limbs and spontaneous sweating.

Etiology and pathology: The pattern often results from insufficiency of the Heart Qi and Heart Yang which causes retardation of Blood circulation. The attack may be induced and the disease aggravated by mental irritation, exposure to Cold after over strain and stress, or excessive indulgence in greasy food and alcoholic drinking, for all of which may elicit accumulation of Phlegm and stagnation of Blood. Stagnation of Blood in the vessel of the Heart creates palpitations and cardiac pain (stabbing pain if stagnation of Blood predominates; stuffy pain if accumulation of Phlegm predominates). As the Heart Meridian of Hand - ShaoYin traverses the shoulder region and the medial aspect of the arm, referred pain there occurs. Stagnation of the Heart Blood may cause retardation of general Blood circulation, which is the cause of cyanosis of the face, Ups and nails, a purplish dark tongue or purplish spots on the tongue and a thready and hesitant pulse or a missed - beat pulse. Deficiency of the Heart Yang and stagnation of the Heart Blood hinder Yang Qi from reaching the four limbs and body surface, and thus inducing Cold limbs and spontaneous sweating.

Small Intestine Patterns of Disharmony

The physiological functions of the Small Intestine are dominating digestion and dividing the "clear" from the "turbid" Therefore the disorders of the Small Intestine are actually included in the disorders of the Spleen. The pattern of pain due to the disturbance of the Qi of the Small Intestine is described here only.

The patterns of the Small Intestine often manifest themselves in disturbance of the digestive function. The deficiency patterns of the Small Intestine are included in the deficiency patterns of the Spleen. Their treatment is directed at the Spleen and Stomach. The Heat pattern of excess type of the Small Intestine is similar to hyperactivity of the Heart Fire. The painful pattern due to disturbance of the Qi of the Small Intestine may be included in the patterns of accumulation of Cold in the Liver Meridian.

Pain due to disturbance of the Qi of the Small Intestine

Clinical manifestations: Acute pain of the lower abdomen, abdominal distension, borborygmus; or bearing down pain in the testes referring to the lumbar region; a white tongue coating and a deep Wiry pulse.

Etiology and pathology: The pattern is often due to improper diet, lack of care in wearing clothing appropriate to the weather, or carrying excessive Weights. These may give rise to obstruction and sinking of the Qi of the Small Intestine. Obstruction of the Qi of the Small Intestine brings on acute pain of the lower abdomen, abdominal distension and borborygmus. Sinking of the Qi of the Small Intestine effects bearing - down pain in the testes referring to the lumbar region. The white tongue coating and the deep, Wiry pulse are both signs of stagnation of Qi.

Urinary Bladder Patterns of Disharmony

The physiological function of the Urinary Bladder is to store and discharge urine. So pathological changes of the Urinary Bladder chiefly manifest as abnormal urination.

The Urinary Bladder is located in the lower abdomen. Its meridian connects with the Kidney with which it is externally - internally related. The main function of the Urinary Bladder is the temporary storage of urine, which is discharged from the body through Qi activity when a sufficient quantity has been accumulated. This function of the Urinary Bladder is performed with the assistance of the Kidney Qi. Disease of the Urinary Bladder will lead to symptoms such as anuria, urgency of micturition and dysuria ; failure of the Urinary Bladder to control urine may lead to frequency of micturition, incontinence of urine and enuresis.

Damp Heat in the Urinary Bladder

Clinical manifestations: Frequency and urgency of urination, burning pain in the urethra, dribbling urination or discontinuation of urination in mid stream; turbid urine, deep yellow in color, hematuria; or stones in the urine; possible lower abdominal distension and Fullness or lumbago; a yellow, sticky tongue coating and a rapid pulse.

Etiology and pathology: This pattern may be due to invasion of exogenous pathogenic Damp Heat which accumulates in the Urinary Bladder. It may also result from excessive eating of hot, greasy and sweet food, leading to downward inFusion of Damp Heat to the Urinary Bladder. Accumulation of Damp Heat impairs the function of the Urinary Bladder, resulting in frequency and urgency of urination, burning pain in the urethra, dribbling urination and yellow urine. Condensed by Heat, the impurities in the urine form stones, which cause sudden discontinuation of urination in mid - stream, turbid urine or stones in the urine. Damp Heat may injure the Vessels and thus hematuria occurs. Blockage of the Urinary Bladder is the cause of lower abdominal distension and Fullness. Since a disorder of a Fu organ may affect its corresponding Zang organ, lumbago appears. A yellow, sticky tongue coating and a rapid pulse are both signs of accumulation of Damp Heat in the interior.

Kidney Patterns of Disharmony

The Kidney functions to store Essence (Jing), serving as the source of reproduction and development ; to dominate Water metabolism, thus maintaining the balance of the body's fluid; to dominate Bones and produce Marrow, thus keeping the Bones healthy and strong; and to open into the ear, the urinogenital orifice and the anus. Therefore, the Kidney is regarded as the Pre-Heaven foundation of life. Pathological changes of the Kidney most often manifest as dysfunction in storing Essence (Jing), disturbance in Water metabolism, abnormality in growth, development and reproduction.

When the Kidney Yin and Kidney Yang are properly stored and kept from leaking, the Kidney functions effectively:

Kidney Qi Deficiency	Kidney Yang Deficiency
Kidney Yin Deficiency	

Kidney Qi Deficiency

Clinical manifestations : Soreness and weakness of the lumbar region and knee joints, frequent urination with clear urine, dribbling of urine after urination or enuresis ; incontinence of urine in severe cases; spermatorrhea and premature ejaculation in men; clear, cold leucorrhoea in women; a pale tongue with white coating and a thready, weak pulse.

Etiology and pathology: This pattern may be due to weakness of the Kidney Qi in old age or insufficiency of the Kidney Qi in childhood. It may also result from overstrain and stress, or prolonged illnesses, both of which may lead to weakness of the Kidney Qi. As the Kidney resides in the lumbar region, when the Kidney Qi is deficient, it may fail to nourish this area and give rise to soreness and weakness of the lumbar region and knee joints. Weakness of the Kidney Qi implies an inability of the Urinary Bladder to control urination, hence frequent urination with clear urine, dribbling after urination, enuresis and incontinence of urine. Deficiency of the Kidney Qi weakens its function of storage, and thus spermatorrhea, premature ejaculation, and clear, cold leucorrhoea. A pale tongue with white coating and a thready, weak pulse are both signs of deficiency of the Kidney Qi.

Kidney Yang Deficiency

Clinical manifestations: Pallor, Cold limbs, soreness and weakness of the lumbar region and knee joints, impotence, infertility, dizziness, tinnitus, a pale tongue with white coating and a deep, weak pulse.

Etiology and pathology: This pattern may be due to a constitutional deficiency of Yang or weakness of the Kidney in old age. It may also be due to a prolonged illness, or to excessive sexual activity, both of which may injure the Kidney and produce deficiency of the Kidney Yang. In Yang deficiency, the warming function of Yang is impaired, hence cold limbs and pallor. Deficiency of the Kidney Yang deprives the Bones, ears, Brain, Marrow of nourishment and may cause soreness of the lumbar region and weakness of the knee joints, dizziness and tinnitus. When the Kidney Yang is insufficient, the reproductive function is impaired with impotence in men, and infertility (due to Cold in the Uterus) in women resulting. A pale tongue with white coating and a deep, weak pulse are both signs of insufficiency of the Kidney Yang.

Kidney Yin Deficiency

Clinical manifestations: Dizziness, tinnitus, insomnia, poor memory, soreness and weakness of the lumbar region and knee joints, nocturnal emission, Dryness of the mouth, afternoon fever, malar flush, night sweating, yellow urine, constipation, a red tongue with little coating and a thready, rapid pulse.

Etiology and pathology: This pattern may be due to a prolonged illness, or to excessive sexual activity. It may also occur in the late stage of febrile diseases. In these cases the Kidney Yin is consumed. Deficiency of the Kidney Yin weakens the Kidney in its function of producing Marrow, dominating Bones and nourishing the Brain; the result is dizziness, tinnitus, poor memory, soreness and weakness of the lumbar region and knee joints. Deficiency of Yin produces endogenous Heat, hence afternoon fever, malar flush, night sweating, Dryness of the mouth, yellow urine and constipation. Disturbance in the interior by Heat of the deficiency type is the cause of nocturnal emission. Disturbance of the Mind by Heat leads to insomnia. A red tongue with little coating and a thready, rapid pulse are both signs of deficiency of Yin leading to endogenous Heat.

Gall Bladder Patterns of Disharmony

The Gallbladder functions, to store and excrete the bile and thus assist in the digestion of food. The Qi of the Gallbladder is closely related to the human emotions. Since the Gallbladder and Liver are extremely and internally related, the two organs are often diseased at the same time.

Damp Heat in the Liver and Gallbladder

Clinical manifestations: Hypochondriac distension and pain, bitter taste in the mouth, poor appetite, nausea, vomiting, abdominal distension, scanty and yellow urine, a yellow, sticky tongue coating and a Wiry, rapid pulse. In addition there may be yellow sclera and skin of the entire body or fever. The occurrence of eczema of scrotum, swelling and burning pain in the testes or yellow foul leucorrhoea with pruritus vulvae suggests Damp Heat in the Liver Meridian.

Etiology and pathology: This pattern may be due to invasion of exogenous pathogenic Damp Heat or to excessive eating of greasy food which produces Damp Heat in the interior. In either case, Damp Heat accumulates in the Liver and Gallbladder. The accumulation of Damp Heat impairs the function of the Liver and Gallbladder in promoting the free flow of Qi, causing hypochondriac pain. The upward overflow of the Qi of the Gallbladder leads to a bitter taste in the mouth. The accumulation of Damp Heat also impairs the function of the Spleen and Stomach in ascending and descending, eliciting poor appetite, nausea, vomiting and abdominal distension. Downward inFusion of Damp Heat into the Urinary Bladder brings on scanty, yellow urine. A yellow, sticky tongue coating and a Wiry, rapid pulse are both signs of Damp Heat in the Liver and Gallbladder. Once the function of the Liver and Gallbladder in promoting the free flow of Qi is impaired, the bile, instead of circulating along its normal, route, spreads to the exterior and results in yellow sclera and skin of the entire body. The presence of Damp Heat induces the Qi to stagnate and fever may appear. Since the Liver Meridian curves around the external genitalia, downward inFusion of Damp Heat along the Liver Meridian may produce eczema of the scrotum, or swelling and pain of the testes; and in women, pruritus vulvae and yellow foul leucorrhoea may result.

Liver Patterns of Disharmony

The Liver functions to promote the free flow of Qi, dominate the tendons and open into the eye. Pathological changes of the Liver mainly manifest themselves in dysfunctions of the Liver in storing Blood and in promoting the free flow of Qi, and in disorders of the tendons

Hyperactivity of Liver Fire	Liver Blood Deficiency
Retention of Cold in the Liver Meridian	Liver Yang Rising
Liver Qi Stagnation	Liver Wind in the Interior

Hyperactivity of Liver Fire

Clinical manifestations: Distending pain in the head; dizziness and vertigo; redness, swelling and pain of the eyes; a bitter taste and Dryness in the mouth; irritability; burning pain in the costal and hypochondriac regions; tinnitus like the sound of waves; yellow urine and constipation; hematemesis, hemoptysis or epistaxis; a red tongue with yellow coating and a Wiry, rapid pulse.

Etiology and pathology: This pattern may be due to obstruction of the Liver Qi turning into Fire with upward disturbance of the Qi and Fire or to excessive indulgence in cigarette smoking, alcoholic drinking or greasy food, which may lead to accumulation of Heat and production of Fire. Since Fire is characterized by upward movement, the effect of the Liver Fire on the head and eyes may produce distending pain in the head, dizziness and vertigo, redness, swelling and pain of the eyes and a bitter taste and Dryness in the mouth. The Liver relates to the emotion of anger and irritability is the consequence of hyperactivity of the Liver Fire. Excessive Liver Fire burns the Liver Meridian and brings about a burning pain at the costal and hypochondriac region. When the Liver Fire attacks the ear along the Gallbladder Meridian, there may be tinnitus, which has abrupt onset, sounds like waves and is not alleviated by pressure. The injury of Blood Vessels by the Liver Fire may produce hematemesis, hemoptysis or epistaxis. Yellow urine, constipation, a red tongue with yellow coating and a Wiry, rapid pulse are all signs of hyperactivity of the Liver Fire in the interior.

Liver Blood Deficiency

Clinical manifestations: Pallor, dizziness and vertigo, blurring of vision, Dryness of the eyes, night blindness, numbness of the limbs, spasms of the tendons, scanty menstrual flow or amenorrhea, a pale tongue and a thready pulse.

Etiology and pathology: This pattern may be due to insufficient production of Blood, to excessive loss of Blood or to consumption of the Liver Blood by a prolonged illness. Deficiency of the Liver Blood deprives the Heat and eyes of nourishment and may result in pallor, dizziness and vertigo, blurring of vision, Dryness of the eyes and night blindness. When the Liver Blood fails to nourish the limbs and tendons, there may be numbness of the limbs and spasms of the tendons. Insufficiency of the Liver Blood empties the sea of Blood, thus bringing on scanty menstrual flow and amenorrhea. A pale tongue and a thready pulse are the consequence of deficiency of Blood.

Retention of Cold in the Liver Meridian

Clinical manifestations: Lower abdominal distending pain, with bearing down sensation in the testes; the scrotum may be contracted; this pain can be aggravated by Cold and alleviated by warmth; the tongue coating is white and slippery and the pulse deep and Wiry.

Etiology and pathology: This pattern is due to invasion of the Liver Meridian by exogenous pathogenic Cold which blocks the Qi and Blood circulation. The Liver Meridian curves around the external genitalia and passes through the lower abdominal region. As Cold is characterized by contraction and stagnation, invasion of the meridian by Cold may block the Qi and Blood circulation and thus leading to pain. Cold disperses with warmth and thus pain is relieved; when Cold accumulates, the pain becomes worse. A white, slippery tongue coating and a deep, Wiry pulse are (both signs of interior Cold)

Liver Yang Rising

Clinical manifestations: Headache with distending sensation in the head, dizziness and vertigo, tinnitus. Hushed face and red eyes, irritability, insomnia with dream - disturbed sleep, palpitations, poor memory, soreness and weakness of the low back and knees, a red tongue and a Wiry, thready and rapid pulse.

Etiology and pathology: This pattern may be due to mental depression, anger and anxiety. They produce obstruction of the Liver Qi which later turns into Fire. The Fire consumes the Yin Blood in the interior and does not allow Yin to restrain Yang. The pattern may also result from constitutional deficiency of the Yin of the Liver and Kidney, in which case, the Liver Yang fails to be restrained. Excessive ascending of the Yang and Qi of the Liver is the cause of headache with distending sensation in the head, dizziness and vertigo and tinnitus. Hyperactivity of the Liver Yang may produce redness of the face and eyes, and irritability. When there is deficiency of Yin leading to excess of Yang, the Mind fails to be nourished and the harmonious state of Yin and Yang is broken. As a result, such symptoms as palpitations, poor memory, and insomnia with dream disturbed sleep ensues. Deficiency of the Yin of the Liver and Kidney deprives the tendons and Bones of nourishment and thus brings on soreness and weakness of the low back and knees. A red tongue and a Wiry, rapid pulse are both signs of deficiency, of Yin leading to hyperactivity of Fire.

Liver Qi Stagnation

Clinical manifestations: Mental depression; irritability; distending or wandering pain in the costal and hypochondriac regions; distension of the breasts; stuffiness in the chest; sighing; epigastric and abdominal distension and pain; poor appetite; belching; or possibly a foreign body sensation in the throat; irregular menstruation and dysmenorrhea in women; a thin, white tongue coating and a Wiry pulse. In prolonged cases, there may be pricking pain in the costal and hypochondriac regions or palpable mass may be present. The tongue is purplish dark in color, or there are purplish spots on the tongue.

Etiology and pathology: The pattern is often due to mental irritation which impairs the function of the Liver in promoting the free flow of Qi and results in stagnation of the Liver Qi, leading to retardation of the Qi circulation, thus presenting mental depression, irritability, distending pain in the costal and hypochondriac regions and breasts, stuffiness in the chest and sighing. Transverse invasion of the Spleen and Stomach by the Liver Qi produces epigastric and abdominal distension and pain, poor appetite and belching. Retardation of the Qi circulation allows Damp to collect and Phlegm may be formed; the Phlegm and Qi may accumulate in the throat, resulting in a foreign body sensation in the throat. Affected by dysfunction of Qi, the circulation of both Qi and Blood is retarded and disharmony of the

Chong and Ren (Conception Vessel) Meridians may result. This can cause irregular menstruation and dysmenorrhea. Long standing obstruction of the Liver Qi, leading to stagnation of Qi and Blood, may elicit palpable masses, accompanied by pricking pain in the costal and hypochondriac regions, a purple tongue or a tongue with purplish spots, and a Wiry pulse.

Liver Wind in the Interior

The occurrence of such symptoms and signs as dizziness and vertigo, convulsion, tremor and numbness, as a part of a process of pathological changes is referred to as Liver wind, which may result from:

> Liver Yang Rising,
>
> Extreme Heat stirring Wind
>
> Liver Blood deficiency

Liver Yang turning into Wind

Clinical manifestations: Dizziness and vertigo, headache, numbness or tremor of the limbs, dysphasia, a red and tremulous tongue and a Wiry, rapid pulse. In severe cases there may be sudden collapse, coma, stiffness of the tongue, aphasia, deviation of the mouth and eye, and hemiplegia.

Etiology and pathology: This pattern often occurs to patients with a constitutional deficiency of Yin and excess of Yang. It may be induced by such factors as drastic emotional changes, overstrain and stress and excessive alcoholic drinking, all of which may Further consume Yin and give rise to abrupt rising of Yang. Subsequently the Liver wind is produced. The disturbance of the head and eyes by the Liver Yang produces dizziness, vertigo and headache. The tendons may be deprived of nourishment by either insufficiency of the Liver Yin or constitutional excess of Phlegm leading to obstruction of Qi and Blood, and this may cause numbness or tremor of the limbs, and dysphasia. Sudden onset of rising Liver Yang may stir up wind and produce upward movement of Qi and Blood, which, in combination with Phlegm Fire, clouds the "clear cavity" and thus creating sudden collapse and coma. Invasion of the meridians by wind Phlegm binders the Qi and Blood circulation and brings on stiffness of the tongue with aphasia, deviation of the mouth and eye and hemiplegia. A red tongue and a Wiry, rapid pulse are both signs of hyperactivity of the Liver Yang.

Extreme Heat stirring wind

Clinical manifestations: High fever, convulsion, neck rigidity, upward staring of the eyes; in severe cases, opisthotonus, coma and lock jaw; a deep - red tongue and a Wiry, rapid pulse.

Etiology and pathology: This pattern may occur in exogenous febrile diseases where excessive pathogenic Heat stirs up the Liver wind. If excessive pathogenic Heat induces high fever, this may scorch the tendons, producing convulsion, neck rigidity, upward string of the eyes and opisthotonos. Disturbance of the Mind by Heat leads to coma. A deep red tongue and a Wiry, rapid pulse are both signs of disorders of the Liver with excessive Heat.

Liver Blood Deficiency producing wind

Deficiency of the Liver Blood deprives the tendons of nourishment and thus stirs up deficiency type wind in the interior. For clinical manifestations, etiology and pathology refer to the pattern of insufficiency of the Liver Blood.

Complicated Patterns of Disharmony

Heart and Spleen Deficiency

Clinical manifestations: Sallow complexion, general lassitude, palpitations, poor memory, insomnia, dream disturbed sleep, reduced appetite, abdominal distension, loose stools; irregular menstruation in women; a pale tongue with thin, white coating and a thready weak pulse.

Etiology and pathology: This pattern may be due to poor recuperation after an illness; chronic hemorrhage; or worry, overstrain and stress. In any case, the Heart Blood is consumed and the Spleen Qi is weakened. On the other hand, a weakness of the Spleen Qi may fail to provide a source for the production of Qi and Blood, and thus make the Heart Blood even more deficient. Deficiency of Qi and Blood causes sallow complexion, general lassitude, a pale tongue with thin, white coating and a thready, weak pulse. Deficiency of the Heart Blood deprives the Heart and Mind of nourishment, eliciting palpitations, poor memory, insomnia and dream disturbed sleep. When deficiency of the Spleen impairs its function of transportation, there may be reduced appetite, abdominal distension and loose stools. Deficiency of Qi and Blood may weaken the Chong Meridian, and manifest as scanty menstrual flow or even amenorrhea. Weakness of the Spleen Qi implies inability of the Spleen in controlling Blood, and thus results in profuse menstrual flow.

Lung and Kidney Qi Deficiency

Clinical manifestations: Asthmatic breathing, shortness of breath, and more exhalation than inhalation, all of which become worse on exertion ; low voice, Cold limbs, blue complexion, spontaneous sweating, incontinence of urine due to severe cough ; a pale tongue with thin coating and a weak pulse of deficiency type.

Etiology and pathology: This pattern is often due to prolonged cough which affects the Lung and Kidney in succession, resulting in deficiency of Qi of both organs. It may also be due to overstrain and stress which injures the Kidney Qi and impairs the Kidney's function of receiving Qi. The Lung controls respiration and the Kidney dominates the reception of Qi. "The Lung is the commander of Qi and the Kidney is the root of Qi." With deficiency of the Qi of the Lung and Kidney, there may be asthmatic breathing, shortness of breath, and more exhalation than inhalation, all of which become worse on exertion. Deficiency of the Lung leads to weakness of Zong (gathering) Qi, causing low voice. Yang Qi, being deficient, fails to warm up the exterior, resulting in Cold limbs and a blue complexion. Deficiency of Qi may cause weakness of Wei (defensive) Yang, which explains spontaneous sweating. Weakness of the Kidney Qi may impair the function of the Urinary Bladder in controlling urine, incontinence of urine in coughing appears. A pale tongue with thin coating and a weak pulse of deficiency type are both signs of deficiency of Yang Qi.

Lung and Spleen Qi Deficiency

Clinical manifestations: General lassitude; cough with proFuse, dilute, white sputum; poor appetite, loose stools; in severe cases, facial puffiness and edema of the feet; a pale tongue with white coating

Etiology and pathology: This pattern is often due to prolonged cough which may cause deficiency of the Lung and later affect the Spleen or the deficiency of the Spleen which weakens the source of the Lung Qi. Deficiency of Qi implies hypofunction of Zang Fu organs that is the reason for general lassitude. Deficiency of Qi does not allow normal distribution of Body Fluids, the accumulation of which forms Phlegm Damp. The retention of Phlegm Damp in the Lung impairs the Lung's function in descending and thus produces cough with proFuse, dilute and white sputum. Dysfunction of the Spleen in transportation manifests as poor appetite and loose stools. Deficiency of both the Lung and Spleen impairs the function of Qi in circulating fluid, resulting in accumulation of harmFul Water and Damp and producing facial puffiness and edema of feet. A pale tongue with white coating and a weak pulse are both signs of deficiency of Qi.

Spleen and Kidney Yang Deficiency

Clinical manifestations: Pallor, Cold limbs; soreness and weakness of the lumbar region and knee joints; loose stools or diarrhea at dawn; facial puffiness and edema of the limbs; a pale swollen delicate tongue with thin white coating and a deep weak pulse.

Etiology and pathology: This pattern is often due to a prolonged illness which consumes Qi and injures Yang, the disease spreading from the Spleen to the Kidney. It may also result from deficiency of the Kidney Yang with the Spleen Yang failing to be warmed and thus producing injury of the Yang Qi of both organs. Dysfunction of the Yang of the Spleen and Kidney in providing warmth causes pallor, Cold limbs and soreness and weakness of the lumbar region and knee joints. Insufficiency of Yang Qi does not allow normal digestion, transportation and transformation of food; the result is loose stools or diarrhea at dawn. Deficiency of Yang Qi implies inability to transport and transform Body Fluids; the result is accumulation of harmFul Water and Damp on the body surface, which manifests as facial puffiness and edema of the limbs. A pale swollen and delicate tongue with thin white coating and a deep, weak pulse are both signs of deficiency of Yang.

Liver and Kidney Yin Deficiency

Clinical manifestations: Dizziness, blurring of vision, Dryness of the throat, tinnitus; Heat sensation in the chest, palms and soles; soreness and weakness of the lumbar region and knee joints; malar flush, night sweating; nocturnal emission; scanty menstrual flow; a red tongue with little coating and a thready, rapid pulse.

Etiology and pathology: This pattern is often due to drastic emotional changes and overstrain and stress which injure Yin Blood; or to a prolonged illness which consumes the Yin of the Liver and Kidney. Deficiency of the Yin of the Liver and Kidney deprives the head and eyes of nourishment and thus produces dizziness, blurring of vision and tinnitus. Deficiency of Yin produces endogenous Heat and thus results in Heat sensation in the chest, palms and soles, malar flush, night sweating, Dryness of the throat, a red tongue with little coating and a thready, rapid pulse. Disturbance by deficiency type Fire in the interior causes nocturnal emission. Deficiency of the Yin of the Liver and Kidney leads to a disturbance of the regulation of the Chong and Ren Meridians, hence the scanty menstrual flow.

Lung and Kidney Yin Deficiency

Clinical manifestations: Cough with a small amount of sputum, or with blood tinged sputum; Dryness of the mouth and throat; soreness and weakness of the lumbar region and knee joints; tidal fever, malar flush, night sweating, nocturnal emission; a red tongue with little coating and a thready, rapid pulse.

Etiology and pathology: This pattern is often due to prolonged cough which injures the Lung, giving rise to insufficiency of the Yin fluid, which spreads from the Lung to the Kidney. It may also result from overstrain and stress, which consumes the Kidney Yin and thus prevents the Kidney Yin from nourishing the Lung. In either case a Yin deficiency of both organs results. Insufficiency of the Lung Yin deprives the Lung of moisture, resulting in cough with a small amount of sputum and Dryness of the mouth and throat. Deficiency of Yin produces endogenous Heat eliciting tidal fever, malar flush and night sweating. Injury of the Lung Vessels by deficiency type Heat may produce Blood - tinged sputum. Insufficiency of the

Kidney Yin brings on soreness and weakness of the lumbar region and knee joints, and nocturnal emission. A red tongue with little coating and a thready, rapid pulse are both signs of deficiency of Yin producing endogenous Heat.

Heart and Kidney not harmonised

Clinical manifestation: Mental restlessness, insomnia, palpitations, poor memory, dizziness, tinnitus, Dryness of the throat, soreness of the lumbar region, spermatorrhea in dreams, tidal fever, night sweating, a red tongue with little coating and a thready, rapid pulse.

Etiology and pathology: The pattern is often due to prolonged illnesses, overstrain and stress, or excessive sexual activity, all of which may injure the Yin of the Heart and Kidney. It may also result from drastic emotional changes leading to obstruction of Qi which turns into Fire. The Heart Fire may become hyperactive in the upper part of the body and fail to inFuse downwards to harmonize the Kidney. The resulting imbalance between the Heart and Kidney disturbs the regulation of Water and Fire. When the Kidney Yin is insufficient, it may fail to rise up to harmonize the Heart. The resulting hyperactivity of the Heart Fire may disturb the Mind and manifest as mental restlessness, insomnia and palpitations. Consumption of the Kidney Essence (Jing) leads to emptiness of the sea of Marrow and produces dizziness, tinnitus and poor memory. Undernourishment of the lumbar region causes soreness of the back. Disharmony between the Heart and Kidney leads to disturbance of deficiency type Fire and produces weakness in controlling the release of sperm with the symptom of spermatorrhea in dreams. A dry throat, tidal fever, night sweating, a red tongue with little coating and a thready, rapid pulse are all signs of deficiency of Yin leading to hyperactivity of Fire.

Liver invading the Stomach

Clinical manifestations: Distension and pain in the costal, hypochondriac and epigastric regions, belching, acid regurgitation, an empty and uncomfortable sensation in the Stomach; mental depression or irritability; a thin tongue coating and a Wiry pulse.

Etiology and pathology: This pattern is often due to injury of the Liver by mental depression or irritation, and injury of the Stomach by irregular food intake or overstrain and stress. The resulting hyperactivity of the Liver and weakness of the Stomach, therefore, leads to disharmony between the Liver and Stomach. Dysfunction of the Liver in promoting the free flow of Qi produces mental depression or irritability, and distension, Fullness and pain in the costal and hypochondriac regions. Invasion of the Stomach by the Liver Qi impairs the descending function of the Stomach, manifesting as distension and pain in the epigastric region, belching, acid regurgitation and an empty and uncomfortable sensation in the Stomach. A Wiry pulse is a sign of disorders of the Liver.

Liver invading the Spleen

Clinical manifestations: Distension, Fullness and pain in the costal and hypochondriac regions; mental depression or irritability; poor appetite, abdominal distension, loose stools; a thin tongue coating and a Wiry pulse.

Etiology and pathology: This pattern is often due to injury of the Liver by mental depression or irritation, or to injury of the Spleen by irregular food intake or overstrain and stress. In both cases, the Liver Qi invades the Spleen transversely, resulting in an imbalance between the two organs. Dysfunction of the Liver in promoting the free flow of Qi produces distension, Fullness and pain in the costal and hypochondriac regions, mental depression or irritability. Invasion of the Spleen by the Liver Qi impairs the Spleen's function of transportation; poor appetite, abdominal distension and loose stools result. A Wiry pulse is a sign of Liver disorders.

Liver Fire invading the Lungs

Clinical manifestations: Burning pain in the costal and hypochondriac regions; paroxysmal cough or even hemoptysis in severe cases; quick temper, irritability, restlessness, Heat sensation in the chest, bitter taste in the mouth; dizziness, red eyes; a red tongue with thin yellow coating and a Wiry, rapid pulse.

Etiology and pathology: This pattern is often due to mental depression leading to obstruction of the Liver Qi which turns into Fire. The upward invasion of the Lung by the Liver Fire results in this pattern. Obstruction of Qi turns into hyperactive Fire and impairs the Liver's function in promoting the free flow of Qi, manifesting as burning pain in the costal and hypochondriac regions, quick temper and irritability. Upward invasion of the Lung by the Liver Qi and Fire impairs the Lungs descending function, leading to paroxysmal cough. Injury of the Vessels of the Lung by Fire and Heat creates hemoptysis. Flaring up of the Liver Fire gives rise to restlessness, Heat sensation in the chest, bitter taste in the mouth, dizziness and red eyes. A red tongue with thin, yellow coating and Wiry, rapid pulse are both signs of hyperactivity of the Liver Fire in the interior.

Practical Chinese Medicine

Section 6

Points

The Meridian, Channels, Collaterals and Acupoints

A General Introduction to Meridians and Collaterals

Jing-Luo, is a general term for the Jing Mai (meridians) and Luo Mai (collaterals), which are the pathways through which the Qi and Blood of human body circulates.

Jing means "go through" or "a path ". They are the main trunks, thick and large. They run longitudinally and interiorly within the body. They include the twelve regular meridians, the eight extra meridians and the twelve divergent meridians.

Luo means "something that connects" or "a net ". They are the branches of the meridians, thin and small. They run transversely and superficially and crisscross and net the whole body. They include the fifteen collaterals, the minute collaterals, and the superficial collaterals.

Many ancient medical books recorded that the meridians and collaterals are the pathways in which the Qi and Blood of human body are circulated. In chapter 23 of Classic on Medical Problems, it says, "The meridians and collaterals transport Qi and Blood and adjust Yin and Yang, in order to nourish the body". In volume 4 of Compendium of Acupuncture and Moxibustion, it says, "The twelve meridians and the fifteen collaterals, which distribute exteriorly on the whole body, are the pathways in which the Blood and Qi circulate. They originate from and are rooted in the Kidney and are the source of life". So we can see that the meridians and collaterals have a close relationship with the activities of human life.

In summary, the meridian and collaterals pertain to the Zang-Fu organs interiorly and link the extremities and joints exteriorly. They run and connect the upper and lower aspects of the body, unifying all parts of the body into an organic whole. They transport the Qi and Blood, nourish the whole body and maintain the harmonious balance of all the functions and activities of the many parts of the body.

The theory of meridians and collaterals is a theoretical doctrine that analyses the course and distribution, physiological function and pathological changes of the meridians of the human body and their relationship with the Zang-Fu organs. It is a fundamental concept in the basic theory of Traditional Chinese Medicine, and the cornerstone theory underlying acupressure, acupuncture and moxibustion. It integrates physiology, pathology, diagnostic theories and treatment principles in Chinese medicine, with the theory of Yin Yang, the five elements and the theory of Zang-Fu, thus forming the theoretical basis of Chinese medicine. For a long time, it has been of great significance in guiding Chinese medical clinical practice in many areas. This is especially so in the practice of acupressure and acupuncture whereby Patterne differentiation, point selection, the needling or stimulation techniques of reinforcing and reducing, and acupuncture anaesthesia are seen as arising from the theory of the meridians and collaterals.

General Introduction to Acupoints

Acupoints are the specific sites through which the Qi of the Zang-Fu organs and meridians is transported to the body surface and through which acupressure, acupuncture and moxibustion and other therapies are applied by external stimulation.

Shuxue (acupoints) are also termed 'Xue', or 'Xue Wei'. 'Shu' means 'transportation' and 'transmission', while 'Xue' means 'hole' or 'gathering'. In the medical literature of the past dynasties, acupoints have had other names such as 'Qi point' and 'aperture'.

Distributed on their related meridian pathways, acupoints are closely linked with the meridians and collaterals. So the acupoints should not be regarded as superficial points alone, but as special sites which connect with each other, and through which the internal tissues and organs are related. The meridians and collaterals connect the whole body, both interiorly and exteriorly, and diseases of the body can be treated by stimulating the acupoints on the body surface to regulate the related meridians, Zang-Fu organs and the circulation of Qi and Blood.

Classification of Acupoints

After the systematic classification, acupoints are classified into three categories:

1) Acupoints of the fourteen meridians

2) Extraordinary points

3) Ashi points

1) Acupoints of the fourteen meridians

The acupoints distributed along the twelve regular meridians and the Du and Ren meridians are called "acupoints of the fourteen meridians", or "meridian points". Through the consequent medical practice of people after the discovery of acupoints, the points were localized and named, becoming increasingly more in number, and further systematised. Since the points are distributed on the course of the fourteen meridians, the points are very closely related to the meridians. They can not only treat the diseases of meridians themselves, but also reflect disorders of the fourteen meridians and the related Zang-Fu organs. The twelve regular meridians are distributed symmetrically in pairs on the left and right sides of the body (309 pairs of points), while the Du and the Ren meridians are single, aligning on the posterior and anterior midlines respectively (24+28 = 52 points). The acupoints of the 14 meridians total 361

2) Extraordinary points

Extraordinary points, also called "extra points", are points with a definite location and a specific name, but are not related to the fourteen meridians. These points are especially effective in the treatment of certain diseases. For instance, Taiyang (EX-HN5) located on the head, is used to treat headache. While Yaoyan (EX-B7) on the waist, is used to treat low back pain. Although scattered over the body, they are still related to the meridian system. For examples, Yintang (EX-NH3) is related to the Du Meridian, and Taiyang is related to the Sanjiao Meridian. From the acupuncture literature of the past dynasties, it can be seen that some of extraordinary points were gradually absorbed into points of the fourteen regular meridians. For instance, UB-43 and GB-31 were formerly extraordinary points in "Prescriptions Worth a Thousand Gold for Emergencies", however they were later attributed as points of the fourteen meridians in Illustrated Manual on the Points for Acupuncture on a New Bronze Figure.

3) Ashi points

Ashi points are also called "tender spots", "sensitive points", "unfixed points", or reflex points. These points have neither specific names nor definite locations. They are neither points of the fourteen meridians nor the extra points. They are the tender spots and other reflexive spots that are used as sites for needling and moxibustion. Ashi points are usually near the affected areas, but not necessarily.

In addition, there are many new points that have been discovered. These points are effective in treating some specific diseases. For instance, Dannang (EX-LE 6) is used to treat diseases of biliary tract, Anmian to treat insomnia, Luozhen (EX-UE) to treat stiff neck, and the point Toothache to treat toothache, etc.

Specific Points

Specific points refer to those of the fourteen meridians that have special properties. Since they have different therapeutic effects, the ancient doctors gave them different names. Knowing the meaning, indications and clinical applications of these points is of importance clinically for point selection. The commonly used specific points are introduced as follows.

The Five Shu Points

Each of the twelve regular meridians has five specific points below the elbows or knees, namely, the Jing (well), Ying (spring), Shu (stream), Jing (river) and He (sea), which are termed five Shu points. It was first stated in Chapter 1 of Miraculous Pivot (Ling Shu) "The points at which Qi springs up are called Jing (well) points; the points where Qi flows copiously are called Ying (spring) points; the points where Qi flows like a stream are called Shu (stream) points; the points where Qi flows through are called Jing (river) points; and the points where Qi gathers are called He (sea) points". But the specific names and the locations of the points were not given in this chapter. In Chapter 2 of Miraculous Pivot, it recorded the individual names and locations of the Jing (well) Ying (spring), Shu (stream), Jing (river) and He (sea) of each meridian except the Heart Meridian of Hand-Shaoyang. This was later compensated in the Compendium of Acupuncture and Moxibustion.

The five Shu points were perceived by the doctors of the past as flowing water, representing the volume of Qi and blood in the meridians. They were respectively given the names of Jing (well), Ying (spring), Shu (stream), Jing (river) and He (sea), to demonstrate that the Qi of meridians flow from the distal extremities to the elbows or knees.

The Jing (well) points are situated on the tips of the fingers and toes where the meridian Qi starts to bubble, just like the origin of water, hence the name Jing (well) points.

The Ying (spring) points are situated distal to the metacarpal-phalangeal joints and the metatarsophalangeal joints where the meridian qi starts to gush, just like a spring, hence the name Ying (spring) points.

The Shu (stream) points are situated proximal to the metacarpal-phalangeal joints and the metatarsophalangeal joints where the meridian Qi flourishes, just like a stream, hence the name Shu (stream) points.

The Jing (river) points are situated above the wrists and ankles where the meridian Qi is pouring abundantly, just like a river, hence the name Jing (river) points.

The He (sea) points are situated near the elbows and knees, where the Qi goes into the body, and gathers in the Zang-Fu organs, just like the confluence of rivers in the sea, and hence the name the He (sea) points.

The Yuan (Source) Points and the Luo (Connecting) Points.

Most of the Yuan (Source) points and Luo (connecting) points are situated near the wrists and ankles. Each meridian and Zang-Fu organ is closely related to the Yuan (Source) points of the meridian.

"Yuan" means source; Yuan (Source) Qi. The Yuan (Source) points are those where the Yuan (Source) Qi of the Zang-Fu and meridian passes and gathers. Disorders of the Zang-Fu organs are usually reflected on the twelve Yuan (Source) points, which are also called the "twelve Yuan".

"Luo" means connecting. Luo (connecting) points are the sites where the fifteen Luo Collaterals branch out from the regular meridians. Most of the Luo (connecting) points are distributed at the intersection of the exteriorly-interiorly related meridians. They have the function of connecting the exteriorly-interiorly related meridians.

The Yuan (Source) Points and Luo (Connecting) Points may be used independently or in combination. The combination of them is called the "host and guest combination," which is applied according to the occurring order of the diseases on the exteriorly interiorly related meridians. When a meridian is first affected, its Yuan (Source) Point is used, while for second affected meridian, its Luo - (Connecting) Point is used. For instance, both the Lung Meridian and the Large Intestine Meridian are diseased, but the former is affected first, Taiyuan (Lu-09), its Yuan (Source) Point is selected as a main point, and Pianli (LI-06), the Luo (Connecting) Point of the Large Intestine Meridian is used as a combining point. On the contrary, if the Large Intestine Meridian is diseased first and then the Lung Meridian, Hegu (LI-04), the Yuan - (Source) Point should be prescribed as a main point, while Lieque (Lu-07), the Luo (Connecting) Point as a combining point. This method is adopted when the externally internally related meridians are affected. And it is known as the combination of the exterior interior points.

The Back Shu Points and the Front Mu Points

The Back Shu Points and the Front Mu Points may be used independently or in combination. Whenever an internal organ is affected, the Back Shu Point or the Front Mu Point pertaining to that organ may be prescribed. The application of both may strengthen the therapeutic effects. For instance, Weishu (UB-21) on the back and Zhongwan (Ren-12) on the abdomen may be selected for gastric disorders; or Pang - guangshu (UB-28) in the sacral region and Zhongji (Ren-03) in the lower abdomen for disorders of the Urinary Bladder.

The Front (Mu) Points

The Front (Mu) Points are those located at the chest and abdomen, where the Qi of the Zang Fu organs is inFused. Since they are situated closely to their respective related Zang Fu organs, any problems of the Zang Fu organs can be seen in the corresponding Front - (Mu) Points. For instance, tenderness may appear in Riyue (GB-24) or Qimen (Liv-14) if the Gallbladder is affected, and if the Stomach is diseased, there is tenderness in Zhongwan (Ren-12). Therefore, the Front - (Mu) Points are mainly applied to treat disorders of the Zang Fu organs and in the local areas. For example, Liver disorders associated with hypochondriac pain may be treated by needling Qimen (Liv-14), and abdominal pain due to Large Intestine disorders may be relieved by needling Tianshu (St-25).

The Back Shu Points and the Front - Mu Points work for diseases of the Zang Fu organs. In addition, they are of different nature of Yin and Yang. The Back - Shu Points located on the back pertain to Yang, while the Front - Mu Points located on the chest and abdomen pertain to Yin. It is stated in the sixty - seventh problem of Classic on Medical Problems, "Diseases of the Zang organs (Yin) are manifested in the Back Shu Points, and the diseases of Fu organs (Yang) arc manifested in the Front Mu Points." Therefore, the Back Shu Points are mainly used to treat the problems of five Zang organs, and the Front Mu Points are mainly effective to the problems of six Fu organs. For example, Xinshu (UB-15) is helpful to the Heart diseases; Ganshu (UB-18) works for the Liver diseases; Zhongwan (Ren-12) is effective to the Stomach diseases and Tianshu (St-25) is good for the Large Intestine diseases. This is one of the methods to treat Yang disease from Yin and vice versa

Internal Organs Front (Mu) Point

Lung	ZhongFu (Lu-01)	Large Intestine	Tianshu (St-25)
Heart	Juque (Ren-14)	Small Intestine	Guanyuan (Ren-04)
Liver	Qimen (Liv-14)	Gallbladder	Riyue (GB-24)
Spleen	Zhangmen (Liv-13)	Stomach	Zhongwan (Ren-12)
Kidney	Jingmen (GB-25)	Urinary Bladder	Zhongji (Ren-03)
Pericardium	Tanzhong (Ren-17)	San Jiao	Shimen (Ren-05)

The Xi - (Cleft) Point

"Xi" means hollow or cleft. The Xi (cleft) points are located at the sites where the Qi of the meridians is deeply converged and accumulated. They are situated below the elbows and knees of four limbs. Each of the twelve regular meridians and of the four extra meridians (Yinwei, Yangwei, Yinqiao and Yangqiao) has a Xi (cleft) point, totally sixteen.

The Lower He - (Sea) Points

Since the large intestine, the small intestine and the San Jiao meridians have their He (sea) points on the upper limbs, the above six points which are situated on the lower limbs, are named the lower He (sea) points to identify the difference.

The Lower He Sea Points of the Six Fu Organs

The lower He (sea) points refer to the six He (sea) points pertaining to the six Fu organs along the three Yang meridians of the foot. They are situated below the knees and the popliteal fossa. They were first noted in chapter 4 of Miraculous Pivot, "The disorders of the six Fu organs can be treated by the He (sea) points".

As it is mentioned in the fourth chapter of Ling Shu (Miraculous Pivot), "The disorders of the six Fu organs can be treated by the He - (Sea) Points." For example, gastric pain and sour regurgitation are treated by Zusanli (St-36); dysentery or appendicitis is treated by Shangjuxu (St-37); biliary pain and vomiting are treated by Yang lingquan (GB-34).

Six Fu - Organs Lower He - (Sea) Point

Stomach Zusanli St-36	Large intestine Shangjuxu St-37
Small intestine Xiajuxu St-39	Gallbladder Yang lingquan GB-34
Urinary Bladder Weizhong UB-40	San Jiao WeiYang UB-39

Methods of Locating Acupoints

1 cun

There are hundreds of points on the human body, each of them having its own location. In order to select the points correctly, we need to locate them. In the clinic, correct location of acupoints is closely related to the therapeutic result. So the ancient doctors emphasized the location of points. In order to locate acupoints accurately, the practitioner must understand the methods of locating acupoints. In modern clinic, the commonly used methods of point location include proportional measurements, finger measurement and simple measurement.

Proportional Measurement

This method utilizes the bones and joints as landmarks to measure various portions of the human body. It locates acupoints by means of respectively dividing the width or length of various portions of the human body into definite numbers of equal units, as the standard for measurement. This measurement is applicable on patients of different sexes, ages and body sizes. This method was supplemented and revised by generations of past dynasties, became a basic standard for point location. The proportional measurements of the commonly used portions of the body are introduced here.

Units of Measurement in Traditional Chinese Medicine

There is a very simple, accurate unit of measurement used in Traditional Chinese Medicine, called the 'CUN'.

1 Cun is the width of the thumb joint - as shown in these diagrams.

Practical Chinese Medicine

The width of the index finger is also used in conjunction with the thumb; for example, 3 thumbs are equal to four fingers or 2 fingers are equal to 1.5 cun.

The measurements are always accurate for each individual. Obviously, **it is essential that the Measurements are those of the person being treated.**

Throughout this manual, to avoid any confusion, measurements are always given in either 'Thumbs' or 'fingers'.

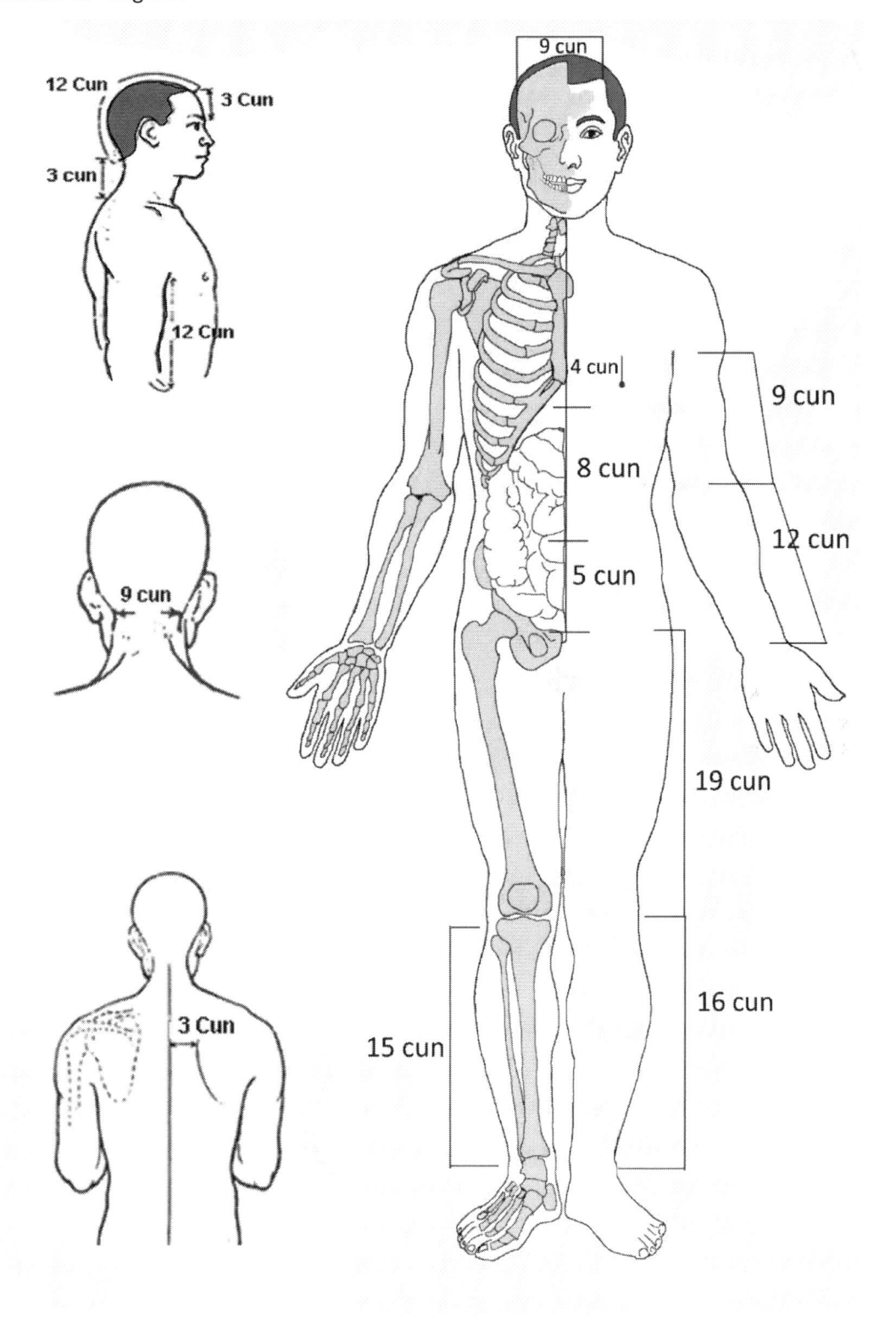

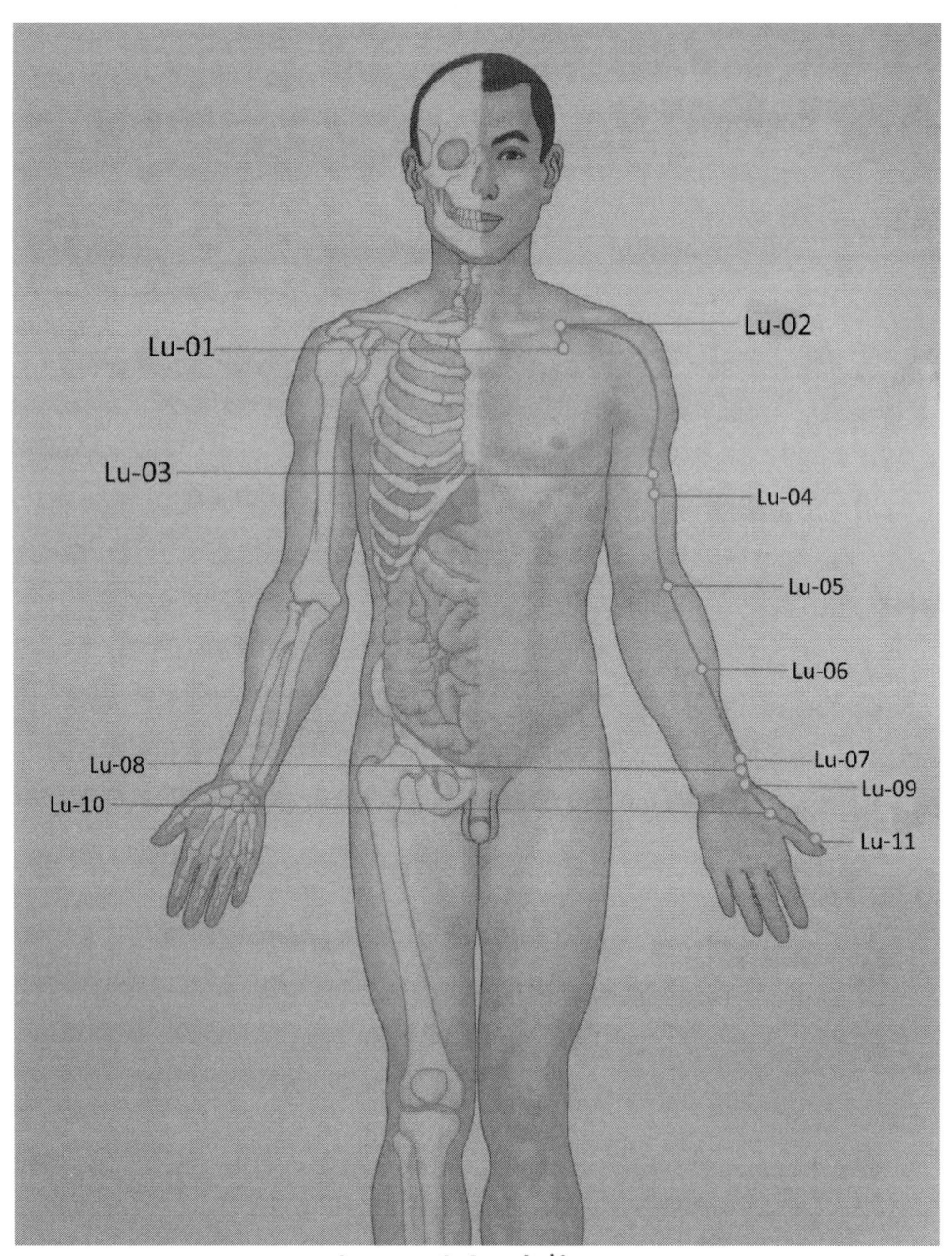

Lung Meridian

Lungs

Lu 01   Zhong Fu

Central Residence

Regulates Lung Qi, stops cough, Stimulates the descending of Lung Qi, Disperses fullness from the chest and stops pain,

1 cun directly below Lu-2. 6 cun lateral to the Ren channel

Lu 02   Yun Men

Cloud door

Disperses fullness from the chest Stimulates the descending of Lung Qi, Stops cough

In the depression below the acromial extremity of the clavicle, 6 cun lateral to the Ren channel.

Lu 03   Tian Fu

On the medial aspect of the

upper arm, 3 cun below the end of axillery fold, on the radial side of m. biceps brachii.

Lu 04   Xia Bai

On the medial aspect of the upper arm, 1 cun below Tain Fu Lu3, on the radial side of m. biceps brachii.

Lu 05   Chi Ze

Foot Marsh

Clears Lung Heat,

Stimulates the descending of Lung Qi, Expels Phlegm from the Lungs, Benefits the Bladder, Relaxes the sinews,

in the transverse cubital crease, on the radial side of the biceps muscle tendon. The point is located with the elbow slightly flexed.

Lu 06   Kong Zui

Biggest Hole

Regulates Lung Qi and causes Lung Qi to descend, Clears Heat, Stops bleeding,

On the ulnar aspect of the forearm, on the line joining Lu-9 and Lu-5, 7 cun above the transverse crease of the wrist.

Lu-07 Lei Que

Broken Sequence

Luo Connecting point, Opening point of Ren Mai, Ma Dan-yang Heavenly Star, Stimulates the descending and dispersing of Lung Qi, Circulates the Defensive Qi and releases the Exterior, Expels exterior Wind, Opens the Directing Vessel, Benefits the Bladder and opens Water passages, Opens the nose, Communicates with the Large Intestine,

At the origin of the styloid process of the radius, 1.5 cun above to the wrist crease. Located point by crossing index finger of one hand over the thumb of other.

Lu 08   Jing Qu

Channel canal

1 cun superior to the transverse crease and Lu-9, on the medial side of the styloid process of the radius, level with the highest spot.

Lu 09   Tai Yuan

Great Deep Pool

Resolves Phlegm,

Regulates Lung Qi, stops cough, Tonifies Lung Qi and Lung Yin, Tonifies (Zong) Gathering Qi, Promotes the circulation of blood and influences the pulse, Clears Lung and Liver Heat,

On the distal crease of the wrist, at the lower border of the trapezium on the radial side.

Lu 10   Yu Ji

Fish Border

Clears Lung Heat Benefits the throat

Proximal to the metacarpophalangeal joint of the thumb on the radial border of the metacarpal bone.

Lu 11   Shao Shang

Lesser Metal

Expels Wind (Exterior & Interior), Stimulates the dispersing and descending of Lung Qi, Benefits the throat, Opens the orifices and promotes resuscitation

On the radial side of the thumb, about 0.1 cun from the corner of the nail.

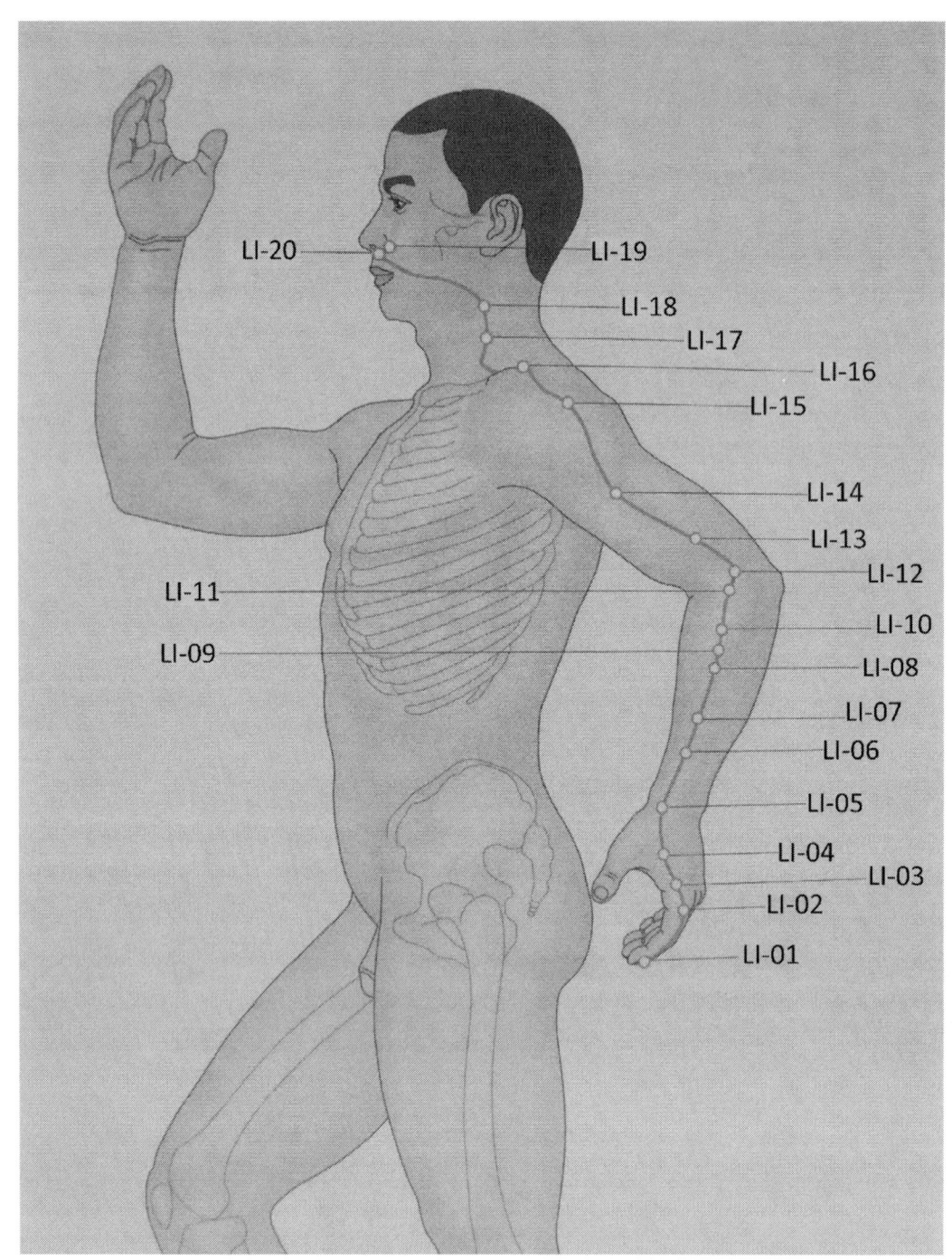

Large Intestine Meridian

Large Intestine

LI 01   Shang Yang

Metal Yang

Clears Heat, Brightens the eyes, Benefits the throat

Calms the mind, Expels Wind and Matters Cold

On the radial side of the index finger, about 0.1 cun posterior to the corner of the nail.

LI 02   Er Jian

Second Interval

Clears Heat

On the radial side of the index finger, distal to the metacarpophalangeal joint, at the junction of red & white skin. Slightly flex finger

LI 03   San Jian

Third Interval

Dispels exterior Wind, Clears Heat, Brightens the eyes, Benefits the throat

When a loose fist is made,

LI 04 HeGu

Joining Valley

Dispels, exterior Wind, Releases the Exterior, Stimulates the dispersing function of the Lungs, Stops pain, Removes obstructions from channel,

Tonifies Qi and consolidates the Exterior, Harmonises ascending and descending,

Midway between the junction of the 1st. & 2nd metacarpal bones and the margin of the web.

LI 05 Yang Xi

Yang Stream

Expels Wind Releases the Exterior Benefits the Throat Stops pain

On the radial side, over the wrist joint between the two tendons of m. extensor pollicis brevis and extensor pollicis longus. Point is in anatomical snuffbox.

LI 06 Pian Li

Slanting passage

Opens the Lung Water passages

With the elbow flexed and the radial side of the arm upward, point is on a line between LI-05 and LI-11, 3 cun above LI-05.

LI 07 Wen Liu

Warm Flow

Clears Heat, Stops pain, Expels Wind, Benefits the throat,

With the elbow flexed and the radial side of the arm upward, point is on a line

on the radial side of the index finger, in a depression proximal to head of the 2nd. metacarpophalangeal joint.

between LI-05 and LI-11, 5 cun above LI-05

LI 08 Xia Lian

With the elbow flexed and the radial side of the arm upward, point is on a line between LI-05 and LI-11, 4 cun below LI-11

LI 09 Shang Lian

With the elbow flexed and the radial side of the arm upward, point is on a line between LI-05 and LI-11, 3 cun below LI-11

LI 10 Shou San Li

Arm 3 Miles

Removes obstructions from channel Tonifies Qi

With the elbow flexed and the radial side of the arm upward, point is on a line between LI-05 and LI-11, 2 cun below LI-11, on the medial aspect of the radius.

LI 11 Qu Chi

Crooked Pond

Expels exterior Wind,

Clears Heat,

Cools Blood, Resolves Dampness, Regulates (Ying) Nutritive Qi and Blood, Benefits the sinews and joints,

When elbow flexed is in the depression at the lateral end of the transverse cubital crease, midway between Lu-05 and lateral epicondyle of the humerus.

LI 12 Zhou Liao

Elbow Seam

With the elbow flexed point is superior to the epicondyle of the humerus, about 1 cun superolateral to LI-11, on the medial aspect of the humerus.

LI 13 Wu Li - Shou

Superior to the epicondyle of the humerus, on a line between LI-11 and LI-15 3 cun above LI-11

LI 14 Bi Nao

Arm and Scapula

Removes obstructions from channel, brightens the eyes, Resolves Phlegm and disperses masses

On the lower border of the deltoid muscle and the medial side of the humerus. 7 cun above LI-11.

LI 15 Jian Yu

Shoulder Transporting point

Benefits sinews, Promotes circulation of Qi in the channels, Stops pain, Expels Wind

Directly below the anterior border of the acromion, on the upper portion of the m. deltoideus, where a depression is formed when the arm is abducted.

LI 16 Ju Gu

Great Bone

Moves Blood locally

Removes obstructions from channel, Opens the chest, Subdues ascending rebellious Qi, Stimulates the descending of Lung Qi, Benefits the joints

In the upper aspect of the shoulder, in the depression between the acromial extremity of the clavicle and the scapular spine.

LI 17 Tian Ding

On the lateral side of the

neck, 1 cun below Neck Fu Tu (L.I.) 18, on the posterior border of m. sternocleidomastoideus.

LI 18   Fu Tu

Support the Prominence

Benefits the throat, Relieves cough, Resolves Phlegm and disperses masses

On the lateral side of the neck, level with the tip of the Adam's apple, between the sternal head and the clavicular head of m. sternocleidomastoideus.

LI 19   He Liao - Nose

Directly below the lateral margin of the nostril 0.5 cun lateral to Du-26

LI 20   Ying Xiang

Welcome Fragrance

Dispels exterior Wind

In the nasolabial sulcus (groove), at the level of the midpoint of the lateral border of ala nasi.

Stomach Meridian

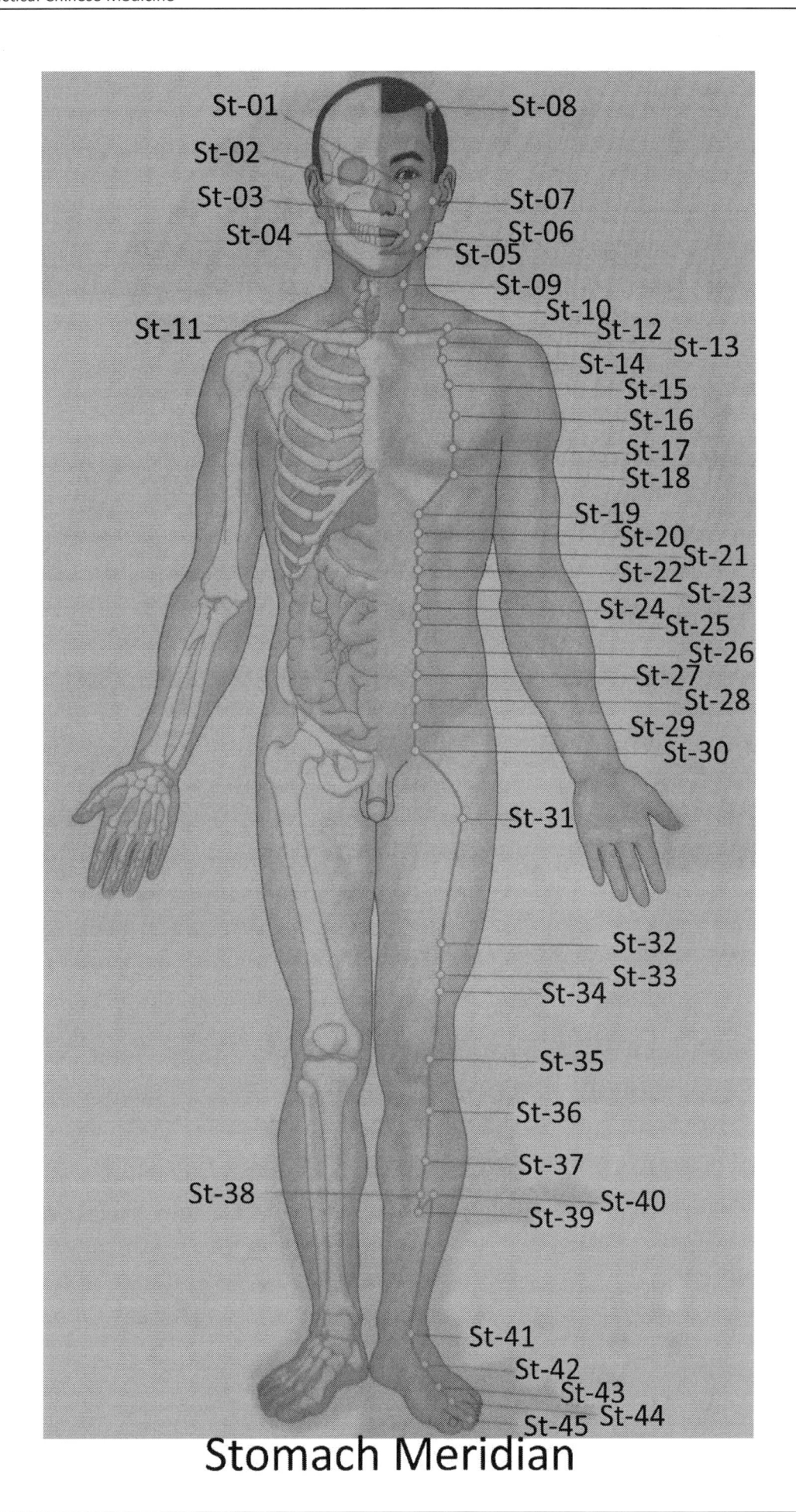

Stomach

St 01   Cheng Qi

Containing Tears

Expels Wind, Brightens the eyes, Stops lacrymation

With the eyes looking straight forward, the point is directly below the pupil, between the eyeball and the infraorbital ridge.

St 02   Si Bai

Four Whites

Expels Wind Brightens the eyes

Below St-01, in the depression at the infraorbital foramen.

St 03   Ju Liao

Big Bone

Expels Wind

Removes obstructions from channel, Relieves swelling

Directly below St-02 at the level of the lower border of ala nasi, on the lateral side of the nasolabial groove.

St 04   Di Cang

Earth Granary

Expels Wind

Removes obstructions from channel, Benefits tendons and muscles

Lateral to the corner of the mouth, directly below St-03

St 05   Da ying

1.3 cun anterior and lower to the angle of mandible, in the groove-like depression appearing when cheek is bulged.

St 06   Jiache

Jaw Chariot

Expels Wind

Removes obstructions from channel

One finger breath anterior and superior to the lower angle of the mandible where m. masseter attaches at the prominence of the muscle when the teeth are clenched.

St 07   Xia Guan

Lower Gate

Removes obstructions from channel Benefits the ear

At the lower border of the zygomatic arch, in the depression anterior to the condyloid process of the mandible. Locate point with mouth closed.

St 08   Tou Wei

Head Support

Expels Wind, Relieves pain, Brightens the eyes, Clears Heat, Stops lacrymation, Relieves dizziness,

0.5 cun within the anterior hairline at the corner of the forehead, 4.5 cun lateral to Du-24

St 09   Ren Ying

Person's Welcome

Regulates Qi, Removes masses, Benefits the throat, Relieves swellings, Benefits High Blood pressure,

Level with the Adams apple, just on the course of the common carotid artery, on the anterior border of m. sternocleidomastoideus

St 10   Shui Tu

1 cun below Renying St 9, on the anterior border of sternocleidomastoid muscle.

St 11   Qishe

At the superior border of the sternal extremity of the clavicle, between the sternal head and the clavicular head of the sternocleidomastoid muscle.

St 12   Que Pen

Empty Basin

Subdues rebellious Qi

In the midpoint of the supraclavicular fossa, 4 cun lateral to the Ren meridian.

St 13   Qi Hu

At the lower border of the middle of the clavical, 4 cun lateral to the Ren meridian.

St 14   Ku Fang

In the 1st. intercostals space, 4 cun lateral to the Ren meridian.

St 15   Wu Yi

In the 2nd. intercostals space, 4 cun lateral to the Ren meridian.

St 16   Ying Chuang

In the 3rd. intercostals space, 4 cun lateral to the Ren meridian.

St 17   Ruzhong

In the 4th. intercostals space, in the centre of the nipple, 4 cun lateral to the Ren meridian.

St 18   Ru Gen

Breast Root

Regulates Stomach Qi Regulates the breast and lactation, Dispels stagnation

In the 5th. intercostals space, directly below nipple, 4 cun lateral to the Ren meridian.

St 19   Bu Rong

6 cun above the umbilicus, 2 cun lateral to Ren-14

St 20   Cheng man

5 cun above the umbilicus, 2 cun lateral to Ren-13

St 21   Liang Men

Beam Door

Regulates the Stomach, subdues rebellious Qi, Stops vomiting, Relieves pain,

4 cun above the umbilicus, 2 cun lateral to Ren-12

St 22   Pass Gate

Restores the descending of Stomach Qi, dissolves accumulations in the epigastria,

3 cun above the umbilicus, 2 cun lateral to Ren-11

St 23   Tai Yi

2 cun above the umbilicus. 2 cun lateral to Ren-10

St 24   Huarou Men

1 cun above the umbilicus, 2 cun lateral to Ren-09

St 25   Tian Shu

Heavenly Pillar

Promotes the function of the Intestines,

Clears Heat, regulates Qi, Relieves retention of food,

2 cun lateral to the centre of the umbilicus.

St 26   Wai Ling

1 cun below the umbilicus, 2 cun lateral to Ren-07

St 27   Da Ju

Big Great

Regulates Stomach Qi

2 cun below the umbilicus, 2 cun lateral to Ren-05

St 28   Shui Dao

Water passage

Benefits urination, Opens the Water passages, Benefits Difficult Urination Syndrome, Regulates menstruation, Stops pain,

3 cun below the umbilicus, 2 cun lateral to Ren-04

St 29   Gui Lai

Returning

Relieves stagnation of Blood

4 cun below the umbilicus, 2 cun lateral to Ren-03

St 30   Qi Chong

Penetrating Qi

Regulates Stomach Qi, Promotes Essence, Tonifies the Sea of Food, Regulates Blood

5 cun below the umbilicus, 2 cun lateral to Ren 2

St 31   Bi Guan

Thigh Gate

Removes obstruction from the channel

At cross point of line directly down from anterio superior iliac spine and line level with lower bor. of symphysis pubis, in depression on lateral side of m. sartorius, when thigh is flexed.

St 32   Fu Tu

Hidden Rabbit

Removes obstruction from channel, Expels Wind Heat

On the line connecting the anterior superior iliac spine and lateral border of the patella, 6 cun above the laterosuperior border of the patella, in m. rectus femoris.

St 33   Yin Shi

When knee is flexed, point is 3 cun above the laterosuperior border of the patella, on line joining laterosuperior border of the patella and the anterior superior iliac spine

St 34   Liang Qiu

Beam Mound

Subdues rebellious Stomach Qi, Removes obstructions from channel, Expels Dampness and Wind, Relieves retention of food, stops pain,

When knee is flexed, point is 2 cun above the laterosuperior border of the patella.

St 35   Du Bi

Calf Nose

Invigorates the channel, Relieves swelling, Stops pain

When knee is flexed, point is at the lower border of the patella, in the depression lateral to the patellar ligament.

St 36   Zu San Li

Three Miles of the Foot

Benefits Stomach and Spleen, Tonifies Qi and Blood, Dispels Cold, Strengthens the body, Brightens the eyes, Regulates Ying and Wei Qi, Regulates the Intestines, Raises Yang,

3 cun below St-35, 1 finger breath from the anterior crest of the Tibia, in the m. tibialis anterior.

St 37   Shang Ju Xu

Upper Great Emptiness

Regulates the function of Stomach and Large

Intestines, Eliminates Damp Heat, Dispels retention of Food, Calms asthma,

3 cun below St-36. 1 finger breath from the anterior crest of the Tibia, in the m. tibialis anterior.

St 38   Tiao Kou

Narrow Opening

Removes obstruction from channel

2 cun below St-37, midway between St-35 and St-41

St 39   Xia Ju Xu

Lower Great Emptiness

Regulates the function of Stomach and Intestines, Eliminates Damp Heat, Eliminates Wind Damp, Stops pain,

3 cun below St-37, 1 finger breath from the anterior crest of the Tibia, in the m tibialis anterior,

St 40   Feng Long

Abundant Bulge

Resolves Phlegm and Damp, Calms asthma, Clears Heat, Calms and clears the mind, Opens the chest,

8 cun superior to the external malleolus. 1 finger breath lateral to St-38

St 41   Jie Xi

Dispersing Stream

Removes obstruction from channel, Eliminates Wind, Clears Heat, Clears the mind, Brightens the eyes

Dorsum of foot, midpoint of transverse crease of ankle joint, level with tip of the external malleolus, in depression between tendons of m. extensor digitorum longus and lallucia longus.

St 42   Chong Yang

Rushing Yang

Tonifies Stomach and Spleen, Calms the Mind, Removes obstruction from channel

Distal to St-41, at the highest point of the dorsum of the foot, in the depression between the 2nd. & 3rd. metatarsal bones and the cuneiform bone.

St 43   Xian Gu

Sinking Valley

Eliminates Wind and Heat, Removes obstruction from channel,

In the depression distal to the junction of the 2nd. & 3rd. metatarsal bones.

St 44   Nei Ting

Inner courtyard

Clears Heat, Eliminates fullness, Regulates Qi, Stops pain, Promotes digestion, Eliminates Wind from the face,

Proximal to the web margin between the 2nd and 3rd toes, in the depression distal and lateral to the 2nd. metatarsodigital joint.

St 45 Li Dui

Sick mouth

Calms the Mind, Brightens the eyes, Clears the Heart, Relieves retention of food,

At the lateral side in the outer corner of the nail of the 2nd. toe.

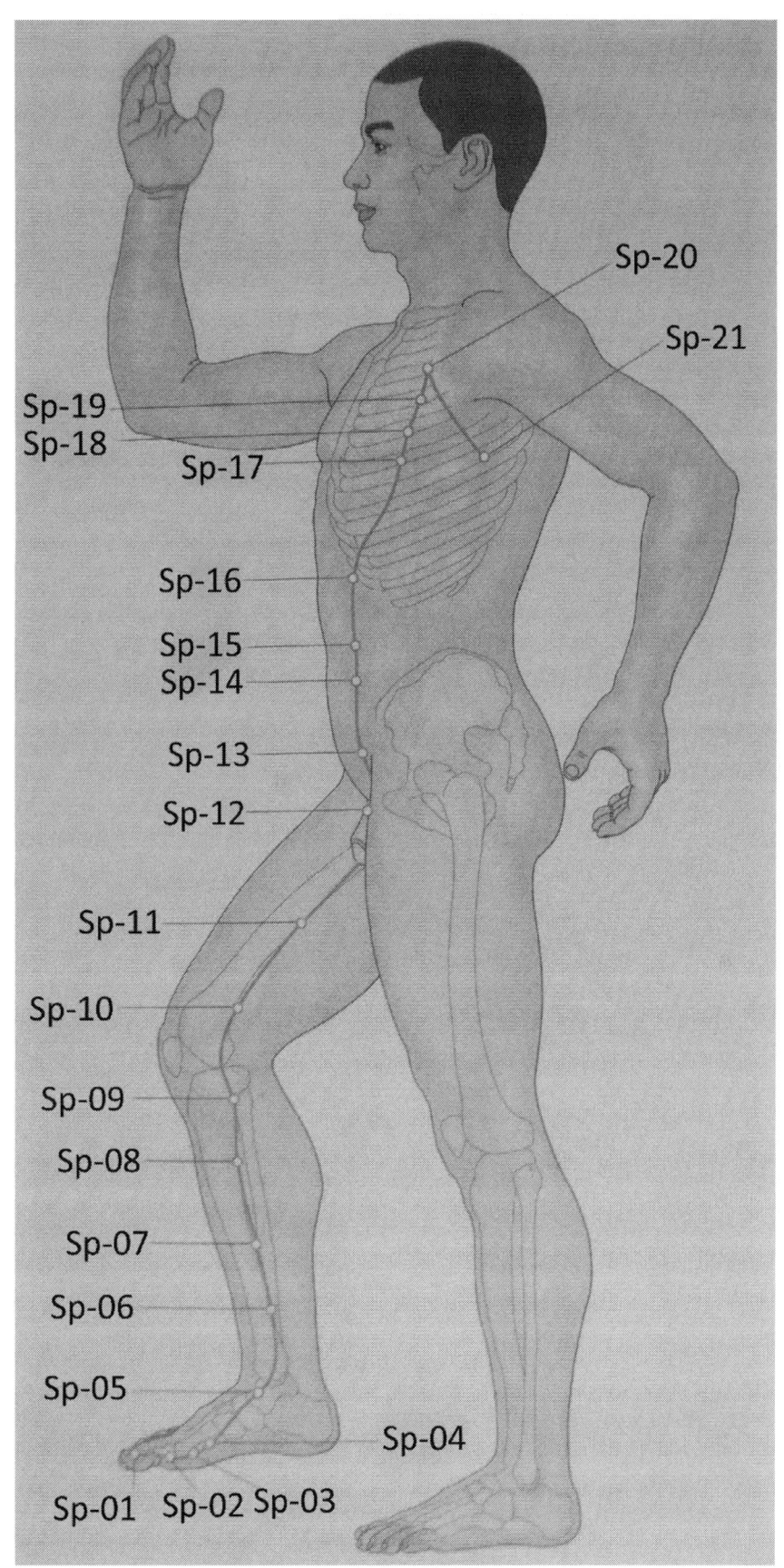

Spleen Meridian

Spleen

Sp 01   Yin Bai

Hidden White

Strengthens the Spleen, Regulates Blood, Calms the Mind.

At the medial corner of the root of the nail of the great toe.

Sp 02   Da Du

Big Capital

Strengthens the Spleen, Promotes digestion, Clears Heat.

On the medial and distal to the 1st. metatarsophalangeal joint.

Sp 03   Tai Bai

Greater White

Strengthens the Spleen, Resolves Damp, Strengthens the spine.

On the medial and proximal to the 1st. metatarsophalangeal joint. at the junction of the red and white skin.

Sp 04   Gong Sun

Minute Connecting channels

Tonifies Stomach and Spleen, Regulates the Penetrating Vessel, Stops bleeding, Dispels fullness, Pacifies the Stomach, Removes obstructions, Regulates menstruation,

In the depression distal and inferior to the base of the 1st. metatarsal bone. 1 cun posterior to Sp3, at the junction of the red and white skin.

Sp 05   Shang Qiu

Gold Mound

Strengthens Stomach and Spleen, Resolves Damp.......

In the depression distal and inferior to the medial malleolus, midway between the tuberosity of the navicular bone and the tip of the medial malleolus.

Sp 06   San Yin Jiao

Three Yin Meeting

Strengthens the Spleen, Resolves Damp, Promotes the function of the Liver and the smooth flowing of Liver Qi, Tonifies the Kidneys, Nourishes Blood and Yin, Benefits urination, Regulates the uterus, Moves Blood and eliminates stasis, Cools Blood, Stops pain, Calms the Mind.

3 cun above the tip of the medial malleolus, near the posterior border of the Tibia.

Sp 07   Lou Gu

3 cun above Sp-06. One finger breath lateral to the posterior border of the Tibia

Sp 08   Di Ji

Earth pivot

Removes obstructions from the channel, Regulates Qi and Blood, Regulates the uterus, Stops pain,

7 cun above Sp-06. One finger breath lateral to the posterior border of the Tibia.

Sp 09   Yin Ling Quan

Yin Mound Spring

Resolves Dampness, Benefits the Lower Burner, Benefits urination, Removes obstructions from the channel.

Is in the depression on the inferior border of the medial condyle of the Tibia at the posterior border of the Tibia.

Sp 10   Xue Hai

Cools the Blood, Removes stasis of Blood, Regulates menstruation, Tonifies Blood.

2 cun above the medial epicondyle of the femur, at the protuberance of the m. vastus medialis.

Sp 11   Ji Men

6 cun above Sp-10 on the line drawn from Sp-10 to Sp-12

Sp 12   Chong Men

Rushing Door

Removes obstructions from the channel, Tonifies Yin.....

Superior to the lateral end of the inguinal groove, on the lateral side of the femoral artery, at the level of the upper border of symphsis pubis, 3.5 cun lateral to Ren-02

Sp 13   Fu She

0.7 cun laterosuperior to Sp-12, 4 cun lateral to the Ren meridian.

Sp 14   Fu Jie

1.3 cun below Sp-15, 4 cun lateral to the Ren meridian, on the lateral side of m. rectus abdominis.

Sp 15   Da Heng

Big Horizontal Stroke

Strengthens the Spleen, Strengthens the Limbs, Resolves Damp, Regulates Qi, Stops pain, Promotes the function of the Large Intestine.

4 cun lateral to the centre of the umbilicus, on the lateral

side of m. rectus abdominis.

Sp 16   Fu Ai

3 cun above Sp-15, 4 cun lateral to Ren-11

Sp 17   Shi Dou

In the 5th. intercostal space, 6 cun lateral to the Ren meridian.

Sp 18   Tian Xi

In the 4th. intercostal space, 6 cun lateral to the Ren meridian.

Sp 19   Xiong Xiang

In the 3rd. intercostal space, 6 cun lateral to the Ren meridian.

Sp 20   Zhou Rong

In the 2nd. intercostal space, 6 cun lateral to the Ren meridian.

Sp 21   Da Bao

General Control

Moves Blood in the Blood Connecting channels

On the mid axillary line, 6 cun below the axilla, midway between the axilla and the free end of the 11th. rib.

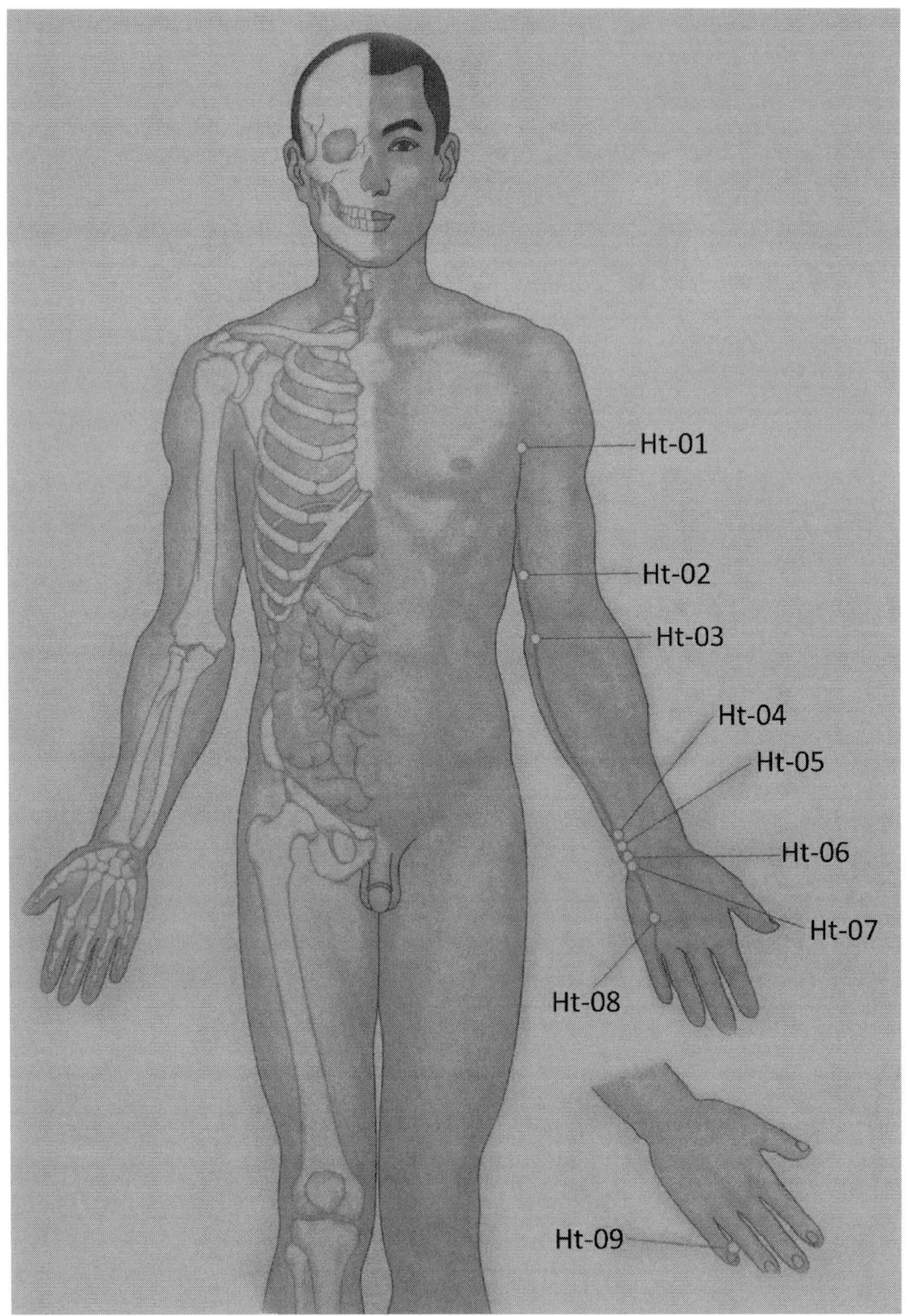

Heart Meridian

Heart

Ht 01   Ji Quan

Supreme spring

Nourishes Heart Yin
Clears Empty Heat

In the centre of the armpit, on the medial side of axillary artery.

Ht 02   Qing Ling

3 cun superior to the medial epicondyle of the humerus, in the groove of the biceps brachii muscle on the ulnar aspect. 3 cun above Ht-03 on a line to Ht-01

Ht 03   Shao Hai

Lesser Yin Sea

Removes obstructions from channel
Calms the Mind
Clears HeatAt the medial end of the transverse cubital crease when the elbow is flexed. or midpoint between P-03 and medial epicondyle of humerus.

Ht 04   Ling Dao

Mind Path

Removes obstructions from channelOn the ulnar side of the wrist, between the tendons of flexor carpi ulnaris muscle and flexor digitorum supersicialis muscle, 2 cun superior to Ht-07.

Ht 05   Tong Li

Inner Communication

Calms the Mind, Tonifies Heart Qi, Opens into the tongue, Benefits the Bladder,

On the ulnar side of the forearm, proximal to the wrist between the tendons of flexor carpi ulnaris muscle and flexor digitorum supersicialis muscle, 1 cun superior to Ht-07.

Ht 06   Yin Xi

Yin Accumulation

Nourishes Heart Yin
Clears Heat
Stops sweating
Calms the MindOn the ulnar side of the wrist, between the tendons of flexor carpi ulnaris muscle and flexor digitorum supersicialis muscle, 0.5 cun superior to Ht-07.

Ht 07   Shen Men

Mind Door

Calms the Mind, Nourishes Heart Blood, Opens the orifices,

Along the most distal skin crease of the wrist on the ulnar side of the flexor carpi ulnaris muscle, on the radial side of the pisiform bone.

Ht 08   Shao Fu

Lesser Yin Mansion

Clears Heart Fire, Heart Empty Heat and Heart Phlegm Fire
Calms the Mind .... Between the 4th & 5th metacarpal bone, posterior to the metacarpo- phalangeal joint, on transverse crease of palm. Point is touched by the tip of the little finger when fist is clenched

Ht 09   Shao Chong

Lesser Yin Rushing

Clears Heat, Subdues Wind, Opens the Heart orifices, Relieves fullness, Restores consciousness, About 0.1 cun posterior to the corner of the vallum unguis on the radial side of the little finger.

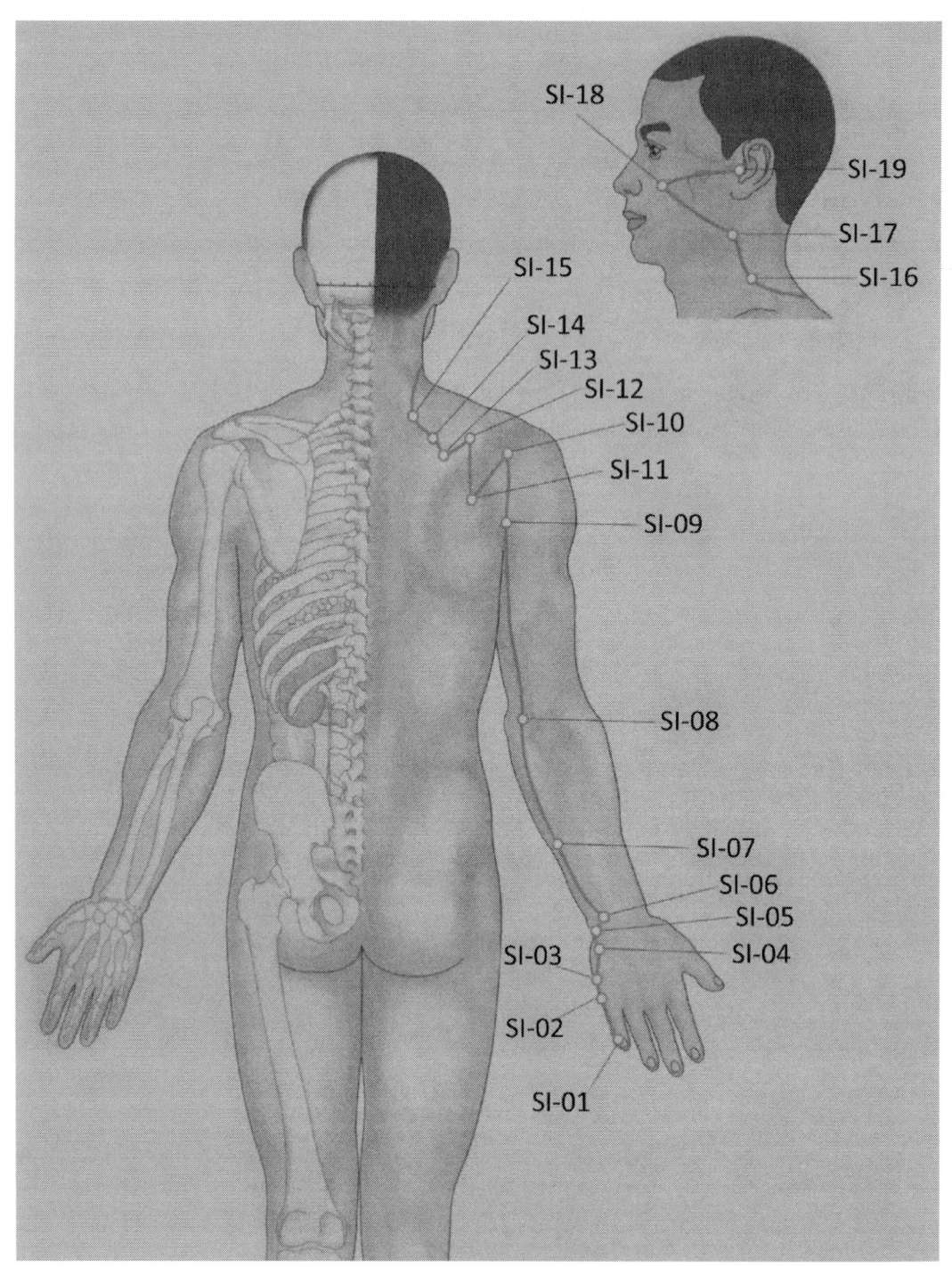

Small Intestine Meridian

Small Intestine

SI 01   Shaoze

Lesser Marsh

Expels Wind Heat,
Subdues Wind,
Opens the orifices,
Removes obstructions from channel,
Promotes lactation and production of milk.

On the ulnar side of the little finger, about 1 fen proximal to the corner of the nail.

SI 02   Qian Gu

Front Valley

Clears Heat.

When a loose fist is made, point is on the Ulnar side, distal to the 5th. metacarpophalangel joint on the junction of the red and white skin

SI 03   Hou Xi

Back Stream

Eliminates interior Wind from Governing (Du) Vessel, Expels exterior Wind, Benefits the sinews, Resolves Dampness, Resolves jaundice, Clears the Mind.

Make loose fist, Point is on the Ulnar side, on the end of the transvease crease, proximal to the 5th. metacarpophalangel joint on the junction of the red and white skin.

SI 04   Wan Gu

Wrist Bone

Removes obstructions from channel
Eliminates Damp Heat.

Distal to the hamate bone on the junction of the red and white skin

SI 05   Yang Gu

Yang Valley

Clears the mind, Removes obstructions from channel,
Expels exterior Damp Heat,

Proximal to the hamate bone, in a depression between the styloid process and the triquetral bone, on the junction of the red and white skin

SI 06   Yang Lao

Nourishing the Old

Benefits sinews
Benefits the eyes
Removes obstructions from channel.

On the head of the ulna where there is a seam when the palms turns to the chest.

SI 07   Zhi Zheng

Branch to Heart Channel

Removes obstructions from channel, Calms the Mind ....

5 cun above the wrist, on the border of the ulna, on a line joining SI-05 and SI-08

SI 08   Xiao Hai

Small Intestine Sea

Resolves Damp Heat
Removes obstructions from channel
Calms the Mind.

When elbow is flexed, In the fossa between the ulnar olecranon and the medial epicondyle of the humerus.

SI 09   Jian Zhen

Upright Shoulder

1 cun above the posterior end of the axillary fold.

SI 10   Nao Shu

Humerus Transporting Point

Straight above SI-09 in the depression below the spine of the scapula.

SI 11   Tian Zong

Heavenly Attribution

1 cun below the midpoint of the lower border of the spine.

SI 12   Bing Feng

Watching Wind

1 cun above the midpoint of the lower border of the spine.

SI 13   Qu Yuan

Bend Wall

On the upper border of the spine, 1 cun lateral to the medial end.

SI 14   Jian Wai Shu

Transport point of Outside of Shoulder

3 cun from Du 13, which is below the spinous process of the 1st. thoracic vertebra.

SI 15   Jian Hong Shu

Transport point of Centre of Shoulder

2 cun from Du 14, which is below the spinous process of the 7th. cervical vertebra.

SI 16   Tian Chuang

Level with the laryngeal prominence, on the posterior border of the sternocleidomastoid muscle.

SI 17   Tian Rong

Heaven Appearance

Resolves Damp Heat, Expels Fire Poison, Removes obstructions from channel..

Level with the angle of the mandible, on the anterior border of the sternocleidomastoid muscle.

SI 18   Quan Liao

Zygoma Crevice

Expels Wind, Relieves pain

On the lower border of the zygomatic bone, directly below the external canthus.

SI 19   Ting Gong

Listening Palace

Benefits the ears

Anterior to the tragus, where a depression is formed when the mouth is open.

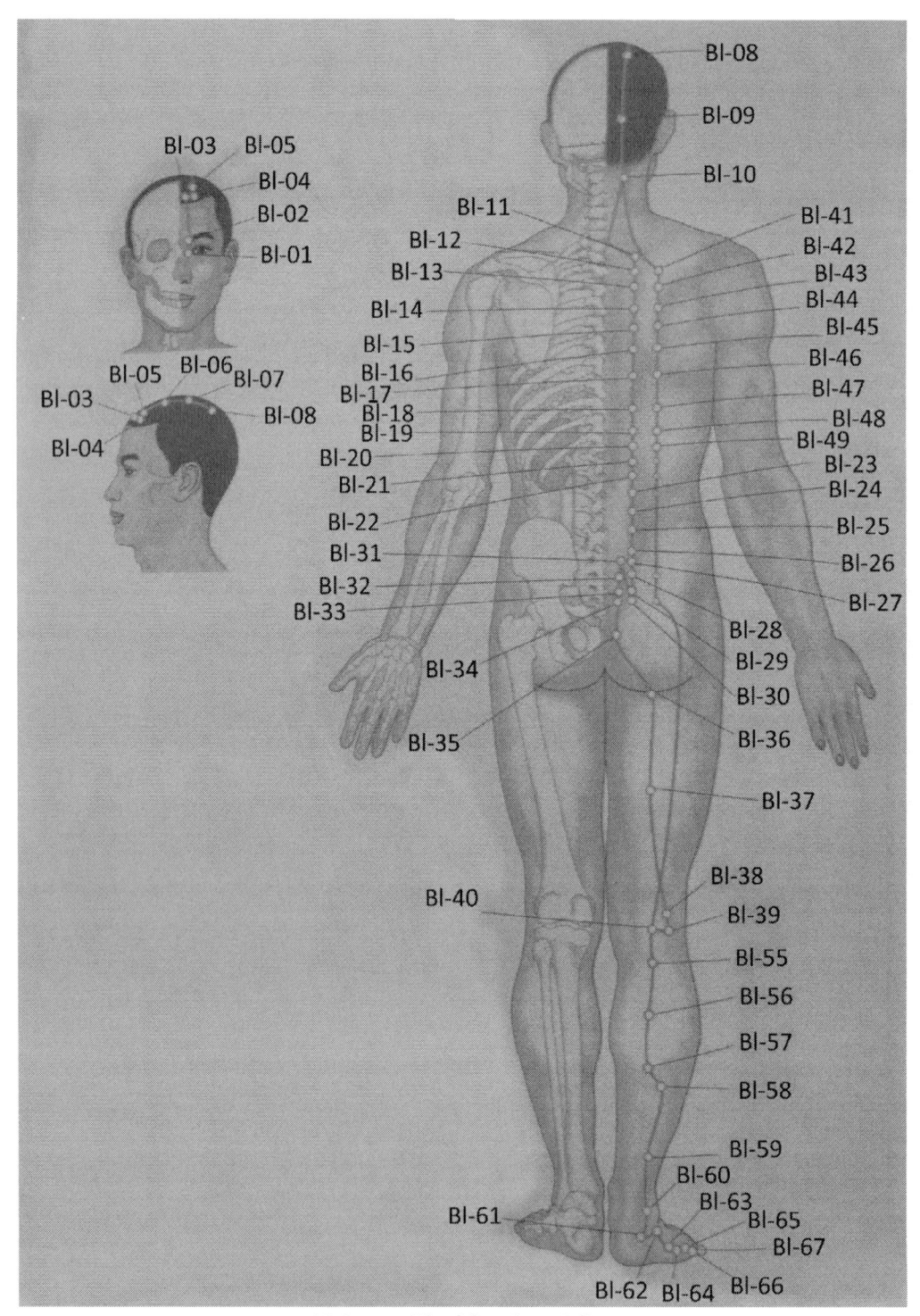

Urinary Bladder Meridian

Urinary Bladder

BL 01　Jing Ming

Eye Brightness

Expels Wind, Clears Heat, Brightens the eyes, Stops pain, Stops itching, Stops lacrymation.

On the margin of the orbit and 0.1 cun superior to the inner cantus.

BL 02　Zan Zhu

Collecting Bamboo

Expels Wind, Brightens the eyes, Soothes the Liver, Removes obstructions from the channel, Stops pain, ...

At the medial end of the eyebrow, on the supra orbital notch.

BL 03　Mei Chong

Directly above UB-02, on the hairline superior to the medial end of the eyebrow, 0.5 cun inside the hairline and midway between DU-24 and Bl-04.

BL 04　Qu Chi

0.5 cun inside the hairline, 1.5 cun lateral to the midline. One third of the distance laterally from DU-24 to ST-8

BL 05　Wu Chi

Five Places

Subdues interior Wind, Restores consciousness

1.5 cun lateral to the midline and 1.5 cun superior to the hairline and directly above UB-04

BL 06　Cheng Guang

1.5 cun lateral to the midline and 1.5 cun superior to Bl-05

BL 07　Tong Tian

Reaching Heaven

Subdues Wind, Clears the nose, Brightens the eyes, Stops convulsions, Opens the orifices.

1.5 cun lateral to the midline and 1.5 cun posterior to Bl-06

BL 08　Luo Que

1.5 cun lateral to the midline and 1.5 cun posterior to Bl-07

BL 09　Yu Zhen

At the superior border of the occipital protuberance and 1.3 cun lateral to Midline or DU-17

BL 10　Tian Zhu

Heaven Pillar

Expels Wind, Clears the brain, Opens the orifices, Soothes the sinews, Brightens the eyes, Removes obstructions from the channel, Invigorates the lower back.

1.3 cun lateral to the midline or DU-15, on the lateral margin of the trapezius muscle. 0.5 cun within the posterior hairline.

BL 11　Da Zhu

Big Reed

Nourishes Blood, Expels Wind, Strengthens bones, Soothes the sinews, Releases the Exterior.

1.5 cun lateral to the inferior spinous process of the 1st. thoracic vertebra. (In the space between it and the lower vertabra)

BL 12　Feng Men

Wind Door

Expels and prevents exterior Wind, Releases the exterior, Stimulates the Lung dispersing function, Regulates Yuan and Wei Qi.

1.5 cun beside the inferior end of the spinous process of the 2nd. thoracic vertebra. (In the space between it and the lower vertabra)

BL 13　Fei Shu

Lung Back Transporting Point

Stimulates the Lung dispersing and descending function, Regulates Lung Qi, Regulates Yuan and Wei Qi, Tonifies Lung Qi, Stops cough, Clears Heat.

1.5 cun beside the inferior end of the spinous process of the 3th. thoracic vertebra on a level with the spine of the scapula.

BL 14　Jue Yin Shu

Terminal Yin Back

Regulates the Heart, Calms the Mind.

1.5 cun beside the inferior end of the spinous process of the 4th. thoracic vertebra.

BL 15　Xin Shu

Heart Transporting Point

Calms the Mind, Clears Heat, Stimulates the brain, Invigorates Blood, Nourishes the Heart, Nourishes Heart Yin.

1.5 cun beside the inferior end of the spinous process of the 5th. thoracic vertebra.

BL 16　Du Shu

Governing Vessel Back Transporting Point

Regulates the Heart, Invigorates Blood.

1.5 cun beside the inferior end of the spinous process of the 6th. thoracic vertebra.

BL 17   Ge Shu

Diaphragm Back Transporting Point

Nourishes Blood, Invigorates Blood, Opens the chest, Removes obstructions from diaphragm, Pacifies Stomach Qi, Tonifies Qi and Blood, Clears Heat, Calms the Mind.

1.5 cun beside the inferior end of the spinous process of the 7th. thoracic vertebra on a level with the inferior angle of the scapula.

BL 18   Gan Shu

Liver Back Transporting Point

Benefits Liver and Gall Bladder, Resolves Damp Heat, Moves stagnant Qi, Benefits the eyes, Eliminates Wind.

1.5 cun beside the inferior end of the spinous process of the 9th. thoracic vertebra

BL 19   Dan Shu

Gall Bladder Back Transporting Point

Resolves Damp Heat in Liver and Gall Bladder, Pacifies the Stomach, Relaxes the diaphragm.

1.5 cun beside the inferior end of the spinous process of the 10th. thoracic vertebra

BL 20   Pi Shu

Spleen Back Transporting Point

Tonifies Spleen and Stomach, Resolves Damp, Nourishes Blood.

1.5 cun beside the inferior end of the spinous process of the 11th. thoracic vertebra

BL 21   Wei Shu

Stomach Back Transporting Point

Regulates and tonifies Stomach Qi, Resolves Damp, Pacifies the Stomach, Relieves retention of food

1.5 cun beside the inferior end of the spinous process of the 12th. thoracic vertebra

BL 22   San Jiao Shu

San Jiao Back Transporting Point

Resolves Dampness, Opens the Water passagesRegulates the transformation of fluids in the lower burner.

1.5 cun beside the inferior end of the spinous process of the 1st. lumbar vertebra

BL 23   Shen Shu

Kidney Back Transporting Point

Tonifies the Kidneys and Nourishes the Kidney Essence, Strengthens the lower back, Nourishes Blood, Benefits the bones and Marrow, Resolves Dampness, Strengthens the Kidney function of reception of Qi, Brightens the eyes, Benefits the ears,

1.5 cun beside the inferior end of the spinous process of the 2nd. lumbar vertebra

BL 24   Qi Hai Shu

Sea of Qi Back Transporting Point

Strengthens the lower back, Removes obstructions from the channel, Regulates Qi and Blood, Tonifying Kidney Yang disperses Cold.

1.5 cun beside the inferior end of the spinous process of the 3rd. lumbar vertebra.

BL 25   Da Chang Shu

Large Intestine Back Transporting Point

Promotes the function of the Large Intestine, Strengthens the lower back, Removes obstructions from the channel, Relieves fullness and swelling.

1.5 cun beside the inferior end of the spinous process of the 4th. lumbar vertebra

BL 26   Guan Yuan Shu

Origin Gate Back Transporting Point

Strengthens the lower back, Removes obstructions from channel

1.5 cun beside the inferior end of the spinous process of the 5th. lumbar vertebra

BL 27   Xiao Chang Shu

Small Intestine Back Transporting Point

Promotes the function of the Small Intestine, Resolves Dampness, Clears Heat, Benefits urination, ...

1.5 cun lateral to the midline of the back, level to the 1st. posterior sacral foramen, in the depression between the medial border of the posterior superior iliac spine and the sacrum.

BL 28 Pang Guang Shu

Bladder Back Transporting Point

Regulates the Bladder, Resolves Dampness, Clears Heat, Stops Pain, Eliminates stagnation, Opens the Water passages in the Lower Burner, Strengthens the loins.

Level with the 2nd. posterior sacral foramen, 1.5 cun lateral to Governing Meridian, in the depression between lower medial border of the posterior superior iliac spine of sacrum

BL 29 Zhong Lu Shu

1.5 cun lateral to the midline of the back at the level of the 3rd. posterior sacral foramen.

BL 30 Bai Huan Shu

White Ring Back Transporting Point

1.5 cun lateral to the midline of the back at the level of the 4th. posterior sacral foramen.

BL 31 Shang Liao

Upper Crevice

Regulates the Lower Burner, Tonifies the Lumbar region and knees, Nourishes the Kidneys

On the 1st. posterior sacral foramen and about midway between the posterosuperior iliac spine and the median line.

BL 32 Ci Liao

Second Crevice

Regulates the Lower Burner, Tonifies the Lumbar region and knees, Nourishes the Kidneys

On the 2nd. posterior sacral foramen and about midway between the posterosuperior iliac spine and the median line.

BL 33 Zhong Liao

Central Crevice

Regulates the Lower Burner, Tonifies the Lumbar region and knees, Nourishes the Kidneys

On the 3th. posterior sacral foramen and about midway between UB-29 and the median line.

BL 34 Xia Liao

Lower Crevice

Regulates the Lower Burner, Tonifies the Lumbar region and knees, Nourishes the Kidneys

On the 4th. posterior sacral foramen and about midway between UB-30 and the median line.

BL 35 Hui Yang

0.5 cun lateral to the median line and level with the superior border of the coccyx.

BL 36 Cheng Fu

Receiving Support

In the middle of the gluteal sulcus, at the posterior midline of the thigh.

BL 37 Yin Men

Huge Gate

6 cun inferior to Cheng Fu, BL 36, and in the centre of the back of the thigh.

BL 38 Fu Xi

Rich for the Vitals Correspondence

On the lateral side of the popliteal fossa, and 1 cun superior to UB-39

BL 39 Wei Yang

Supporting Yang

Opens the Water passages in the Lower Burner, Stimulates the transformation and excretion of fluids in the Lower Burner, Benefits the Bladder.

On the lateral side of the popliteal fossa, beside UB-40 at the inner margin of the biceps femoris muscle.

BL 40 Wei Zhong

Supporting Middle

Clears Heat, Resolves Dampness, Relaxes the sinews, Removes obstructions from the channel, Cools Blood, Eliminates stasis of Blood, Clears Summer Heat.

In the middle of the popliteal fossa.

BL 41 Fu Fen

3 cun lateral to the lower end of the spinious process of the 2nd. thoracic vertebra. (In the space between it and the lower vertabra)

BL 42 Po Hu

Door of the Corporeal Soul

Stimulates the descending of Lung Qi, Regulates Qi, Clears Heat, Stops cough and asthma, Subdues rebellious Qi.

3 cun lateral to the lower end of the spinious process

of the 3th. thoracic vertebra.

BL 43   Gao Huang Shu

Vitals

Tonifies Qi of the whole body, Strengthens Deficiency, Nourishes Essence, Nourishes Lung Yin, Invigorates the Mind, Stops cough and calms asthma.

In the depression of the medial border of the scapula, 3 cun lateral to the lower end of the spinous process of the 4th. thoracic vertebra.

BL 44   Shen Tang

Mind Hall

Calms the Mind

3 cun lateral to the lower end of the spinous process of the 5th. thoracic vertebra.

BL 45   Yi Xi

3 cun lateral to the lower end of the spinous process of the 6th. thoracic vertebra.

BL 46   Ge Guan

3 cun lateral to the lower end of the spinous process of the 7th. thoracic vertebra.

BL 47   Hun Men

Door of the Ethereal Soul

Regulates Liver Qi, Roots the Ethereal Soul.

3 cun lateral to the lower end of the spinous process of the 9th. thoracic vertebra.

BL 48   Yang Gang

3 cun lateral to the lower end of the spinous process of the 10th. thoracic vertebra.

BL 49   Yi She

Thought Shelter

Tonifies the Spleen Stimulates memory and concentration.

3 cun lateral to the lower end of the spinous process of the 11th. thoracic vertebra.

BL 50   Wei Cang

3 cun lateral to the lower end of the spinous process of the 12th. thoracic vertebra.

BL 51   Huang Men

Vitals Door

Regulates the Triple Burner, Ensures the smooth spread of the Triple Burner Qi to the Heart region.

3 cun lateral to the lower end of the spinous process of the 1st. lumbar vertebra.

BL 52   Zhi Si

Room of Will Power

Tonifies the Kidneys, Strengthens the back, Reinforces the will power,

3 cun lateral to the lower end of the spinous process of the 2nd. lumbar vertebra.

BL 53   Bao Huang

Bladder Vitals

Opens the Water passages in the Lower Burner, Stimulates the transformation and excretion of fluids.

3 cun lateral to the midpoint of the 2nd. sacral vertebra.

BL 54   Zhi Bian

Lowermost Edge

In the depression 3 cun lateral to the sacral hiatus or spinous process of the 4th sacral vertebra.

BL 55   He Yang

2 cun inferior to UB-40, where the two heads of the gastrocnemius muscle meet.

BL 56   Cheng Jin

Midway between UB-55 and UB-57 in the centre of the belly of the gastronemius muscle.

BL 57   Cheng Shan

Supporting Mountain

Relaxes the sinews, Invigorates Blood, Clears Heat, Removes obstructions from the channel.

Inferior to the belly of the gastronemius muscle, midway between UB-40 and the upper border of the calcaneum.

BL 58   Fei Yang

Flying Up

Removes obstructions from the channel, Strengthens the Kidneys.

7 cun superior to UB-60, posterior to the fibula, at the lateral side of the gastronemius muscle.

BL 59   Fu Yang

Instep Yang

Removes obstructions from the channel, Invigorates the Yang Heel Vessel, Strengthens the back.

3 cun superior to UB-60, posterior to the fibula.

BL 60   Kun Lun

Kunlun (Mountains)

Expels Wind, Removes obstructions from the

channel, Relaxes the sinews, Clears Heat, Invigorates Blood, Strengthens the back

In the depression, midway between the tendo calcaneus and the lateral malleolus.

BL 61   Pu Shen

Servants Aide

Inferior to the external malleolus, posterior to the calcanueum, or 2 cun directly below UB-60.

BL 62   Shen Mai

Ninth Channel

Removes obstructions from the channel, Benefits the eyes, Relaxes sinews, Opens the Yang Heel Vessel, Clears the Mind, Eliminates interior Wind.

In the depression 0.5 cun below the lower border of the external malleolus, directly below the tip. In the depression inferior to the lateral malleolus.

BL 63   Jin Men

Golden Door

Clears Heat, Stops pain

1 cun inferior and distal to UB-62, in the depression below cuboid bone.

BL 65   Shu Gu

Binding bone

Removes obstructions from the channel, Clears Heat, Eliminates Wind.

On the posterior lateral part of the head of the 5th. metatarsal bone, at the external aspect of the foot.

Bl 64   Jing Gu

Capitol Bone

Clears Heat, Eliminates Wind, Calms the Mind, Clears the brain, Strengthens the back.

On the inferior border of the tuberosity of the 5th. metatarsal bone, at the external aspect of the foot.

Bl 66   Tong Gu

Passing Valley

Clears Heat, Removes obstructions from the channel, Eliminates Wind,

In the depression on the anterior lateral part of the 5th. metatarso- phalangeal joint.

BL 67   Zhi Yin

Reaching Yin

Eliminates Wind, Removes obstructions from the channel, Invigorates Blood, Clears the eye

About 0.1 cun posterior to the lateral corner of the vallum unguis of the little toe.

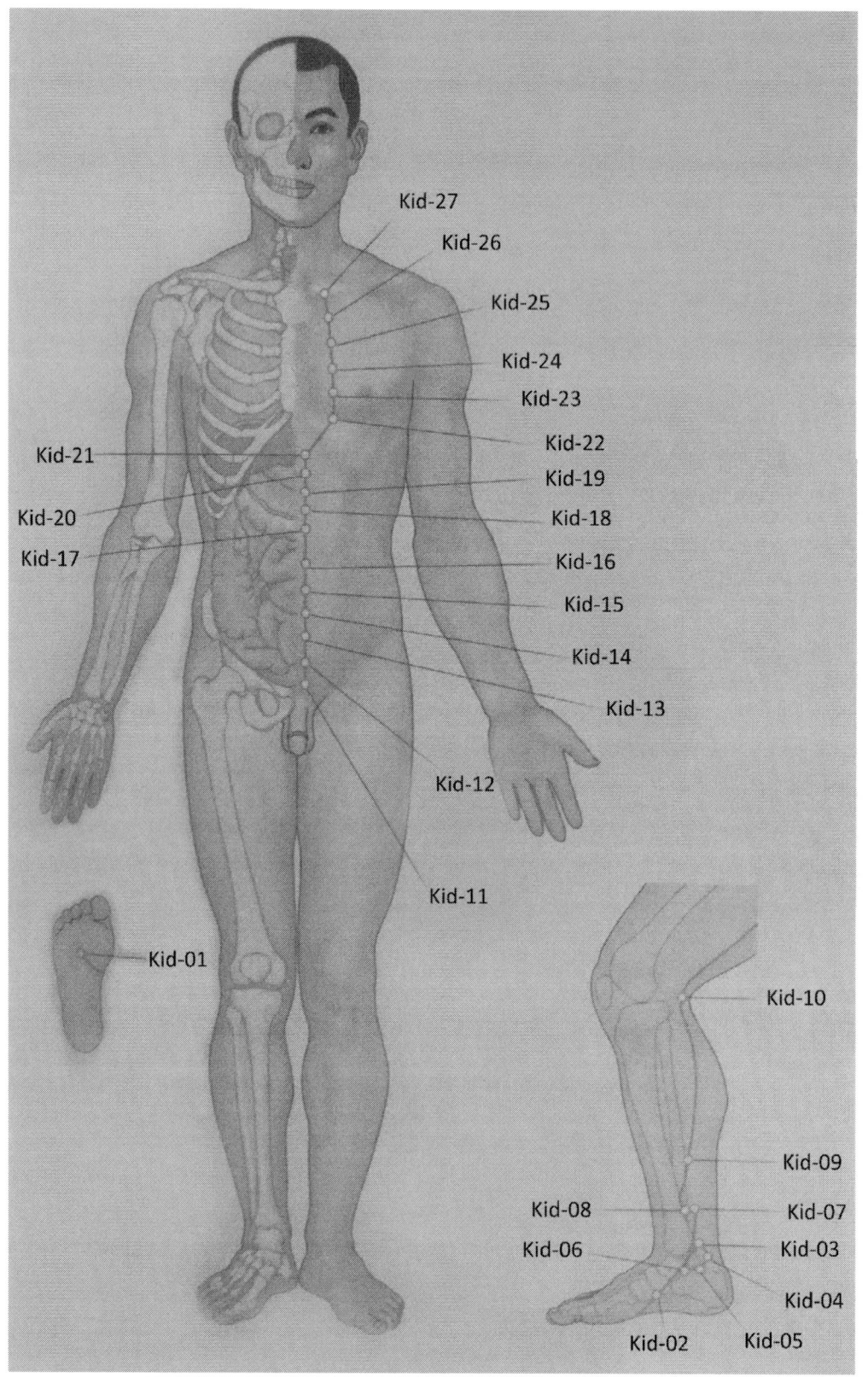

Kidney Meridian

Kidney

K 01   Yong Quan
Bubbling Spring

Tonifies Yin, Clears Heat, Subdues Wind, Subdues Empty Heat, Calms the Mind, Restores consciousness, Clears the brain.

On the sole, in the depression when the foot is in plantar flexion, approx. at the junction of the anterior third and posterior two thirds of the sole.

K 02   Ran Gu
Blazing Valley

Clears Empty Heat, Invigorates the Yin Heel Vessel, Cools Blood

Anterior and inferior to the medial malleolus, in the depression on the lower border of the tuberousity of the navicular bone.

K 03   Tai Xi
Greater Stream

Tonifies the Kidneys, Benefits Essence, Strengthens the lower back and knees, Regulates the uterus

In the depression between the medial malleolus and the tendo calcaneus, at the level with the tip of the medial malleolus.

K 04   Da Zhong
Big Bell

Strengthens the back, Lifts the spirit,

Posterior and inferior to the medial malleolus, in the depression medial to the attachment of tendo calcaneus.

K 05   Shui Quan
Water Spring

Benefits urination, Promotes circulation of Blood, Stops abdominal pain, Regulates the uterus,

1 directly below Tai Xi K3, in the depression anterior and superior to the medial side of the tuberousity of the calcaneum.

K 06   Zhao Hai
Shining Sea

Nourishes Yin, Benefits the eyes, Calms the Mind, Invigorates the Yin Heel Vessel, Cools Blood, Benefits the throat, Promotes the function of the uterus, Opens the chest

In the depression of the lower border of the medial malleolus, or 1 cun below the medial malleolus.

K 07   Fu Liu
Returning Current

Tonifies the Kidneys, Resolves Damp, Eliminates oedema, Strengthens the lower back, Regulates sweating

2 cun directly above K-03, on the anterior border of tendo calcaneus.

K 08   Jiao Xin
Meeting the Spleen channel

Removes obstruction from the channel, Stops abdominal pain, Removes masses, Regulates menstruation

0.5 cun anterior to K-07, 2 cun above K-03 posterior to the medial border of tibia.

K 09   Zhu Bin
Guest Building

Calms the Mind, Tonifies Kidney Yin, Opens the chest, Regulates the Yin Linking Vessel.

5 cun directly above Tai Xi K3, at the lower end of the belly of m. gastrocnemius, on the line drawn between K-03 and K-10.

K 10   Yin Gu
Yin Valley

Expels Dampness from the Lower Burner, Tonifies Kidney Yin.

With knee flexed, the point is on the medial side of the popliteal fossa, between tendons m. semitendinosus & semimembranosus at the level with UB-40

K 11   Heng Gu
Transverse Bone

5 cun below the umbilicus, on the superior border of symphysis pubis, 0.5 cun lateral to Ren-02.

K 12   Da He
Great Brightness

4 cun below the umbilicus, 0.5 cun lateral to Ren -03.

K 13   Qi Xue
Qi Hole

Tonifies Kidney Yin and Essence, Removes obstruction from channel,

3 cun below the umbilicus, 0.5 cun lateral to Ren-04.

K 14   Si Man
Four Full

2 cun below the umbilicus, 0.5 cun lateral to Ren-05.

K 15   Zhong Zhu - abdo

Middle Flowing Out

1 cun below the umbilicus, 0.5 cun lateral to Ren-07.

K 16   Huang Shu

Vitals Transporting Point

Removes obstruction from the channel, Tonifies the Kidneys, Benefits the Heart,

0.5 cun lateral to the umbilicus level with Ren-08.

K 17   Shang Qu

Merchant Crooked

2 cun above the umbilicus, 0.5 cun lateral to Ren-10.

K 18   Shi Guan

Stone Border

3 cun above the umbilicus, 0.5 cun lateral to Ren-11.

K 19   Yin Du

Yin Capital

4 cun above the umbilicus, 0.5 cun lateral to Ren-12

K 20   Tong Gu

Through The Valley

5 cun above the umbilicus, 0.5 cun lateral to Ren-13

K 21   You Men

Dark Gate

6 cun above the umbilicus, 0.5 cun lateral to Ren-14

K 22   Bu Lang

Walking On The Verandah

In the 5th. intercostal space, 2 cun lateral to the Ren channel.

K 23   Shen Feng

Mind Seal

Tonifies the Kidneys, Calm the Mind.

In the 4th. intercostal space, 2 cun lateral to the Ren channel.

K 24   Ling Xu

Spirit Burial Ground

Tonifies the Kidneys, Calm the Mind

In the 3rd. intercostal space, 2 cun lateral to the Ren channel.

K 25   Shen Cang

Mind Storage

Tonifies the Kidneys, Calm the Mind

In the 2nd. intercostal space, 2 cun lateral to the Ren channel.

K 26   Yu Zhong

Amidst Elegance

In the 1st. intercostal space, 2 cun lateral to the Ren channel.

K 27   Shu Fu

Transporting point Mansion

Stimulates the Kidney function of reception of Qi, Subdues rebellious Qi, Stops cough, Calms asthma, Resolves Phlegm,

In the depression on the lower border of the clavicle, 2 cun lateral to the Ren channel.

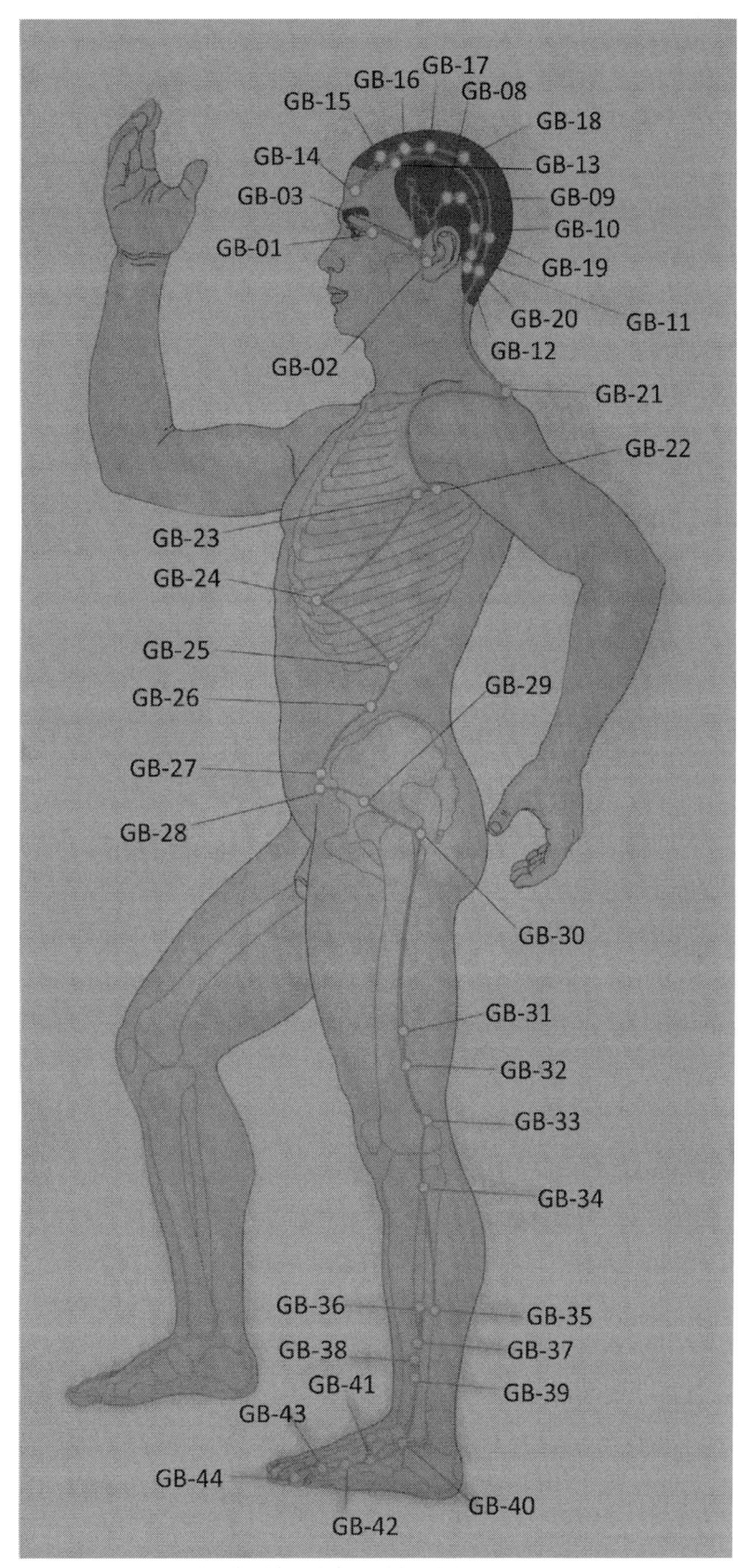

Gall Bladder Meridian

Gall Bladder

GB 01   Tong Zi Liao
Pupil Crevice

Expels Wind Heat, Clears Fire, Brightens the eyes, Local point,

0.5 cun lateral to the outer cantus, in the depression on the lateral side of the orbit.

GB 02   Ting Hui
Hearing Convergence

Removes obstructions from channel, Benefits the ears, Expels exterior Wind,

Anterior to the intertragic notch, at the posterior border of the condyloid process of the mandible. located when mouth is open.

GB 03   Shang Guan

In the front of ear, on the upper border of the zygomatic arch, in the depression directly above St-07

GB 04   Han Yan

Within the hairline of the temporal region, at the junction of the upper 1/4 and the lower 3/4 of the distance between St-08 and GB-07

GB 05   Xuan Lu
Hanging Skull

Within the hairline of the temporal region, midway of the border line connecting St-08 and GB-07

GB 06   Xuan Li
Deviation from Hanging Skull

Removes obstructions from channel, Benefits the ear, Local point, Within the hairline of the temporal region, at the junction of the lower 1/4 and the upper 3/4 of the distance between St 8 & GB7

GB 07   Qu Bin

Directly above the posterior border of the pre-auricular hairline, about one finger breath anterior to SJ-20

GB 08   Shuai Gu
Leading Valley

Removes obstructions from channel, Benefits the ear,

Superior to the apex of the auricle, 1.5 cun within the hairline,

GB 09   Tian Choung
Penetrating Heaven

Removes obstructions from channel, Subdues rising Qi, Eliminates interior Wind, Calms spasms, Calms Mind,

Directly above the posterior border of the auricle, 2 cun within the hairline, about 0.5 cun posterior to GB-08

GB 10   Fu Bai

Posterior and superior to the mastoid proces, midway of the curve line drawn from GB-09 and GB-11

GB 11   Qiao Yin - head

Posterior and superior to the mastoid process, on a line between GB-10 & GB-12

GB 12   Wan Gu - head

Eliminates Wind, Calms spasms, Subdues rising Qi, Calms the Mind, In the depression posterior and inferior to the mastoid process.

GB 13   Ben Shen
Mind Root

Calms the Mind, Eliminates Wind, Gathers Essence to the head, Clears the brain,

0.5 cun within the hairline of the forehead, 3 cun lateral to Shenting (Du 24).

GB 14   Yang Bai

Eliminates exterior Wind, Subdues rising Qi, ...

On the forehead, 1 cun directly above the midpoint of the eyebrow.

GB 15   Tou Lin Qi
Falling Tears

Regulates the Mind, Balances the emotions,

Directly above Yang Bai, 0.5 cun within the hairline, midway between Du-24 and St-08

GB 16   Muc Huang

1.5 cun posterior to GB-15 on the line connecting GB-15 to GB-20

GB 17   Zheng Ying

1.5 cun posterior to GB-16 on the line connecting GB-15 to GB-20

GB 18   Cheng Ling
Spirit Receiver

Calms the Mind, Clears the brain, 1.5 cun posterior to GB-17 on the line connecting GB-15 to GB-20

GB 19   Nao Kong

Directly above Feng chi (GB 20) at the level with Nao hu (Du 17), on the lateral side of the external occipital protuberance.

GB 20   Feng Chi
Wind Pond

Eliminates Wind, interior and exterior, Subdues Liver Yang, Brightens the eyes, Benefits the ears, Clears Heat, Clears the brain, ...

In the depression between the upper portion of m. sternocleidomastoideus and m. trapezius, on the same level with Du-16

GB 21 Jian Jing

Shoulder Well

Relaxes sinews, Promotes lactation, Promotes delivery.

Midway between Du-14 and the acromion, at the highest point of the shoulder.

GB 22 Yuan Ye

On the mid axillary line when tthe arm is raised, 3 cun below the axilla.

GB 23 Zhe Jin

1 cun anterior to GB-22, approx. at the level with the nipple.

GB 24 Ri Yue

Resolves Damp Heat, Promotes the function of the Gall Bladder and the Liver,

3 ribs below the nipple, in the 7th. intercostal space.

GB 25 Jing Men

On the lateral side of the abdomen, on the lower border of the free end of the 12th. rib.

GB 26 Dai Mai

Girdle Vessel

Regulates the uterus, Resolves Damp Heat, Regulates the Girdle Vessel,

Directly below the free end of the eleventh rib where Liv-13 is located, at the level with the umbilicus.

GB 27 Wu Shu

In the lateral side of the abdomen, anterior to the superior iliac spine, 3 cun below the level of the umbilicus.

GB 28 Wei Dao

Anterior and inferior to the anterior superior iliac spine, 0.5 cun anterior and inferior to GB-27

GB 29 Ju Liao - femur

Removes obstructions from the channel,

In the depression of the midpoint between the anterosuperior iliac spine and the great trochanter.

GB 30 Huan Tiao

Jumping Circle

Removes obstructions from the channel, Tonifies Blood and Qi, Resolves Damp Heat,

At the junction of the lateral 1/3 and the medial 2/3 of the distance between the great trochanter and the hiatus of the sacrum. Patient lying on side with thigh flexed.

GB 31 Feng Shi

Wind Market

Expels Wind, Relaxes the sinews, Strengthens the bones, Relieves itching,

On the midline of the lateral aspect of the thigh, 7 cun above the transverse crease. With patient standing with the hands close to sides, the point is where tip of finger touches.

GB 32 Zhong Du - femur

On the lateral aspect of the tigh, 5 cun above the transverse popliteal crease, between m. vastus lateralis and m. biceps femoris.

GB 33 Xi Yang Guan

Knee Yang gate

3 cun above Yang ling quan (GB 34) lateral to the knee joint, between the tendons of m. biceps femoris and the femur.

GB 34 Yang Ling Quan

Yang Hill Spring

Promotes the smooth flow of Liver Qi, Resolves Damp Heat, Removes obstructions from the channel, Relaxes the sinews, Subdues rebellious Qi,

In the depression anterior and inferior to the small head of the fibula. 2 cun inferior to the knee

GB 35 Yang Jiao

Yang Crossing

Relaxes the sinews, Removes obstructions from the channel, Stops pain,

7 cun above the tip of the external malleolus, on the posterior border of the fibula.

GB 36 Wai Qui

Outer Mound

Removes obstructions from the channel, Stops pain

7 cun above the tip of the external malleolus, on the anterior border of the fibula.

GB 37 Guang Ming

Brightness

Brightens the eyes, Expels Wind, Clears Heat, Conducts Fire downwards,

5 cun above the tip of the external malleolus, on the anterior border of the fibula.

GB 38 Yang Fu

Yang Aid

Subdues Liver Yang, Clears Heat, Resolves Damp Heat,

4 cun above and slightly anterior to the tip of the external malleolus, on the anterior border of the fibula, between m. extensor digitorum longus and m. peronaeus brevis.

GB 39 Xuan Zhong

Hanging Bell

Benefits Essence, Nourishes Marrow, Eliminates Wind,

3 cun above the tip of the external malleolus, in the depression between the posterior border of the fibula and the tendons of m. peronaeus longus and brevis.

GB 40 Qui Xu

Mound Ruins

Promotes the smooth flow of Liver Qi

In the depression on the lateral side of the tendon of m. extensor digitorum longus, anterior and inferior to the external malleolas.

GB 41 Zu Lin Qi

Falling Tears (foot)

Resolves Damp Heat, Promotes the smooth flow of Liver Qi, Regulates the Girdle Vessel

In the depression distal to the junction of the 4th. and 5th. metatarsal bones, on the lateral side of the tendon of m. extensor digiti minimi of the foot.

GB 42 Di Wu Hui

Between the 4th. and 5th. metatarsal bones, on the medial side of the tendon of m. extensor digiti minimi of foot.

GB 43 Xia Xi

Stream Insertion

Subdues Liver Yang, Benefits the ears, Resolves Damp Heat

On the dorsum of the foot, between the 4th. and 5th. toe, proximal to the margin of the web.

GB 44   Qiao Yin - zu

Orifice Yin (foot)

Subdues Liver Yang, Benefits the eyes, Calms the Mind ...

On the lateral side of the 4th. toe, about 0.1 cun posterior to the corner of the nail.

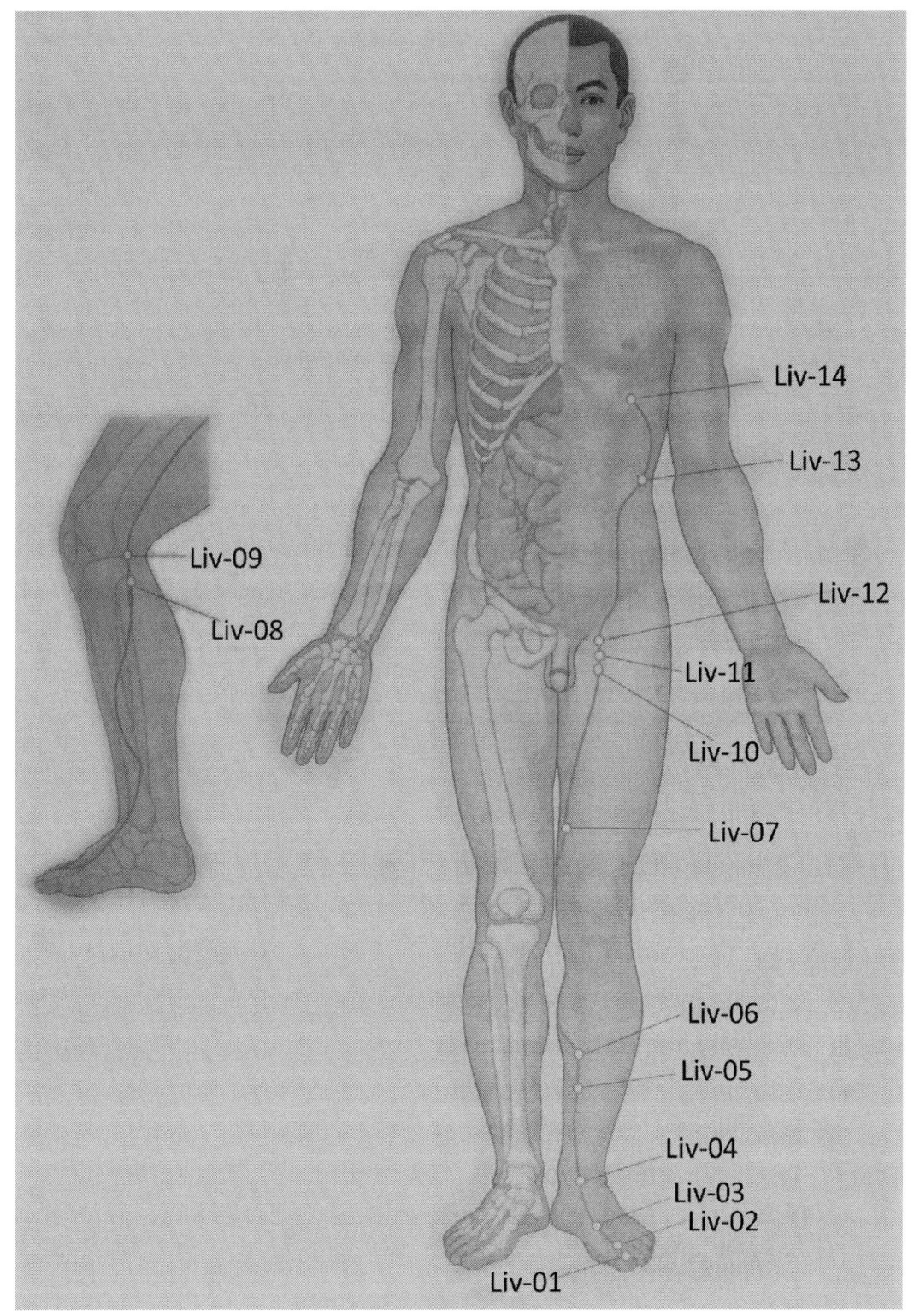

Liver Meridian

Liver

Liv 01 Da Dun

Big Thick

Regulates menstruation, Resolves Damp Heat, Promotes the smooth flow of Liver Qi, Restores consciousness,

On the lateral side of the dorsum of the terminal phalanx of the great toe, between the corner of the nail and the interphalangeal joint

Liv 02 Xing Jian

Temporary In-Between

Clears Liver Fire, Subdues Liver Yang, Cools Blood, Subdues interior Wind

On the dorsum of the foot between the first and second toe, proximal to the margin of the web.

Liv 03 Tai Chong

Bigger Rushing

Subdues Liver Yang, Expels interior Wind, Promotes the smooth flow of Liver Qi, Nourishes Liver Blood and Liver Yin, Regulates menstruation, Calms the Mind, Calms Spasms

On the dorsum of the foot, in the depression distal to the junction of the first and second metatarsal bones.

Liv 04 Zhong Feng

Middle Seal

Promotes the smooth flow of Liver Qi in the Triple Burner

1 cun anterior to the medial malleolus, midway between Sp-05 and St-41, in the depression on the medial side of the tendon of m. tibialis anterior.

Liv 05 Li Gou

Gourd Ditch

Promotes the smooth flow of Liver Qi, Resolves Damp Heat,

5 cun above the tip of the medial malleolus, on the medial aspect and near the medial border of the tibia.

Liv 06 Zhong Du - Foot

Middle Capital

Promotes the smooth flow of Liver Qi, Resolves Damp Heat

7 cun above the tip of the medial malleolas, on the medial aspect and near the medial border of the tibia.

Liv 07 Xi Guan

Knee Gate

Posterior and inferior to the medial condyle of the tibia, in the upper portion of the medioal head of m. gastrocnemius, 1 cun posterior to Sp-09.

Liv 08 Qu Quan

Spring and Bend

Benefits the Bladder, Resolves Dampness from the Lower Burner, Relaxes the sinews, Nourishes Liver Blood

With Knee flexed, in depression above the medial end of transverse popliteal crease, posterior to medial epicondyle of femur, on the anterior part of insertion of m. semitendinosus & m. semimembranosus

Liv 09 Yin Bao

4 cun above the medial epicondyle of the femur, between m. vastus medialis and m. sartorius.

Liv 10 Wu Li - femur

3 cun directly above Qi chong S30, on the lateral border of m. abdutor longus.

Liv 11 Yin Lian

2 cun directly above St-30, on the lateral border of m. abdutor longus.

Liv 12 Ji Mai

Inferior and lateral to the pubic spine, 2.5 cun lateral to the Ren meridian, at the inguinal groove lateral and inferior to St-30.

Liv 13 Zhang Men

Chapter Gate

Promotes the smooth flow of Liver Qi, Relieves retention of food, Benefits the Stomach and Spleen

On the lateral side of the abdomen, below the free end of the 11th floating rib.

Liv 14 Qi Men

Cycle Gate

Promotes the smooth flow of Liver Qi, Benefits the Stomach, Cools Blood, ...

Directly below the nipple, in the sixth intercostals space.

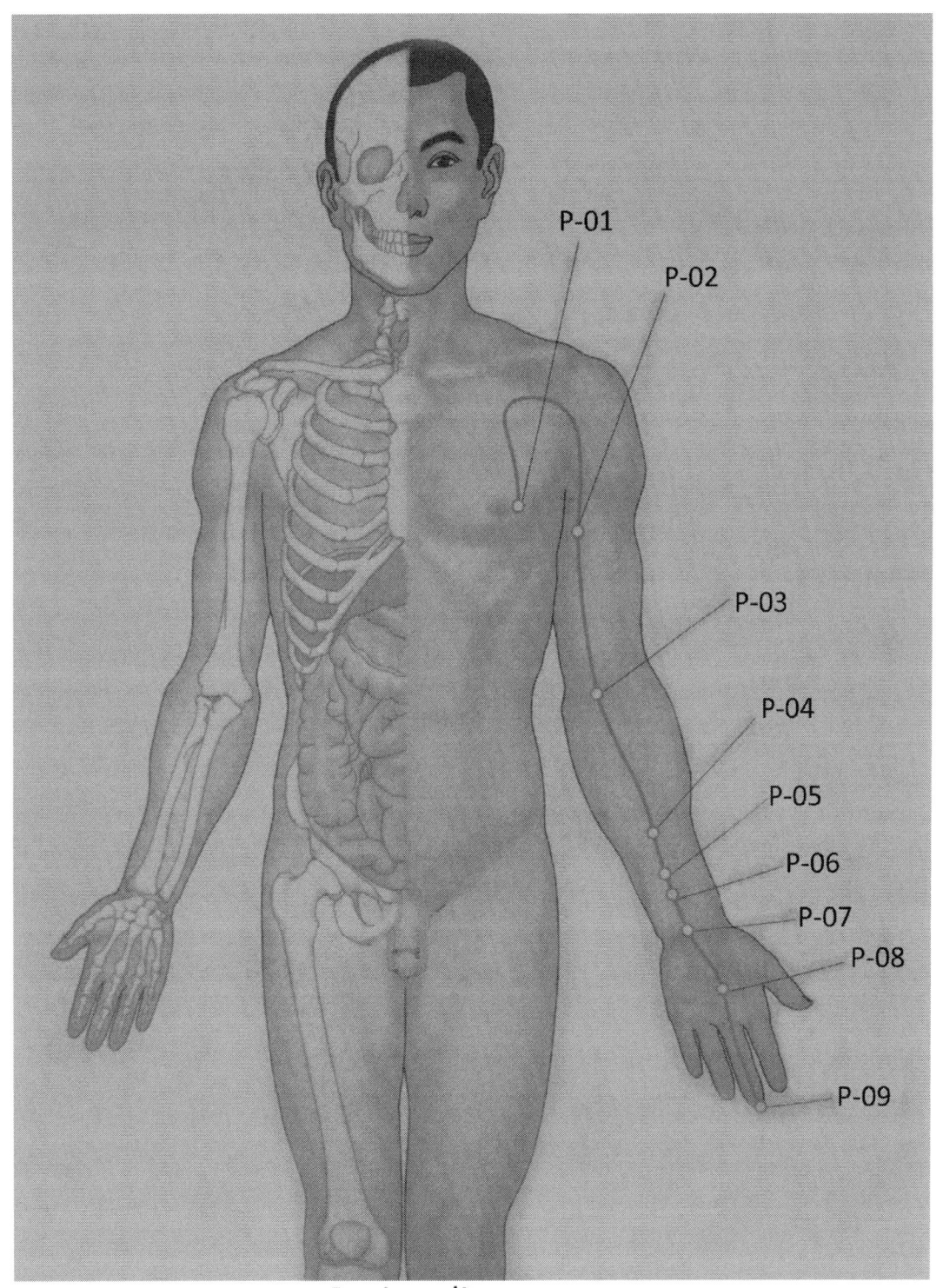

Pericardium

Pericardium

P 01   Tian Chi
Heavenly Pond

1 cun lateral to nipple, in the 4th. intercostal space.

P 02   Tian Quan

2 cun below the end of the anterior axillary fold, on the belly of the m. biceps brachii

P 03   Qu Ze
Marsh on Bend

Pacifies the Stomach, Clears Heat, Cools Blood, Expels Fire Poison, Opens the orifices, Stops convulsions, Moves Blood and dispels stasis, Calms the Mind,

On the transverse cubital crease, on the ulnar side of the tendon of the m. biceps brachii.

P 04   Xi Men
Cleft Door

Removes obstructions from the channel, Stops pain, Calms the Heart, Opens the chest, Regulates Heart Blood, Cools the Blood, Strengthens the Mind

5 cun above the transverse crease of the wrist on the cleft of the tendons of m. palmaris longus and m. flexor carpi radialis

P 05   Jian Shi
Spirit Messenger

Resolves Phlegm in the Heart, Regulates Heart Qi, Opens the chest, Regulates the Stomach, Clears Heat

3 cun above the wrist crease on the cleft of the tendons of m. palmaris longus and m. flexor carpi radialis

P 06   Nei Guan
Inner Gate

Opens the chest, Regulates Heart Qi and Blood, Regulates and clears the Triple Burner, Calms the Mind, Regulates Terminal Yin, Harmonizes the Stomach Qi and clears heat.

2 cun above the wrist crease on the cleft of the tendons of m. palmaris longus and m. flexor carpi radialis

P 07   Da Ling
Great Hill

Calms the Mind, Clears Heat, Tonify Heart

Directly in the wrist crease on the cleft of the tendons of m. palmaris longus and m. flexor carpi radialis

P 08   Lao Gong
Labour Palace

Clears Heart Fire, Calms the Mind,

On the transverse crease of the palm, between 2nd. & 3rd. metacarpal bones. When fist is clenched, point is just below tip of middle finger.

P 09   Zhong Chong
Centre Rush

Clears Heat, Restores consciousness, Expels Wind,

In the centre of the tip of the middle finger.

San Jiao Meridian

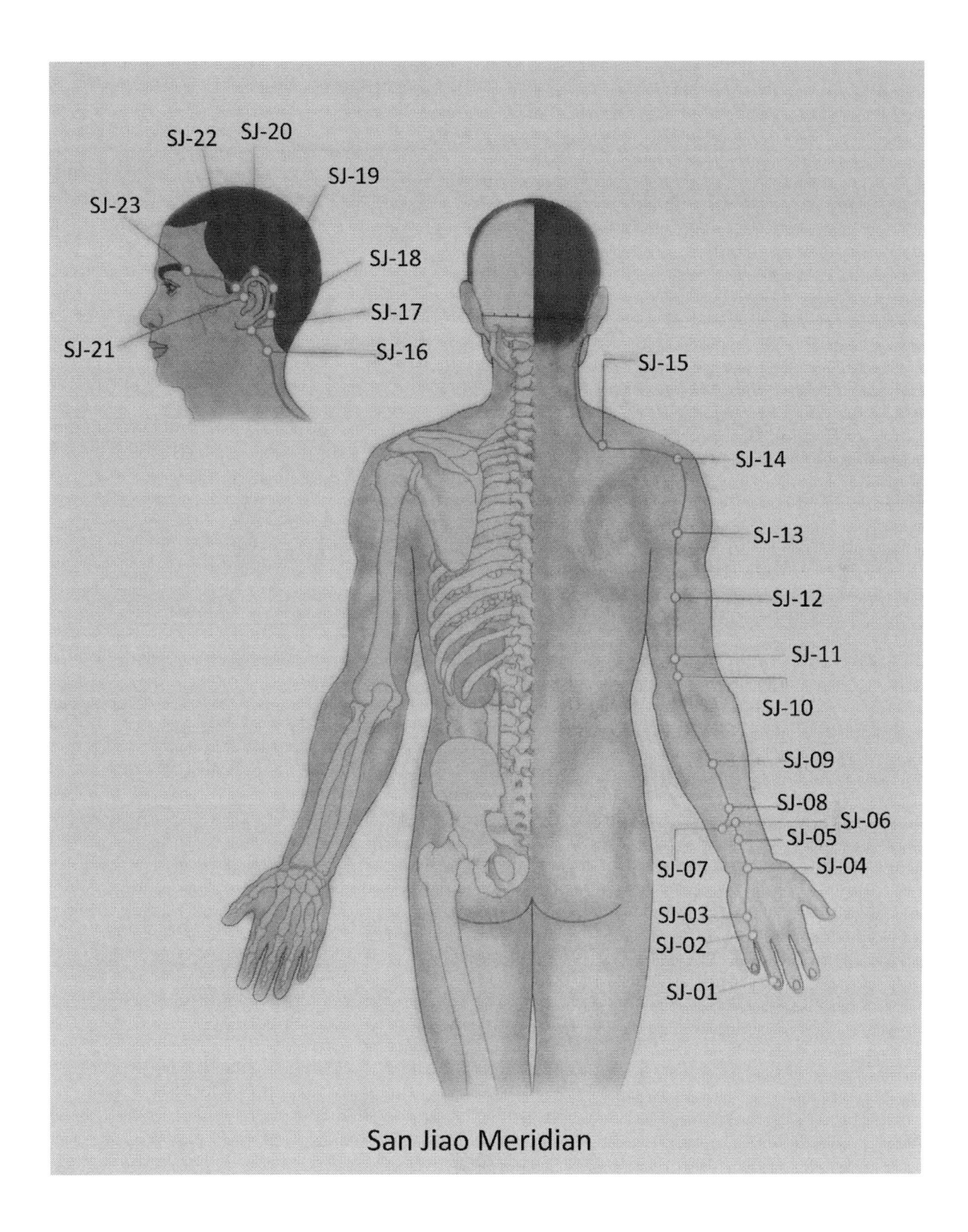

San Jiao

SJ 01   Guan Chong

Gate Rush

Clears Heat, Expels Wind, Invigorates Blood, Restores Consciousness, Stops convulsions

On the lateral side of the ring finger, about 0.1 cun posterior to the corner of the nail.

SJ 02   Ye Men

Fluid Door

Clears Heat, Expels Wind, Benefits the ears, Removes obstructions from the channel

When fist is clenched, point is located in the depression proximal to the margin of the web between the ring and small finger.

SJ 03   Zhong Zhu

Middle Islet

Clears Heat, Expels Wind, Benefits the ears, Removes obstructions from the channel, Regulates Qi, Lifts the Mind

When fist is clenched, point is on the dorsum of the hand between the 4th. & 5th. metacarpal bones, in the depression proximal to the metacarpophalangeal joint

SJ 04   Yang Chi

Yang Pond

Tonifies Yuan Qi, Relaxes sinews, Removes obstructions from the channel, Clears Heat, Regulates the Stomach, Promotes fluid transformation, Benefits Original Qi, Tonifies Penetrating and Directing vessels

On the transverse crease of the dorsum of wrist, in the depression lateral to the tendon of m. extensor digitorum communis.

SJ 05   Wai Guan

Outer Gate

Expels Wind Heat, Releases the Exterior, Removes obstructions from the channel, Benefits the ears, Subdues Liver Yang

2 cun above SJ-04, between the radius and ulna.

SJ 06   Zhi Gou

Branching Ditch

Regulates Qi, Removes obstructions from the channel, Removes obstructions from the Large Intestine, Clears Heat, Expels Wind

3 cun above SJ-04 between the radius and ulna, on the radial side of m. extensor digitorum

SJ 07   Hui Zong

Converging Channels

Removes obstructions from the channel, Benefits the eyes and ears, Stops pain,

At the level with SJ-07, about one finger breath lateral to SJ-06, on the radial side of the ulna.

SJ 08   San Yang Luo

Connecting Three Yang

Clears Heat, Removes obstructions from the channel,

4 cun above SJ-04, between the radius and ulna.

SJ 09   Si Du

Four Rivers

On the lateral side of the forearm, 5 cun below the olecranon, between the radius and ulna.

SJ 10   Tian Jing

Heavenly Well

Relaxes tendons, Resolves Dampness and Phlegm, Dispels "masses", Clears Heat, Dispels stagnation, Regulates Nutritive and Defensive Qi

When elbow is flexed, point is in depression about 1 cun superior to the olecranon.

SJ 11   Qing Leng Yua

1 cun above Tian jing SJ 10, when the elbow is flexed.

SJ 12   Xiao Luo

On the line joining the olecranon and SJ-14, midway between SJ-11 and SJ-13.

SJ 13   Nao Hui

Shoulder Convergence

On the line joining the olecranon and JSJ-14, on the posterior border of m. deltoideus.

SJ 14   Jian Liao

Shoulder Crevice

Posterior and inferior to the acromion, in the depression about 1 cun posterior to LI-15, when the arm is abducted.

SJ 15   Tian Liao

Heavenly Crevice

Midway between GB-21, and SI-13, on the posterior angle of the scapula.

SJ 16   Tian You

Posterior and inferior to the mastoid process, on the posterior border of m. sternocleidomastoideus, almost level with SI-17, and UB-10.

SJ 17   Yi Feng

Wind Screen

Expels Wind Heat, Benefits the ears,

Posterior to the lobule of the ear, in the depression between the mandible and mastoid process.

SJ 18   Qi Mai

In the centre of the mastoid process, at the junction of the middle and lower third of the curve formed by SJ-17, and SJ-20, posterior to the helix.

SJ 19   Lu Xi

Posterior to the ear, at the junction of the upper and middle third of the curve formed by SJ-17, and SJ-20, posterior to the helix.

SJ 20   Jiao Sun

Directly above the ear apex, within the hairline.

SJ 21   Er Men

Ear Door

In the depression anterior to the supratragic notch and slightly superior to the condyloid process of the mandible above SI-19 & GB-02,

SJ 22   He Liao - Ear

Anterior and superior to Er men SJ 21, at the level with the root of the auricle, on the posterior border of the hairline of the temple, where the superficial temporal artery passes.

SJ 23   Si Hu Kong

Silk Bamboo Hole

Expels Wind, Brightens the eyes, Stops pain

In the depression at the lateral end of the eyebrow.

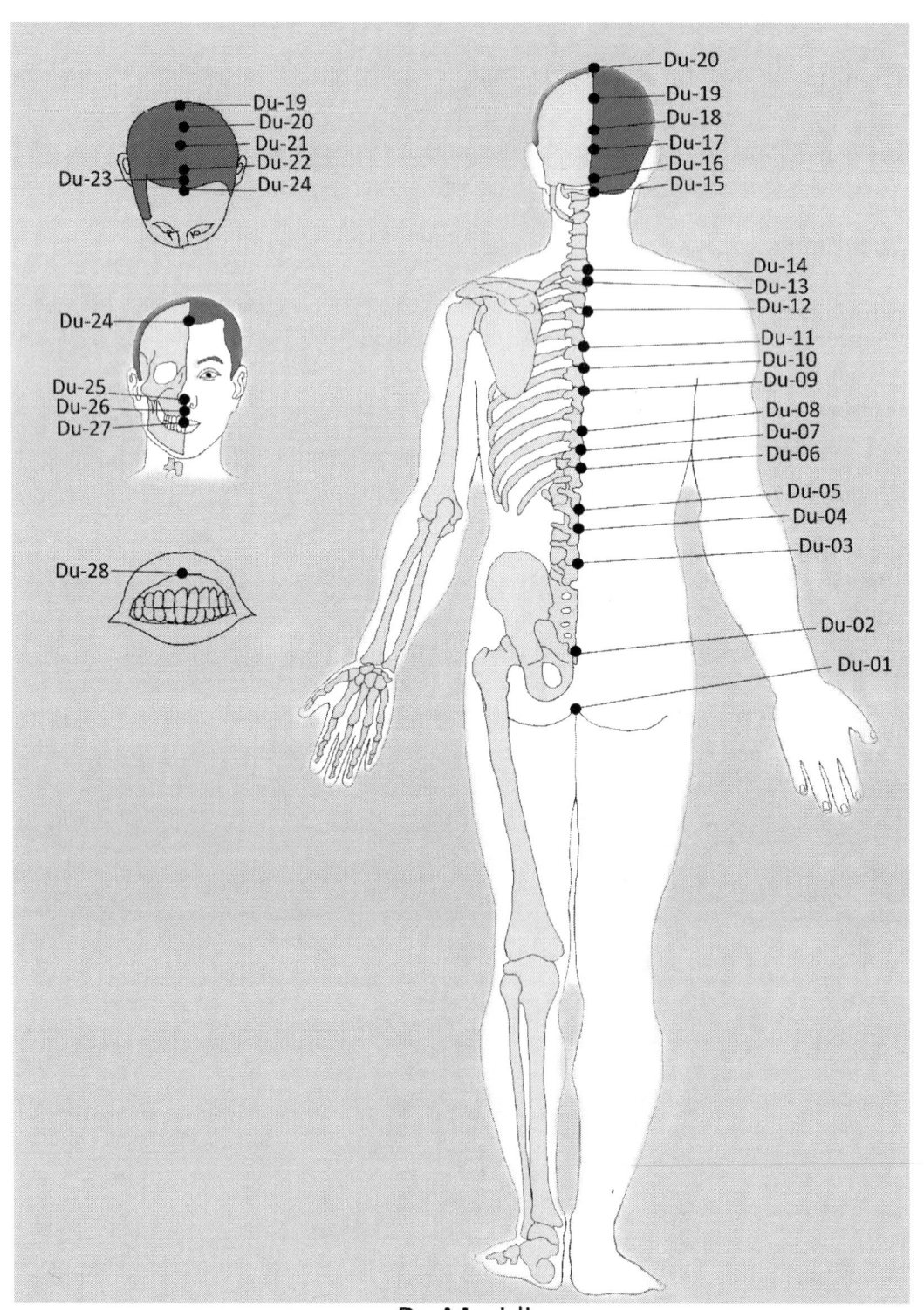

Du Meridian

Du

Du 01 Chang Qiang

Long Strength

Regulates Governing and Directing Vessels, Resolves Damp Heat, Calms the Mind, prolasped anus

Midway between the coccyx and the anus.

Du 02 Yao Shu

Lumbar Shu

Extinguishes interior Wind, Calms spasms and convulsions, Strengthens the lower back

In the hiatus of the sacrum.

Du 03 Yao Yang Quan

Lumbar Yang Gate

Strengthen the lower back, Tonifies Yang, Strengthens the legs, Local point

Below the spinous process ofd the 4th. lumbar vertebra, at a level with iliac crest.

Du 04 Ming Men

Gate of Life

Tonifies Kidney Yang, Nourishes Original Qi, Warms the Gate of Vitality, Expels Cold, Strengthens the lower back, Benefits Essence

Below the spinous process of the 2nd. lumbar vertebra.

Du 05 Xuan Shu

Suspended Pivot

Below the spinous process of the 1st. lumbar vertebra.

Du 06 Ji Zhong

Centre of the Spine

Below the spinous process of the 11th. thoracic vertebra.

Du 07 Zhong Shu

Central Pivot

Below the spinous process of the 10th. thoracic vertebra.

Du 08 Jin Suo

Tendon Spasm (Sinew Contraction)

Relaxes the sinews, Eliminates interior Wind.

Below the spinous process of the 9th. thoracic vertebra.

Du 09 Zhi Yang

Reaching Yang

Regulates Liver & Gall Bladder, Moves Qi, Opens the chest and diaphragm, Resolves Damp Heat

Below the spinous process of the 7th. thoracic vertebra.

Du 10 Ling Tai

Spirit Tower

Below the spinous process of the 6th. thoracic vertebra.

Du 11 Shen Dao

Mind Way (Spirit Pathway)

Regulates the Heart, Calms the Mind, Clears Heart Fire

Below the spinous process of the 5th. thoracic vertebra.

Du 12 Shen Zhu

Body Pillar

Eliminates interior Wind, Tonifies Lung Qi, Calms spasms, Strengthens the body.

Below the spinous process of the 3rd. thoracic vertebra.

Du 13 Tao Dao

Kiln Way (Way of Happiness)

Clears Heat, Clears Wind Heat, Releases the interior, Regulates the Lesser Yang

Below the spinous process of the 1st. thoracic vertebra.

Du 14 Da Zhui

Big Vertebra

Clears Heat, Releases the Exterior, Expels Wind, Regulates Ying and Wei Qi, Clears the Mind, Tonifies Yang, General Anti Inflammatory,

Below the spinous process of the 7th. cervical vertebra and above the 1st. thoracic vertebra.

Du 15 Ya Men

Gate to Dumbness (muteness)

Clears the Mind, Stimulates speech

At the midpoint of the nape. 0.5 cun above the posterior hairline.

Du 16 Feng Fu

Wind Palace

Eliminates Wind, Tonifies Lung Qi, Clears the Mind, Benefits the brain

Directly below the external occipital protuberance, At the midpoint of the nape. 1 cun above the posterior hairline.

Du 17 Nao Hu

Brain Window

Eliminates Wind, Benefits the brain, Clears the Mind.

1.5 cun above Du-16, On the

upper border of the occipital protuberance.

Du 18   Qiang Jian

Unyielding Space

On the midline of the head, 1.5 cun above Du-17, midway between Du-16 and Du-20.

Du 19   Hou Ding

Behind the Crown (Posterior Vertex)

Calms the Mind

1.5 cun above Du-18.

Du 20   Bai Hui

Hundred Meetings

Clears the Mind, Lifts the spirit, Tonifies Yang, Strengthens the ascending function of the Spleen, Eliminates interior Wind, Promotes resuscitation

Midpoint of the line connecting the two apexes of the ears.

Du 21   Qian Ding

In Front of the Crown

1.5 cun anterior to Du-20.

Du 22   Xin Hui

Fontanelle Meeting

1.5 cun anterior to Du 21.

Du 23   Shang Xing

Upper Star

Opens the nose

1 cun within the anterior hairline, on the midsagittal line of the head.

Du 24   Shen Ting

Courtyard of the Mind

Calms the Mind ....

0.5 cun within the anterior hairline, on the midsagittal line of the head. Distance between anterior hairline and glabella (Yin Tang) is 3 cun

Du 25   Su Liao

White Crevice

On the tip of the nose.

Du 26   Ren Zhong

Middle of the Person

Promotes resuscitation, Benefits the Lumbar spine,

A little above the midpoint of the philtrum, near nostrils. At the upper .33 of the philtrum.

Du 27   Dui Duan

Extremity of the Mouth

At the tip of the philtrum, on the median tubercle of the upper lip, at the junction of the skin and upper lip.

Du 28   Yin Jiao - mouth

Gum Intersection

At the junction of the gum and the frenulum of the upper lip.

Ren Meridian

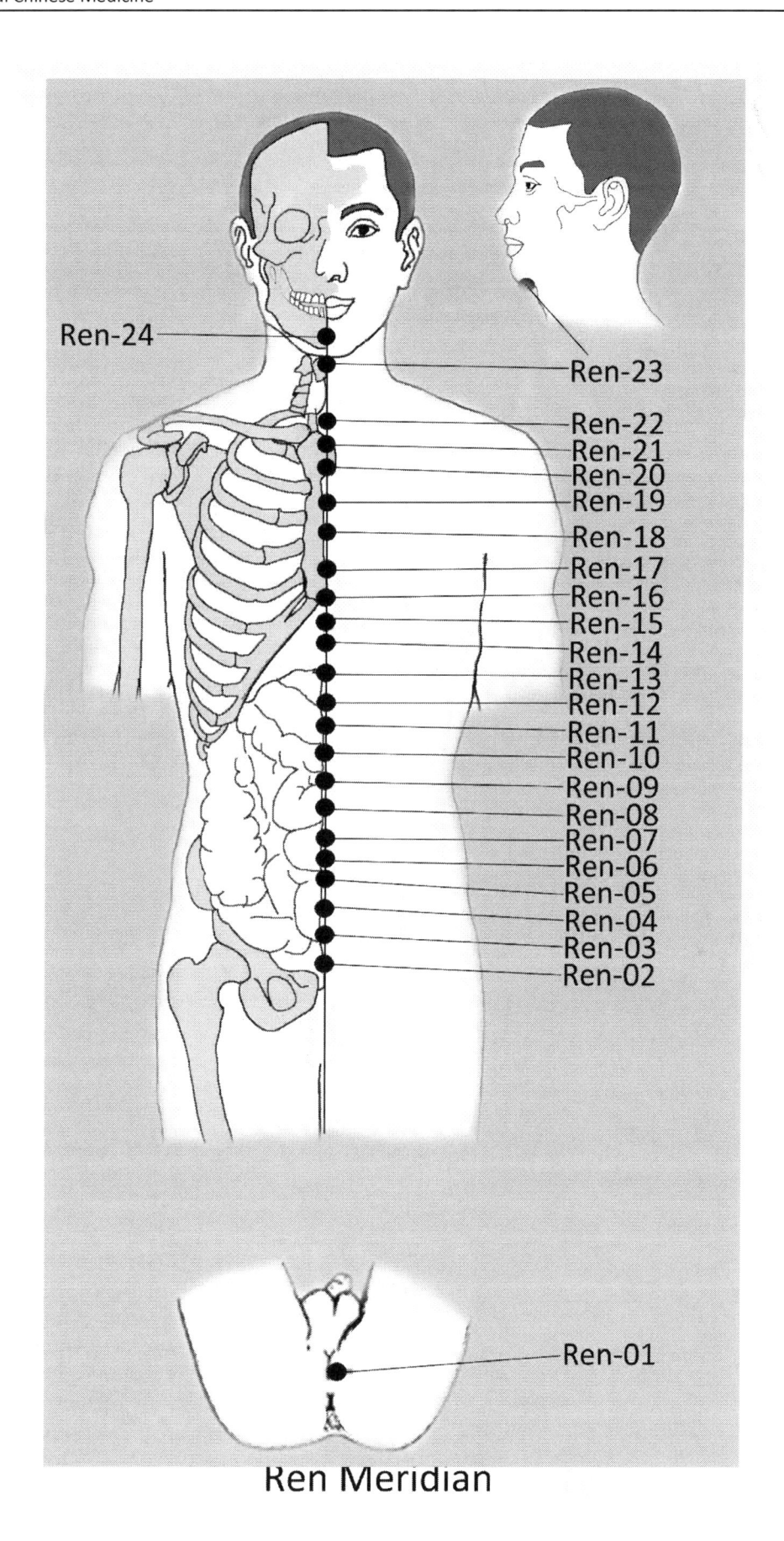

Ren

Ren 01 Hui Yin

Meeting of Yin

Nourishes Yin, Promotes resusitation, Resolves Damp Heat, Benefits Essence

In the centre of the perineum, midway between the anus and the scrotum or posterior labial commissure of vulva.

Ren 02 Qu Gu

Curved Bone

At the superior border of the symphysis pubis, on the midline of the abdomen. 5 cun inferior to the umbilicus.

Ren 03 Zhong Ji

Middle Extremity

Resolves Damp Heat, Promotes the Bladder function of Qi transformation, Clears Heat

1 cun above Ren 2, 4 cun inferior to the umbilicus.

Ren 04 Guan Yuan

Gate of Original Qi

Nourishes Yin, Strengthens Yang, Regulates the uterus, Benefits Original Qi, Tonifies the Kidneys, Calms the Mind, Roots the Ethereal Soul.

3 cun inferior to the umbilicus.

Ren 05 Shi Men

Stone Door

Strengthens Original Qi, Promotes the transformation and excretion of fluids in the Lower Burner, Opens the Water passages

1 cun above Ren 4, 2 cun inferior to the umbilicus.

Ren 06 Qi Hai

Sea of Qi

Tonifies Qi and Yang, Regulates Qi, Tonifies Original Qi, Resolves Dampness,

1.5 cun inferior to the umbilicus.

Ren 07 Yin Jiao - abdomen

Yin Crossing

Nourishes Yin, Regulates the uterus

1 cun below the umbilicus.

Ren 08 Shen Que

Main Palace

Rescues Yang, Strengthens the Spleen, Tonifies Original Qi

In the centre of the umbilicus.

Ren 09 Shui Fen

Water Seperation

Promotes the transformation of fluids, Controls the Water passages

1 cun above the umbilicus.

Ren 10 Xia Wan

Lower Epigastrium

Promotes the descending of Stomach Qi, Relieves stagnation of food, Tonifies the Spleen,

2 cun above umbilicus.

Ren 11 Jian Li

Building Mile

Promotes the rotting and ripening of the Stomach, Stimulates the descending of Stomach Qi

3 cun above the umbilicus.

Ren 12 Zhong Wan

Middle of Epigastrium

Tonifies Stomach and Spleen, Resolves Dampness, Regulates Stomach Qi, Improves digestion

4 cun above the umbilicus.

Ren 13 Zhang Wan

Upper Epigastrium

Subdues rebellious Stomach Qi

5 cun above the umbilicus.

Ren 14 Ju Que

Great Palace

Subdues rebellious Stomach Qi, Calms the Mind, Clears the Heart

6 cun above the umbilicus

Ren 15 Jiu Wei

Turtledove Tail

Calms the Mind, Benefits Original Qi

below the xiphoid process, 7 cun above the umbilicus, locate point in supine position with arms uplifted.

Ren 16 Zhong Ting

Central Courtyard

Local point for Liver Qi Stagnation

1 cun above Ren 15, level with the lower border of the sternum body. On the midline of the sternum, at the level of the 5th. intercostal space.

Ren 17 Shan Zhong

Middle of Chest

Tonifies Qi, Regulates Qi, Dispels fullness from chest, Clears the Lungs, Resolves

Practical Chinese Medicine

Phlegm, Benefits the diaphragm and the breasts, Stimulates production of milk

Between the nipples, level with the 4th intercostals space.

Ren 18 Yu Tang

Jade Hall

1 rib above Ren 17, level with the 3rd. intercostals space.

Ren 19 Zi Gong - Chest

Purple Palace

1 rib above Ren 18, level with the 2nd. intercostals space.

Ren 20 Hua Gai

Magnificent Canopy

1 rib above Ren 19, on the anterior midline, at the midpoint of the sternal angle, at the level with the 1st. intercostals space.

Ren 21 Xuan Ji

Jade Pivot

1 rib above Ren 20, on the anterior midline, in the centre of the manubrium sterni.

Ren 22 Tian Tu

Heaven Projection

Stimulates the descending of Lung Qi, Resolves Phlegm, Clears Heat, Stops cough, Benefits the throat, Soothes asthma

In the centre of the suprasternal fossa.

Ren 23 Lian Quan

Corner Spring

Dispels interior Wind, Promotes speech, Clears Fire, Resolves Phlegm, Subdues rebellious Qi ....

Between the Adam's apple and the mandible, in the depression of the upper border of the hyoid bone

Ren 24 Cheng Jiang

Saliva Receiver

Expels exterior Wind

In the depression in the centre of the mentolabial groove, under the lower lip.

Extra Points

EP B 01 Ding Chuan

Stopping asthma

Expels exterior Wind, Calms asthma

0.5 cun lateral to Du-14.

EP B 02 Hua Tua Jia Ji

Hua Tuo back-filling point

Varies according to each point

A group of 34 points on both sides of the spine 0.5 cun from the midline in correspondence of the intervertebral spaces from the 1st thoracic to the 5th Lumbar vertebra.

EP B 03 Wei Wan Xia Shu

1.5 cun lateral to the lower border of the spineous process of the 8th. thoracic vertebra.

EP B 04 Pi Gen

3.5 cun lateral to the lower border of the spineous process of the 1st. lumbar vertebra.

EP B 05 Xia Ji Shu

Below the spineous process of the 3rd. lumbar vertebra.

EP B 06 Yao Yi

3 cun lateral to the lower border of the spineous process of the 4th. thoracic vertebra.

EP B 07 Yao Wan

In the depression, 4 cun lateral tp the lower border of the spineous process of the 4th. thoracic vertebra.

EP B 08 Shi Qi Zhui Xia

Below the 17th vertebra, Removes obstructions from the challel, Benefits the backOn the midline of the back below the tip of the 5th lumbar vertebra.

EP B 09 Yao Qi

2 cun above the tip of the coccyx.

EP B 10 Jing Gong

Palace of Essence

Tonifies the Kidney Essence

On the back, 0.5 cun lateral to the point Bl-52

EP B 11 Yi Shu

Directly below T8, 1.5 cun lateral

EP CA 01 Zi Gong Xue

Palace of Child

Tonifies and warms Original Qi, Regulates menstruation, Calms the fetus

On the abdomen, 3 cun lateral to Ren-3

EP HN 01 Si Shen Cong

Four Mind Hearing

Subdue interior Wind

A group of four points at the vertex, 1cun in front, behind, left and right of the point Du-20.

©James O'Sullivan

EP HN 02   Dang Yang

1 cun within the natural hairline, directly above the puple, while the patient is looking straight ahead.

EP HN 03   Yin Tang

Seal Hall

Eliminates Wind, Stops convulsions, Calms the Mind, Promotes sleep,

On the midline of the body in between the two eyebrows

EP HN 04   Yu Yao

Fish Spine

Clears Heat, Removes obstructions from channel, Brightens the eyes

In the middle (midpoint) of the eyebrow.

EP HN 05   Tai Yang

Greater Yang

Eliminates Wind, Clears Fire,

In a depression 1 cun posterior to the midpoint, between the lateral end of the eyebrow and the outer canthus.

EP HN 06   Er Jian

Ear Shoulder

At the apex of the ear, when the ear is folded.

EP HN 07   Qiu Ho

At the junction of the lateral 0.25 and medial 0.75 of the inferior border of the orbit.

EP HN 08 Shang ying xian

Below the nose bone, in the depression of the upper end of the nasolabial sutcus.

EP HN 09 Nei Ying Xiang

At the upper end of the nostrils.

EP HN 10   Ju Quan

At the centre of the tongue.

EP HN 11   Hai Quan

Open the mouth and roll the tongue, on the lingual frenulum.

EP HN 12   Jin Jin

On the vein at the left side of the frenulum of the tongue.

EP HN 13   Yu Ye

On the vein at the right side of the freulum of the tongue.

EP HN 14   Yi Ming

1 cun behind the point Yi feng. which is posterior to the lobule of the ear, in the depression between the mandible and mastoid process.

EP HN 15 Jing Bai Lao

1 cun lateral to the midline of the back, 2 cun above Da Zhui Du-14.

EP LL 01   Kuan Gu

1.5 cun bilateral to the point St 34. When knee is flexed, St-34 is 2 cun above the laterosuperior border of the patella.

EP LL 02   He Ding

In the depression of the middle of the upper border of the patella.

EP LL 03 Bai Chong Wo

1 cun above Sp 10.

EP LL 04   Nei Xi Yan

In the depression interior to the patella ligement.

EP LL 05   Xi Yan

Knee eyes

Expel Wind, Benefit the knees

Two points in the depressions medial and lateral to the patellar ligaments. The lateral Xi Yan is identical to St-35

EP LL 06 Dan Nang Xue

Gall Bladder point

Resolves Damp Heat from the Gall Bladder.

1 cun below Yang Ling Quan GB-34.

EP LL 07   Lan Wei Xue

Appendix point

Stops abdominal pain, Resolves Damp Heat.

On the Stomach channel between ST-36 and ST-37, on the right leg only. Tender!

EP LL 08   Nei Huai Jian

At the apex of the medial malleolas.

EP LL 09 Wai Huai Jian

At the apex of the lateral malleolas.

EP LL 10   Ba Feng

Eight Winds

Relax the sinews, Expel Wind Damp, Invigorate Blood

On the dorsum of the foot, on the webs between the five toes, proximal to the margins of the webs.

EP LL 11   Du Yin

At the sole surface, on the

midpoint of the transverse crease of the distal phalangeal joint of the 2nd. toe.

EP LL 12   Qi Dian

At the tip of each toe, above 0.1 cun to the nail. 10 points in total.

EP UL 01   Zhou Jian

At the apex of the ulnar olecranon.

EP UL 02   Er Bai

4 cun above the palmer transverse crease of the wrist, one point is on the ulnar side of the tendon of flexor carpi radialis muscle, and the other on the radial side.

EP UL 03   Zhong Quan

On the back of the wrist, in the depression between the points LI-5 and SJ-4.

EP UL 04   Zhong Kui

In the midpoint of the transverse crease of the proximal phalangeal joint of the middle finger. At the dorsum of the hand.

EP UL 05   Da Gu Kong

In the midpoint of the transverse crease of the phalangeal joint of the thumb. At dorsum of hand.

EP UL 06   Xiao Gu Kong

In the midpoint of the transverse crease of the proximal phalangeal joint of the small finger. At the dorsum of the hand.

EP UL 07   Yao Tong Dian

Two points on the dorsum of the hand. on the radial side and ulnar side of the tendon of the extensor digitorum communis mescle. 1 cun before the transverse crease of the wrist.

EP UL 08   Wai Lao Gong

On the dorsum of the hand between the 2nd. and 3rd. metacarpo phalangeal joint.

EP UL 09   Ba Xie

Eight Pathogenic Factors

Relax the sinews, Expel Wind Damp Invigorate BloodOn the dorsum of the hand, on the webs between the five fingers of both hands. 8 points

EP UL 10   Si Feng

Four cracks

Expel Wind, Resolve Dampness, Promote digestion

On the palmer surface, in the transverse creases of the proximal interphalangeal joints of the four fingers, excluding the thumb.

EP UL 11   Shi Xuan

Ten declarations

Clear Heat, Subdue interior Wind, Open the orifices

On the tips of the ten fingers, about 0.1 cun distal to the nails. 10 points

EP UL 12   Jian Nei Ling

Inner shoulder mound

Removes obstructions from channel, Expels Dampness and Cold

Midway between the end of the anterior axillary fold and LI-15
or directly opp. SI-09,

EP UL 13   Tian Mei

Heavenly Path

Midway between Lu-07 and LI-05

N-HN-54   An Mian

Peaceful Sleep

Calms the Spirit, Soothes the Liver

Behind the ear, midway between GB-20 and SJ-17, Posterior and slightly superior to GB-12,

Made in United States
Troutdale, OR
12/28/2023